SECRET JOURNEYS

SUNY Series in Feminist Criticism and Theory
Michelle Massé, Editor

SECRET JOURNEYS

The Trope of Women's Travel in American Literature

MARILYN C. WESLEY

State University
of New York
Press

Excerpts from "At the Fishhouses," "The Bight," "Brazil, January 1, 1502," "Filling Station," "Santarém," "Over 2,000 Illustrations and a Complete Concordance," "Questions of Travel" from *The Complete Poems 1927–1979* by Elizabeth Bishop. Copyright © 1979, 1983 by Alice Helen Methfessel. Reprinted by permission of Farrar, Straus & Giroux, Inc.

Chapter 4 reprinted from *Women's Studies: An Interdisciplinary Journal* 26.1 (1997): 59–72.

Chapter 5 reprinted from *Colby Quarterly* 31.4 (Dec. 1995).

Chapter 7 reprinted from *Southern Studies: An Interdisciplinary Journal of the South* 4.3 (Fall 1993).

Published by
State University of New York Press, Albany

Production by Susan Geraghty
Marketing by Patrick Durocher

Printed in the United States of America

For information, address State University of New York Press, State University Plaza, Albany, N.Y., 12246

Library of Congress Cataloging-in-Publication Data

Wesley, Marilyn C.
Secret journeys : the trope of women's travel in American literature / Marilyn C. Wasley.
p. cm. — (SUNY series in feminist criticism and theory)
Includes bibliographical references and index.
ISBN 0-7914-3995-X (hc : alk. paper). — ISBN 0-7914-3996-8 (pb : alk. paper)
1. American literature—History and criticism. 2. Travel in literature. 3. Travelers' writings, American—History and criticism. 4. Feminism and literature—United States—History. 5. Women travelers—United States—Historiography. 6. Women and literature—United States—History. 7. Women travelers in literature. I. Title. II. Series.
PS169.T74W47 1998
810.9'355—dc21 97-47577
CIP

10 9 8 7 6 5 4 3 2 1

for my mother
Flora Clarke

CONTENTS

PREFACE

By the 1970s the woman traveler in American literature had come of age. No longer depicted as the Victorian lady discreetly chaperoned about European monuments of high culture or the frightened immigrant come to join her husband in the new land, in influential works like *Fear of Flying* by Erica Jong and *Surfacing* by Canadian author Margaret Atwood she had embarked on extended voyages of self-fulfillment; in novels of the running-away-from-home genre like *Mama Doesn't Live Here Anymore* she was being portrayed as the emergent feminist bent on escape from patriarchal domesticity, and in science fiction by such writers as Joanna Russ, Ursula Le Guin, and Marge Piercy she was presented as a time traveler exploring new social options in locations where, to paraphrase another sci-fi hit of the decade, "no woman had ever gone before."

Today, *Indiscreet Journeys*, *Maiden Voyages*, *Half the Earth*, and *Women Travel*, collections of historic and contemporary fiction and nonfiction about women's travels, are available from commercial publishers, and women writers like Louise Erdrich, Anne Tyler, and Alice Walker make use of the female journey narrative in such widely acclaimed novels as *The Beet Queen*, *Breathing Lessons*, and *The Color Purple*.

But long before these overt representations of freedom and reform became a part of popular culture, there had been a covert trope of women's travel operating throughout American literature. The purpose of this study is to tell the story of women's secret journeys as they have been told, frequently, but fragmentarily, in that literature. From the seventeenth century to the present, representations of the woman traveler have provided expressions of contradiction of the dominant culture and projections of ethical and political alternatives. To read about her journeys is to uncover a complex and dynamic pattern of women's agency and revolution.

Through the examination of the trope of women's travel in American literature, *Secret Journeys* develops a feminist narrative theory intended to replace a model of feminine victimization with that of feminist capability. American feminist criticism has progressed through several stages: an initial concern with defining the often negative images of women in masculinist literature; the study of women's traditions in literature; an effort to discover in women's writing strategies of resistance to dominant ideologies; and the theoretical identification of themes and forms of female ability, engagement, and initiative. Drawing on a range of concepts from anthropology to postmodernism—feminist and African American studies, narrative psychology, postcolonial studies, and the critical insights of Pierre Macherey, Michel de Certeau, Jacques Lacan, Marjorie Homans, Mary Louise Pratt, and many other scholars—*Secret Journeys: The Trope of Women's Travel in American Literature* defines a figure which, through the narrative enactment of the journey, deconstructs and reconstructs the conventional female self and her place in the world and delineates through the trope of women's travel a model of challenge and enterprise that has always been there.

I wish to thank colleagues Thomas Beattie, Thomas J. Travisano, and Margaret Schramm for their helpful suggestions, Hartwick College for the economic assistance of Trustee Research Grants, the Stevens-German Hartwick College Library for research assistance, and to acknowledge the support, encouragement, and editorial assistance of my husband Norman Wesley, without which this work would not have been possible.

INTRODUCTION

The Secret Journey: The Trope of Women's Travel in American Literature

When William Bradford, the Pilgrim chronicler of English settlement in the New World, recounted in chapters 9 and 10 of *Of Plymouth Plantation* the story "Of Their Voyage, and How They Passed the Sea; And of Their Safe Arrival in Cape Cod" and "Showing How They Sought out a Place of Habitation and What Befell Them Thereabout," he failed to mention an important event: somehow during the interval between casting anchor on November 11, 1620, and the debarkation on December 16, he lost his first wife. In his admiring "Life of William Bradford" in *Magnalia Christi Americana*, Cotton Mather explained that Bradford's "dearest consort accidentally falling overboard, was drowned in the harbour" (111), but Samuel Eliot Morison contended in a 1952 introduction to Bradford's text that Dorothy May Bradford, debilitated from the voyage, probably killed herself rather than face the hazards of the unknown shore (xxiv). Dorothy's enigmatic absence symbolizes the trope of the women's travel in American literature: at very least the restoration of her more complicated story would change the official account and question dominant concepts of progress and purpose inscribed by the masculine journey; at most her occluded narrative might configure tentative patterns of alternative development. The ploys, gaps, and misdirections of her secret voyage, like the devices of fiction, provoke and open a way for new understanding.

Travel has always been what Eric J. Leed in *The Mind of the Traveler* designates "'a gendering activity,' a source of behaviors and representations definitive of masculinity in many cultures and periods" (217). The male "Spermatic Journey" of acquisition and aggrandizement he elucidates is predicated on a fundamental opposition: "There is no free and mobile male without the unfree and sessile female, no knight without the lady, no father without the mother." Yet, he notes, the significant "dialectics of gendering may go unobserved in travel literature, dominated as it is by male activities, while the journeys of women are secret, necessitated, or accomplished through the agency of men" (221). For Leed, the defining activity of male travel is secured through cultural imposition of its binary opposite: woman's stability within the domestic sphere. Women's journeys, "necessitated" by compulsion or motivated by choice, either participate in the prerogatives of men or they are unrevealed, like that of Dorothy May Bradford. Thus the literary representation of the "secret" journey is a trope for the signification of alternative.

Man in motion is the dominant image of Western thought. From Columbus to John Glenn, from Odysseus to The Lone Ranger, accounts of travel have served as vehicles for our deepest notions of progress and purpose. And in American culture this preoccupation is especially prominent.[1] Pilgrims, pioneers, immigrants, expatriates, Okies, Arkies, hikers, bikers—America is and has been a nation on the move. Its predominant genres, according to Janis P. Stout in *The Journey Narrative in American Literature*—accounts of exploration, narratives of escape, quests, home-seeking journeys, and rootless wanderings—reflect this obsession. But the history of masculine travel has been, as recent scholarship confirms, a history of imperialism. By the start of World War I, Edward Said observes, "Europe and America held 85 percent of the earth's surface in some sort of colonial subjugation" (71). This enormous and vicious ongoing project of Western imperialism was supported by a culture in which actual travel and the figures and stories it fostered played the crucial role of defining the "new" world as alien and exploitable. As Mary Louise Pratt explains in *Imperial Eyes: Travel and Transculturation* (1991), accounts of travel have been instrumental in what Said describes as the "undeterred and unrelenting Eurocentrism" that "accumulated experiences, territories, peoples, histories; it studied them, classified them, verified them; but above all, it subordinated them to the culture and the very idea of white Christian Europe" (72).

The role of the traveling woman in that literature is problematic. There are, after all, differences between leading and following, setting out and going along for the ride, a significant difference between writing and being written about, and these differences are frequently assigned by gender. As Annette Kolodny demonstrates in *The Lay of the Land*, American expansion has been characteristically depicted as the subjugation of an acquiescent female continent by a domineering male explorer.[2] Some women, however, struggling to define their own sense of experience as consciousness rather than conquest, have developed divergent narrative patterns. One such pattern, figurative accounts of what Leed calls the "secret" journeys of women travelers, is a significant feature of American literature. The textual journeys I consider in this study are not literally hidden from view, but their radical challenges to dominant social values organized by gender and conveyed by culture have not been fully recognized. The trope of women's travel in fiction and nonfiction, prose and poetry, as represented by the variety of examples I consider, functions as a structure for the expression of difference—from feminine restriction, political circumstance, and imperialist expectations—that conveys alternative possibility for development rather than the exploitation symbolized by the contrastive adventure of the male traveler frequently invoked or implied in these texts. In works that have often been assigned to conventional genres that obscure its centrality, the secret journey, always a figure of deconstruction, is further developed by American women writers as a varied means of reconstruction of attitude and circumstance.

British women travel writers of the nineteenth and early twentieth centuries analyzed by Sara Mills in *Discourses of Difference* (1991) narrated their experiences in locations outside England through descriptions of foreign landscapes and peoples and constructions of subjective responses to unfamiliar circumstances. Central to Mills's analysis of nineteenth- and early twentieth-century British women's travel writing is the complex interplay between the "discourses of femininity and colonialism": women travel writers "were at one and the same time part of the colonial enterprise, and yet marginalized within it" (106). For Karen R. Lawrence in *Penelope Voyages* (1994), travel writing by British women in a variety of genres treats "the tension between a desire for escape and a sense that one can never be outside of a binding cultural network" (19). Also fundamental are issues related to the representation of "the self and the other" (26). Such themes suggest that British women travelers have used the topos of women's travel to negotiate an uncertain position between the social status of the male traveler as the agent of empire and the native Other, whose imputed degradation was the ideological premise for the ongoing intervention of colonial governance. The trope of women's travel as represented by the American texts of this study, however, differs significantly. Like their British counterparts American women travelers are engaged in discourses of difference, but because they move within their own country, these differences are not negotiated through encounters with a clearly defined alien Other environment or person. With the exception of Harriet Livermore's missionary travel, Mary Rowlandson's encounter with her Indian captors, and Elizabeth Bishop's global excursions, the American woman traveler I consider contends with the implications of her anomalous status from within the contradictions of local experience and familiar communities.[3]

In each chapter I have traced what Leed calls "the dialectics of gendering" in encounters between the codes of female stasis and the challenges of feminine movement in a wide assortment of political, historical, psychological, and literary conditions of specific "home" cultures. Thus, this study of the trope of women's travel treats neither patterns of evolution nor influence. It concentrates instead on the varying effects of the secret journey as a means of change. Occurring early and late, across experience, class, and race, the figure of women's travel I define is apparently born again and again in differing cultural and social contexts out of the historically specific but constantly renewable ideology of woman's stability that supports the central metaphor of men's travel. Texts of secret journey challenge gendered ideologies based on feminine stability and masculine movement to mediate a wide range of social and psychic circumstances from the colonial Indian wars of Mary Rowlandson's account to the contemporary one-parent family of Marilynne Robinson's novel. Whether the portrayal of the woman traveler originates in experience, as is the case of Harriet Jacobs's report of escape from slavery, or is an evident distortion of actuality, as in John Greenleaf Whittier's *Snow-Bound*, or is an imaginative construction, as in Eudora Welty's short fiction, the trope of women's travel is an innovative, contradictive, and dynamic response to the recurring tension between imposed ideological stasis and gendered freedoms.

To read the trope of women's travel as the locus of deconstruction and reconstruction produces new meaning from a variety of illustrative canonical American texts: John Greenleaf Whittier's *Snow-Bound*, Mary Rowlandson's *A Narrative of the Captivity and Restauration of Mrs. Mary Rowlandson*, Willa Cather's *The Professor's House*, Edith Wharton's *Summer*, Harriet Jacobs's *Incidents in the Life of a Slave Girl*, Sarah Orne Jewett's *The Country of the Pointed Firs*, Marilynne Robinson's *Housekeeping*, Eudora Welty's short fiction, and Elizabeth Bishop's poetry. Specifically, through enacting subversive movement, as in Whittier's famous poem, the woman traveler repatterns understanding by contradicting the assumptions and challenging the oppositions that structure the gendered social world. As evidenced by Mary Rowlandson, the narrative of her travel provides a construct through which to articulate concepts that can be imagined only outside of existing cultural systems, and the protagonist's gothic journey, as employed by Willa Cather and Edith Wharton, discovers strategies for representing meanings suppressed within existing cultural systems. The record of her stasis, like the account of Harriet Jacobs's extraordinary confinements, suggests the hidden powers of the socially marginal to create spaces of empowerment within the dominant order, while the story of her journey, as in Sarah Orne Jewett's writing, organizes alternative ethical patterns within her community. Her movements, as in Marilynne Robinson's novel, introduce an alternative psychology and philosophy of feminine agency. The phenomenal record of her repeated excursions, as Eudora Welty's short fiction demonstrates, formulates social, psychological, and narrative patterns of transformative processes. And meditations on her travels generate the radical mode of travel writing as categorical revision introduced by Elizabeth Bishop.

Representations of women's travel, are, as Mills contends, complex and various, but the secret journeys of this study share a capacity for challenging dominant expectations and a potential for epistemological reorganization addressed through the diverse objectives of exemplary American texts. In taking her figurative journey, the woman traveler moves out of her traditional position as object of masculine culture, and her active career controverts the fundamental opposition of masculine mobility in an exterior area to feminine restriction to a domestic space. Not only does the metaphor of her journey inscribe a place for women in the world, but by challenging the range of privileges and restrictions authorized by gendered spatial orders, the trope of the woman's journey is a narrative reconstruction of the meanings of that world. As her own subject, the woman traveler goes beyond subversion to construction of alternative possibility.

The nonchronological arrangement of chapters illustrates specific reconstructive effects of tropes of women's travel operating in a variety of circumstances. The first section defines the deconstructive trope of the woman traveler through a succinct example of the way in which the debarred possibility of female travel in the social ideology of the nineteenth century signals disturbing contradiction in a male text, which, although rooted in the particulars of John Greenleaf Whittier's situation, is, I believe, indicative of the discursive scandal typically introduced by this figure. In the dominant culture, the woman traveler is an emblem of significant deviation from the gendered norm, which makes her presentation a powerful instrument of contravention of values. It is this effect that women writers have deployed for the radical purposes ensuing sections examine.

The next group of chapters analyzes the creation of alternatives through the inscription of journeys in Mary Rowlandson's seventeenth-century captivity narrative, modern novels by Willa Cather and Edith Wharton, and Harriet Jacobs's nineteenth-century slave narrative. These formally, historically, racially, and socially diverse works are related in that a focus on thematics of movement and stasis operates to overturn the conventionalized expectations reinforced by the lenses of standard genres or periods. In each case, the enactment of journey reveals values unavailable within the terms of the dominant culture.

Whereas a generic focus on women's travel suggests the possibility of alternative social vision or arrangement in texts by Rowlandson,

Cather, Wharton, and Jacobs, in the next two chapters—on the early modern and contemporary novels of Sarah Orne Jewett and Marilynne Robinson—the articulation of the narrative trope of woman's travel, in contrast to male travel narrative as presented by these texts, actively promotes mature and cooperative female communities rather than dependent mother-daughter relationships. Similarly, the last group of chapters explores literary modes of redefinition in Eudora Welty's project in her short fiction—to establish the delicate balance between conserving cultural stability and claiming the possibility for personal development—and in Elizabeth Bishop's creation of a postmodern poetics of travel as epistemological redemption. In these chapters the emphasis is on how personal, social, and political transformation may be effected through tropes of travel.

Through this arrangement I trace in differing situations the narrative trope of women's journey through its several key modes of deconstruction and reconstruction: (1) the contravention of dominant ideological values, (2) the presentation of conceptual values unencoded or unaddressed in political or literary culture, (3) the development of mature social arrangements of women, and (4) the definition of modes of transformation. The trope of women's travel is a dynamic means of expressing contradictions within, alternatives to, ambivalence about, and reformations of varied controlling conditions.

The summary effect of this discussion of diverse effects of the trope of women's travel is to demonstrate that the canon of American literature contains figurative representation of female capability,[4] recoverable through careful attention to the narrative trope of the woman traveler, which challenges received expectations. But my intention is not so much to provide a thematic survey of the use of the trope of women's travel in American literature as to use the study of that trope as an exemplar of another way to read that literature. Feminist literary studies have provided valuable strategies for reading literature centering on the feminine domestic experience; *Secret Journeys* strategizes the effects of feminine adventure outside the home as a radical trope that can change the world. The metaphoric secret journey crosses many theoretical territories (and sometimes contending areas)—feminisms, colonial studies, American literature, black studies, poststructuralism, Marxism, psychoanalysis, anthropology—divergent perspectives brought together to create a practice of narrative construction, which I describe in the concluding chapter as a method of reading the operation of transformation.

In a practical sense, there have always been women who traveled and many who have written about that experience. In the belief that narrative constructions shape reports of experience, I have chosen texts for study that illustrate the imaginative construction of woman's travel as discursive metaphor[5] rather than the actualities of journey. I omit generic travel works by such American women writers as Sarah Kemble Knight, Margaret Fuller, Carolyn Kirkland, Edith Wharton, and many others in favor of unexpected representations of women's travel in different genres in order to concentrate on the invention of alternatives in a variety of situations through a range of formal commitments and textual innovations. I have analyzed texts in which the representation of the woman traveler is a central and insurgent, although frequently unobserved, attribute, texts in which women's travel serves as a trope of female agency, and I have adapted appropriate theoretical methods of examining the special meanings the narrative of the traveling woman reveals.

The selection of texts is, of course, partly a reflection of my own interests and enthusiasms. More important, these texts provide apt examples of the properties that they are used to illustrate. Further, to view these nongeneric travel texts in the novel light of the trope of women's travel frequently illuminates new meanings the way that the revelation of a secret sometimes clarifies familiar situations. But there is another principle of selection that should be explicitly defined. Quite simply, I teach all of these texts in general college surveys of American literature, often on the basis of their inclusion in widely distributed anthologies. The selected texts are, like Whittier's *Snow-Bound*, representatives of the traditional canon, or, like Harriet Jacobs's slave narrative, popular additions to an emerging canon. Therefore, in addition to providing interesting individual illustrations of my contentions, collectively my selections also demonstrate a powerful argument for the pertinence of my conclusions to the general cultural practice we term *American literature.*

I have chosen works from the traditional or emerging canons of American literature because it seems particularly important to me as an educator to find ways to confront the stereotypes and assumptions my own profession has promoted. The traditional dichotomy of masculine adventure and feminine domestic literature largely omits the critique of imperial politics and of social restriction afforded by the categorical challenge of the traveling woman. To read the secret journey as narrative strategy is to read American literature as critical engagement with the assumptions and practices of American experience organized by the gendered hierarchy of masculine world and feminine home. As Judith Fetterly argues in "'Not in the least American': Nineteenth-century Regionalism," the institution of American literature has privileged stories of boys' pursuit of freedom, reluctantly admitted "novels whose business it is to negotiate the marriage of girls," and largely omitted almost everything else (890).[6] By circumventing the exclusivity of masculine agency and subverting the restriction of feminine domesticity, the trope of women's travel can and does represent alternative perspectives and issues.

In an influential article, Janet Wolff declares that the metaphor of travel is so gender exclusionary as to be an inappropriate vehicle for projects of cultural analysis. Nevertheless, she concludes that an alternative strategy might be the "reappropriation" of travel metaphors, a practice "which both exposes the explicit meanings in play and produces the possibility of subverting those meanings by thinking against the grain" (235–36). The trope of the woman traveler provides a means of thinking against the grain. As refuser and transgressor[7] of the conventional account of woman's place in the world in a variety of literary and historical contexts, as tentative deviser of her own destiny through movement on her own terms, as an alternative to the masterplots of imperial conquest and domestic stasis—the woman traveler is important in both canonical and noncanonical fiction and nonfiction and poetry. The strategic deployment of motion and stasis in her narrative functions as a sign of contradiction which questions, either consciously or unconsciously, basic assumptions of her differing cultures and tentatively structures that figurative realignment of known and unknown which may alter perception to change reality.

PART I

Contravention of Values

CHAPTER 1

The Not Unfeared, Half-Welcome Guest: The Woman Traveler in John Greenleaf Whittier's Snow-Bound

A later episode in the Renaissance epic of exploration, invasion, and occupation, the story of the American colonies is consistently a story of travel. Fifteenth- and sixteenth-century accounts of discovery are followed by seventeenth-century histories of English settlement, sermons expounding the analogy between Puritan and Biblical migration, personal records of physical travel and spiritual quest, and the captivity narratives Richard Slotkin called "the dark analogue of exploration" (19). The eighteenth century further develops the travel narrative through popular genres of the story of the hunt and the pioneer adventure. By the nineteenth century, an age that witnessed the dominance of shipping and the beginning of railroads, Western emigration and Eastern immigration, the trope of male travel was readily available for the representation of masculine experience. It provides the central organizing structure for all of Melville; for Whitman's "Song of Myself"; for Thoreau's *Week on the Concord and Merrimack Rivers* and "Travels in the Maine Woods"; for Poe's only novel, *The Narrative of the Voyage of A. Gordon Pym of Nantucket*; for Richard Henry Dana, Jr.'s *Two Years Before the Mast*; for Francis Parkman's *The Oregon Trail*; for John James Audubon's *Ornithological Biography on the Dakota Prairies*; for Mark Twain's *Life on the Mississippi* and *Huckleberry Finn*, to name only the most prominent examples. During the same period Hawthorne's "damned mob of scribbling women" was primarily engaged in first producing domestic novels and later "local color" literature, forms dependent on female residence in a single location. Evidently, literature as formally gendered in terms of movement played an important role in the creation and maintenance of the ideology of separate masculine and feminine spatial spheres. The appearance in 1866 of *Snow-Bound*, an important male work celebrating stasis, is, therefore, notable, and the anomalous appearance of a traveling woman in that poem clearly significant. John Greenleaf Whittier's treatment of the historical Harriet Livermore, whose travels to Palestine inform his ambivalent portrait of her, demonstrates the deconstruction of conventional values through the trope of the woman traveler.

The title of John Greenleaf Whittier's *Snow-Bound* foregrounds the issue of movement, but whereas Emerson's poem "The Snow-Storm," acknowledged as a source of inspiration in the epigraph to the poem, stresses unrestrained motion,[1] Whittier's work, as a comparison of titles illustrates, accentuates immobility. Where Emerson celebrates activity, Whittier memorializes constraint. And yet the most intriguing section of his poetic masterwork ambiguously introduces a moving woman as his "not unfeared, half-welcome guest" (l. 520). Whittier's treatment of the historic Harriet Livermore in *Snow-Bound* reveals the complexity of both masculine identity and of feminine representation in the male literature of the day. His trope of the woman traveler at once confutes his self-inscription within the terms of his own public and private experience and configures the woman in motion as problematic and contradictory. By virtue of her both frightening and appealing movement Harriet expresses thematically Whittier's unacknowledged contradictions of the psychological, political, and cultural ideologies he consciously endorses and formally elides the gendered polarities that organize his world.[2]

In the narrative plot of the poem—the recollection of a domestic gathering during a winter storm—there is no compelling reason for Harriet's presence. She is neither a member of the family like the mother, father, brother, sisters, uncle, and maiden aunt nor a boarder like the school teacher. Daughter of a wealthy judge who served a term in the U.S. Senate, Harriet shares neither the social class nor the homely interests of the others ("Rebuking with her cultured phrase / our homeliness of words and ways" l. 521). And it appears highly unlikely that she would have set off on a two-mile walk to visit the Whittier farm in the threatening weather portending a blizzard recounted in the first fourteen lines of the poem. The only possible reason for her inclusion is her difference from the household, and, I suspect, the poet's unacknowledged attraction to the implications of that difference.

The emphatic constraint of the poem is related to its central purpose: the nostalgic celebration of domesticity recalled from Whittier's youthful experience. In his review of *Snow-Bound* at its publication, James Russell Lowell praised it for glowing with the "light of the old homestead's hearth, whose flickering benediction touches tremulously those dear heads of long ago that are now transfigured with a holier light," noting sadly that the pleasant "scenes and manners" of the poem were swiftly being displaced by "the rapid changes of our national habit": "Already, alas! even in farmhouses, backlog and forestick are obsolescent" (42).

Whittier himself subtitled the poem an "idyll" and was inspired to compose it only after the deaths of his mother in 1857, his older sister, Mary, in 1861, and his younger sister, Elizabeth, in 1864. *Snow-Bound*, which resurrects these figures, is dedicated to the stasis of the past, not the movement of the present; but the little space of domestic warmth recollected in the poem is tellingly framed by active forces, the twin "storms" of the exterior natural and social worlds. The wind blows, the snow falls and drifts, the sleet pelts, while the family, "Shut in from all the world without" (l. 155),[3] enjoys its static harmony around a kitchen fire, temporarily out of the reach of the Doctor's call of "Duty," "the stir of hall and street," the "traffic calling loud for gain," even the "week-old news" (ll. 661–709), which marches into the Whittier home again as soon as the roadway is clear.

Not surprisingly, the family portraits eulogize as well as portray Whittier's lost relatives:

> There, too, our elder sister plied
> Her evening task the stand beside;
> A full rich nature, free to trust,
> Truthful and almost sternly just,
> Impulsive, earnest, prompt to act,
> And make her generous thought a fact,
> Keeping with many a light disguise
> The secret of self sacrifice.
> O heart sore-tried! thou hast the best
> That Heaven itself could give thee,—rest.
> (ll. 378–87)

It is lines like these that most connect Whittier to a reading public which, according to Jayne K. Kribbs, required poetry to "sound a moral note, touch the common soul, comfort an aching heart, and spread the gospel of eternal love" (xxvi). William Sloane Kennedy's reverential description of the Whittier family in his 1892 biography of the poet, for example, like these exemplary lines, is the stuff of consoling legend: "The family life of the Whittiers on the old farm was made delightful, notwithstanding the hard work by the perpetual cheerfulness, humor and wit, and calm and trustful piety of all its members. The cheeriness of atmosphere is insisted upon by all acquaintances of the family" (19).

This portrait of Whittier's sister Mary, marked by prescribed sentimentality and immobility, contrasts, however, the specificity and equivocal movement of Harriet's description. Whittier recounts his elder sister's "full rich nature," but the truthfulness and stern justice attributed to her in the very next lines suggest the conscious curtailment of that nature. Harriet is also notable for the richness of her "nature passionate and bold" (l. 515), but where Mary's character is abstractly defined and deliberately restricted, Harriet's unrestrained luxuriance of spirit and body finds concrete expression:

> Another guest that winter night
> Flashed back from lustrous eyes the light.
> Unmarked by time, and yet not young,
> The honeyed music of her tongue
> And words of meekness scarcely told
> A nature passionate and bold,
> Strong, self-concentred, spurning guide,
> Its milder features dwarfed beside
> Her unbent will's majestic pride.
> (ll. 509–18)

Harriet's "lustrous eyes" and sweet tongue are complemented by "lithe limbs" (l. 524), "white teeth" (l. 525), and "tapering hand and rounded wrist" (l. 537) in ensuing lines. Even her lips and feet merit the poet's attention in easily the most sensuous verse Whittier ever penned.

Unlike Mary, who though "impulsive" has corrected this defect with laudable "self-sacrifice," Harriet with her "unbent will," clearly proud and impetuous, remains self-centered beyond the control of any would-be guide. Finally, Mary is safely "at rest," but Harriet is threateningly lively. Compared to a jungle beast, she has "pard-like, treacherous grace" and dangerous flashing teeth (l. 523). Her volatile intensity of character and feature is further expressed in one of the best lines of the poem in which the poet observes the "sharp heat lightnings of her face" (l. 528).

Whereas the section about the "elder sister" is built on the grammatical pattern of unspoken contravention—the unvoiced "buts" that eliminate or abridge her primary inclinations—the eighty-line section on "the not unfeared, half-welcome guest" is organized around the rhetorical strategy of combining contradictory qualities:

> She blended in a like degree
> The vixen and the devotee
> Revealing with each freak or feint
>   The temper of Petrucio's Kate,
> The rapture of Siena's saint.
> (ll. 533–37)

Among the polarities the full presentation of Harriet elides are young/old, meek/bold, asexual/sexual, weak/strong, self-sacrificing/self-concentred, dependent/independent, connected/isolated, humble/proud, disguised/obvious, dead/alive, safe/dangerous, subdued/intense, forgiving/angry, sweet/shrill. Evidently Harriet's character cannot be categorized within the classifications through which the poet is used to evaluating the world. Not only has Harriet moved in literal space, but by so doing she seems to have overrun the semantic landmarks of figurative space as well. This reading of Harriet conforms to Barbara Johnson's explanation of deconstructive practice in *A World of Difference* (1987): "Instead of a simple 'either/or' structure," which is well exemplified by the portrayal of Mary, "deconstruction attempts to elaborate a discourse that says *neither* 'either/or' *nor* 'both/and' nor even 'neither/nor'" (12–13). To question any of the organizing terms of binary certainty puts others into question as well. The deconstructive strategy of deliberate grammatical confusion at work in the presentation of Harriet demonstrates that her unacceptable feminine movement is a threat, as well, to all the gendered structures of meaning of the social world Whittier is ostensibly trying to reinvent.

It is a world in which both women have suffered, Whittier avers, but whereas the sister, apostrophized as "O heart sore-tried!" is clearly admired for the sanctioned and definitive exclusions of her life, Harriet, who pursues a "troubled path" (l. 563), is excoriated for the dangerous inclusions of hers. The poet implicitly blames Harriet for her sexual force while he explicitly chastises her for the unchecked expression of prohibited emotion. Her feminine hand, for example, "Had facile power to form a fist" (l. 539); her saintly facial features could also "scowl and pout" (l. 543); even her "sweet voice" (l. 544) could "shrill" a "social battle cry" (l. 545). The elder sister exhibits both the rewards and punishments of the woman's ideological place. Harriet's sexuality, anger, and power slights those rewards and punishments to abrogate sexual positioning.

WOMEN'S WORK

To understand that positioning we must consider briefly the other females of the household. Unlike the elder sister, whose "evening task" is somehow not concrete enough to merit naming, "Our mother" is presented in terms of her constant feminine work: "she turned the wheel / Or run the new-knit stocking heel" all the while she entertained the fireside listeners with memories of her girlhood (ll. 256–57). Only at the conclusion of the evening "with care our mother laid her work aside," and then only to "express / Her grateful sense of happiness / For food and shelter, warmth and health" (ll. 604–607), domestic ends to which her own tasks have made material contribution. Even the more fanciful Aunt Mercy is marked by "years of toil and soil and care" (l. 372), but Whittier's younger sister Elizabeth, whose loss he has most recently suffered, is thoroughly etherealized: "I cannot feel that thou art far, / Since near at need the angels are" (ll. 432–33). All the female members of the household are romanticized, but the younger generation significantly more so than the elder.

This difference is consistent with the changes in feminine role precipitated by industrialization. It is important to distinguish between women's function in the home-based economy of seventeenth- and eighteenth-century America and the market economy that developed throughout the nineteenth century. In both periods the home was the woman's province, but the meaning and function of that home varied significantly. According to historian Mary Ryan, in colonial America,

> It was the wife's duty, with the assistance of the daughter and women servants to plant the vegetable garden, breed the poultry, and care for the dairy cattle. She transformed milk into cream, butter and cheese, and butchered livestock as well as cooked the meals. Along with her daily chores the husbandwoman salted, pickled, preserved, and manufactured enough beer and cider to see the family safely through the winter.
>
> Still, the woman's work was hardly done. To clothe the colonial population, woman not only plied the needle but operated wood carders, spinning wheels—participated in the manufacture of thread, yarn and cloth as well as apparel. Her handwrought candles lit the house; medicines of her manufacture restored the family to health; her homemade soap cleansed her home and family. (qtd. by Ehrenreich and English 8)

But in the nineteenth century, when most of women's previous production was being manufactured within a market economy segregated from the household, the middle-class home was the location of female duties not so much physical as ideological. John Ruskin defined its function:

> This is the true nature of home—it is the place of peace; of shelter, not only from all injury, but from all terror, doubt and division. In so far as it is not this, it is not home; so far as the anxieties of the outer life penetrate into it, and the inconsistently minded, unknown, unloved, or hostile society of the outer world is allowed . . . to cross the threshold it ceases to be a home; it is then only a part of the outer world which you have roofed over and lighted fire in. (qtd. by Ehrenreich and English 23)

The portrayal of the older generation of women in *Snow-Bound* looks back to the earlier pattern of the family as the productive center of its own sustenance. The sketches of Whittier's spiritualized sisters, however, the failing members of his own generation, are shaped according to the nineteenth-century ideology of "the angel in the house." That neither pattern is adequate to present needs is evident in the idyllic placement of the poem between the onslaughts of both society and nature. Harriet Livermore, the frightening guest, corresponds to the threat from outer forces. Like the interfering storm and the intruding society, she is described in terms of movement in contrast to the static security of the family group. In fact, more than half the lines in the section describing Harriet are devoted to her travels.

> She has wandered
> Through Smyrna's plague-hushed thoroughfares,
> Up sea-set Malta's rocky stairs,
> Gray olive slopes of hills that hem
>   Thy tombs and shrines, Jerusalem,
> Or startling on thy desert throne
> The desert Queen of Lebanon. . . . (ll. 549–54)

That her activity is to be viewed with alarm is evident in the poet's attitude: she follows a "troubled path" through a "wayward life" that Whittier cannot approve or even understand:

> Nor is it given us to discern
> . . . .
> The sorrow with the woman born
> What forged her cruel chain of moods,
> What set her feet in solitudes
>   And held the love within her mute
> What mingled madness in the blood,
> . . . .
> . . . hid within the folded bud
>   Perversities of flower and fruit.
> (ll. 567–78)

Despite his confessed confusion, however, the poet does manage to suggest that Harriet is sad, loveless, reckless, and insane. In the poem, religious concern masks Whittier's condemnation; he invokes a "Merciful and compassionate" (l.586) God to understand all human weakness. But in the introductory note he appended to *Snow-Bound* in later editions, the historical woman is not so cautiously depicted:

> The "not unfeared, half-welcome guest" was Harriet Livermore, daughter of Judge Livermore, of New Hampshire, a young woman of fine natural ability, enthusiastic, eccentric, with slight control over her violent temper, which sometimes made her religious profession doubtful. She was equally ready to exhort in school-house prayer meetings and dance in a Washington ball-room, while her father was a member of congress. She early embraced the doctrine of the Second Advent, and felt it her duty to proclaim the Lord's speedy coming. With this message she crossed the Atlantic and spent the greater part of a long life in traveling over Europe and Asia.[4] She lived some time with Lady Hester Stanhope,[5] a woman as fantastic and mentally strained as herself, on the slope of Mt. Lebanon but finally quarrelled with her in regard to two white horses with red marks on their backs which suggested the idea of saddles, on which her titled hostess expected to ride into Jerusalem with the Lord.[6] A friend of mine found her, when quite an old woman, wandering in Syria with a tribe of Arabs, who with the Oriental notion that madness is inspiration, accepted her as their prophetess and leader.[7] At the time referred to in *Snow-Bound* she was boarding at the Rocks village two miles from us. (398–99)

Harriet dominates the poet's consciousness in the introduction just as she does in the penultimate section of the poem, but here he was even more concerned to negate her appeal. Almost every sentence but the last—which repositions her in her home environment—condemns her. Throughout, Whittier contradicts initial neutral ascription with eventual negative interpretation. In the first sentence, for example, Harriet's "natural" enthusiasm deteriorates into eccentricity. Her early exhortations to prayer culminate in unbridled fanaticism, and, finally, her uninhibited travel is presented as serving hysterical delusion.

At least one of her relatives was moved to protest what he perceived as an attack on an unprotected woman's precious reputation. In 1884, the Rev. S. T. Livermore of Bridgewater, Massachusetts, published a vindication. According to William Sloane Kennedy's account, which quotes him, the outraged cleric calls the "'epithets heaped upon her' in that poem 'an assault upon a pious female's character,' and the portrait of her 'a cruel caricature,' and hints that he would like to use the 'flexors and extensors of his right arm in her protection'" (29).

Another chapter is added to the disputed characterization by an 1879 letter from Whittier in which he confided to a friend that in 1829 Harriet had stayed at a Philadelphia boarding house frequented by the poet where she was alternately "an agreeable and interesting guest" and "a violent-tempered woman of indomitable will." "I do not think I have exaggerated her character in 'Snow-Bound,'" he asserts, also noting, "Even then she was a noble-looking woman" (31).

THE VOLCANO AND THE ICEBERG

All of Whittier's statements about Harriet Livermore, finally, say a great deal more about his contradictions than her history. Unlike his nineteenth-century following, the most astute of John Greenleaf Whittier's modern critics have concentrated less on the consoling simplicities of his sentiment and more on the intriguing complexities of his character. The "only fresh light I can throw upon him," said Perry Miller in 1964, "is simply that Whittier is a more complicated figure, both as a man and as a writer, than he appears as one of the five monumental 'household poets' of nineteenth century America" (207). Edward Wagenknecht's 1967 biography found in Whittier "A Portrait in Paradox," and in 1971 Robert Penn Warren cited *Snow-Bound* as a summary poem that recapitulates the focal issues of Whittier's life: "In love, politics, and poetry, he was constantly being involved in a deep inner struggle. . . . He was, to no avail, trying to break out of the 'past' of his childhood into the 'future' of manhood—to achieve, in other words, a self" (54–55). Harriet Livermore is the ambivalent symbol of that central struggle. In a word, she is physically and morally *unbounded* in opposition to the *bounds* Whittier may have tried to evade, but evidently needed to maintain.

Coming at the end of the Civil War and the great campaign for abolition to which Whittier had devoted thirty years, *Snow-Bound* significantly does not attempt to establish any new order, but instead extols former virtues. *Snow-Bound* beats a strategic retreat on several fronts: from the present to the past, from the social to the sentimental, from the public to the personal, from poetry as call to abolitionist action to poetry as a sign of domestic refuge. Only Harriet, "A woman tropical, intense" (l. 531) in contrast to the frozen world that occasions Whittier's pastoral withdrawal, hints at the ambiguity of this course.

The obvious political capitulation is more than matched by the psychological resignation and literary abdication the poem also implies. All his life Whittier had been accounting for his failure to turn any of his numerous flirtations into marriages by citing the burden of an aging mother and invalid sister. But in 1866 when his only obligation was to his own needs, he reimagines the comfort of just those confining relationships. Yet we know he was clearly attracted to women. He confessed to many school-boy crushes, and his young manhood included several near engagements. He wrote from Boston in 1829 that he enjoyed looking at young women to "catch the dark brilliancy of their fine eyes and observe the delicate blush stealing over their cheeks." "There are a good many pretty girls here at the Athenaeum—and I like to sit there and remark on the different figures that go floating by me," but even in this youthful passage he is quick to transmute flesh into something else by imagining those "figures" as "aerial creatures just stooping down to our dull earth" (qtd. by Wagenknecht 82).

Although a woman friend commented that she had "always been impressed by the mingled iceberg and volcano" in his character (Miller 216), Whittier chose to live according to the dictates of the colder option. Wagenknecht insists that he "never experienced sexual intercourse" (81). Just before writing *Snow-Bound*, when Whittier was nearly sixty, he had finally managed to extricate himself from a longstanding relationship with Elizabeth Lloyd with whom he shared a physical union of sorts: "Both suffered from severe headaches, but they found if they massaged each other's brows the headaches would go away . . . and he proposed to her" (Warren 45).

But the most important quasi-marriage of his life was of the angelic sort with his other Elizabeth, the "youngest and dearest" sister of *Snow-Bound* (l. 396). In an 1884 memorial, Mrs. Harriet Prescott Spoffard wrote in *Harper's Magazine* that "Mr. Whittier's sister Elizabeth, sympathizing with him completely, of a rare and fastidious taste, and of delicate dark-eyed beauty, was long a companion and must have made the want of any other less keenly felt than by lonely men in general. The bond between the sister and brother was more perfect than of any we have ever known" (qtd. by Kennedy 28). Harriet Livermore can be seen as the subconscious "volcano" to Elizabeth Whittier's actual "iceberg."

Just as the nineteenth-century ideology of the "angel in the house" was founded on the physical and moral exclusions of women by the market economy, its maintenance demanded a related series of personal exclusions. The increasing isolation of the nuclear family in this period made intense family relationships the basis of personality, and in Mark Poster's view, this kind of experience produced "a systematic exchange on the child's part of bodily gratification for parental love" (177), a repression of physical pleasure that "led to sexual incapacities for both men and women. . . . Among the bourgeoisie, women were viewed as asexual beings, as angelic creatures beyond animal lust. When internalized, this image of women led to profound emotional conflicts" (168).[8]

But the explanations for Whittier's repressive choices must go beyond the psychological to the ideological. One explanation for Whittier's ideological choices may lie in Ann Douglas's theory of *The Feminization of the American Culture*. In her view the split between the market and the home separated women from whatever economic power they had formerly possessed and also disempowered two groups of men, the clergy and the writers, who increasingly allied themselves with the feminine sphere of "influence." If women's function was, according to Douglas, to become the agents of virtue expressed as emotionalism, innocence, and religious conformity, they were good at their work. Their views dominated the explosion of periodicals and books espousing their ideology. Since Whittier always longed for literary fame, his enthusiasm for domestic virtues in *Snow-Bound* may reflect his alliance with popular feminine influence. Douglas argues that a gentle Christianity of maternal values replaced the patriarchal Calvinism of an earlier age. Whittier's heritage of inner light, women's equality, and pacifism was suddenly closer to feminized mainstream doctrine. Unfortunately, this comfortable shift inevitably substituted the conformity of what Douglas defines as sentimental culture for the intellectual independence of Quaker history. The isolation of John Greenleaf Whittier the Quaker abolitionist was, upon the publication of *Snow-Bound*, replaced by the celebrity of Whittier the high priest of familial piety.

Harriet, however, expresses Whittier's equivocal and unacknowledged resistance to domestic virtue. Ruskin argued that if any guest "inconsistently minded, hostile, unloved" is merely "allowed" to "cross the threshold," then the sacred family space "ceases to be a home," becoming "only a part of the outer world you have roofed over and built a fire in." It is more than curious, then, that Harriet Livermore, whom Whittier carefully constructed to exhibit just these home-wrecking traits, should be enjoying the family's hospitality. The very pattern of Harriet's structuration in *Snow-Bound* as a unit combining opposite terms marks her as "inconsistently minded." I have sketched her figuration of power and anger, and Warren provides conclusive evidence of hostility. As a young woman, Harriet had converted to Whittier's Quaker religion, but in a dispute over the Friends' doctrine, Harriet slammed a Sister with a piece of stovewood, thus ending her membership in that pacifistic sect. Finally, despite his own evident fascination, Whittier tried to set Harriet "unloved" safely outside the limits of affection by predicting "ill to him whom Fate / Condemned to share her love or hate" (ll. 559–30). Nevertheless, he not only let her "cross the threshold," he placed her at the family hearth just as it is pressed into service as the type of perfect domesticity. Can he have been subverting his own ideology, turning the family farm into just another "part of the outside world" he has futilely "built a fire in"?

In "Home as Region," Theano S. Terkleni, provides a geosocial explanation that applies to Whittier's metaphoric structure. More than a location, home, he explains, is a "culturally constructed" and "historically contingent" (324) means to identification. Spatializing a self in relation to an excluded Other is a strategy for asserting control of a changing situation: "More often than not, home does not become an issue until it is being lost or changed. . . . Whatever term is used to identify the antithesis of home, an indisputable tension exists between the two poles of the dialectic. This tension often takes the form of a struggle between staying home or moving on" (326). The disturbing figure of Harriet's travels is Whittier's attempt to cope with his own changing personal and historical circumstances.

Harriet, it must be understood, is no isolated example. Whittier repeatedly returned to the related issues of movement, stasis, and woman in his most accomplished writing. In *Margaret Smith's Journal*, his only novelistic work, he imagined the response of a female English diarist on a tour through colonial America.[9] The woman's physical movement was matched by her mental agility regarding an allegation of witchcraft, the plight of the Indians, and the disrepute of the Quakers, which placed her outside the moral immobility of Puritan cant, as Whittier portrays it. However, because she travels in the company of relatives and finally returns to the safety of her home and family, Margaret Smith escapes the painful ambiguities of Harriet Livermore.

But despite Margaret's positive placement, two of Whittier's most famous poems about movement and women seem to offer negative asides on his own life. "Maud Muller"—the source of what are perhaps Whittier's best known lines, "For of all sad words of tongue or pen, / The saddest are these: 'It might have been'" (49)—is a rueful story of roads not taken. In this poem it is "the judge" who is moving and a beautiful farm girl who remains stationary. Their brief meeting on a country lane generates in her an "unrest" related to the lively life of the town she sees below her, while he is deeply attracted to her rustic grace.

> But he thought of his sisters, proud and cold,
> And his mother, vain of her rank and gold.
> So, closing his heart, the judge rode on,
> And Maud was left in the field alone.
> (47)

The poem may signal Whittier's regret for his own lost chances.

His well-known ballad "Skipper Ireson's Ride" (55) can be understood as a dialect version of Whittier's predicament. In the poem Skipper Ireson is tarred and feathered for sailing past the suppliant crew of a foundering vessel. Unlike the poet, who maintained loyal connection with his own family, the Skipper abandoned the shipwrecked sons, brothers, husbands, and lovers of the mothers, sisters, wives, and maids—those women of Marblehead who have punished him "fur his hord heart." The gross indignity of Ireson ("Body of turkey, head of owl, / Wings a-droop like a rained on fowl"), in addition to his inner anguish, may be a guilty projection in response to Whittier's need to escape his home, significantly rendered as travel, an ignominious Skimmington "ride" perpetrated by women. In both poems, masculine movement is intolerable and connected to deep and conflicted issues of loyalty to family members. Mobility is imaginable only, it seems, when it is projected farther away from the ambivalence of male allegiance onto a female Other, and even then it is presented as a dubious enterprise.

If the trope of the woman traveler challenges the "feminization" of Whittier's psyche, it also undercuts what we might term the "masculinization" of his literary expression. Through the description of the tales of the residents in the Whittier home, *Snow-Bound* presents an index of the narrative formulas that had been available to the poet and his culture. In his introduction Whittier defines "storytelling" as a necessity in the world of his "boyhood" and itemizes the available resources:

> My father when a young man had traversed the wilderness to Canada, and could tell us of his adventures with Indians and wild beasts and of his sojourn in the French villages. My uncle was ready with his record of hunting and fishing and, it must be confessed, with stories he half-believed, of witchcraft and apparitions. My mother, who was born in the Indian-haunted region of Somerworth, New Hampshire, between Dover and Portsmouth, told us of the inroads of the savages, and the narrow escape of her ancestors. (398)

These are the inherited genres of the mobile male—the hunt, the fight, the flight to the wilderness—which culminate for Nina Baym in a privileged masculine myth: the adversarial confrontation between the unencumbered American man and a restrictive feminine social world (131–32). David Leverenz argues in *Manhood and the American Renaissance* that the aggressive masculinity of American story alienated American authors of the mid-nineteenth century because their literary labors were judged as less manly than the imaginary exploits of traditional heroes, and that the canonical male writers of the period responded by representing the conundrums of American manhood through "destabilizing their narrations" (18).

Whittier's trope of the woman traveler may be similarly understood as a device that destablizes the male narratives that precede it. In the sequence of the poem, the stories related to traditional masculine genres tendered by family members culminate in an evocation of Whittier's own heroic employment of literature in the service of the ideals of abolition as a model for the future:

> A careless boy that night he seemed;
>   But at his desk he had the look
> And air of one who wisely schemed,
>   And hostage from the future took
>   In trained thought and lore of book

Large-brained, clear-eyed—of such as he
Shall Freedom's young apostles be,
Who following in War's bloody trail
Shall every lingering wrong assail.
(ll. 480–88)

As described in the militant diction of the next passage, the anticipated warrior of peace, modeled on Whittier himself, would do nothing less than equalize injustice, dispel ignorance, and reunite the North and South. Paradoxically, however, the masculine potency of this heroic paragon is immediately followed, and thereby possibly rescinded, by the contradictive section devoted to Harriet Livermore. Just as her troubling evasion of gender restriction questions Whittier's accession to codes of domesticity, it may also suggest his lack of comfortable alignment with the gendered narratives of masculine action he has invoked in preceding passages.

Whittier's example indicates that in the male text of the mid-nineteenth century the traveling woman may be employed as a complex sign contradicting the family, literary, and social systems of the period.[10] Her potential for such disturbance may also be discerned, I suspect, in Madeline Usher's brief but unsettling return in Poe's "The Fall of the House of Usher" and in the duplicitous freedom of Hawthorne's Hester in *The Scarlet Letter* and Zenobia in *The Blithedale Romance*. If Douglas is right, the male writer, strongly identified with the family-centered sexual and economic restrictions of the static middle-class female sphere, devised the moving woman as an expression of his own conflicted insertion into that gendered territory. And if Leverenz is correct, the moving woman may be included as one of a number of structural strategies male writers employed to destabilize the literary hegemony of a mythic American manhood.

The trope of the woman traveler, so understood, is the signal of desire, and its renunciation. Although she is alienated from the domestic community, the writer saves her a special place by the fire. Thus, the moving woman functions as the occluded Other of the male text, and her masculine/feminine instability deconstructs literary, social, and psychological strictures defined by gender and elides the oppositional categories from which those strictures are created. To discover "the not unfeared, half-welcome guest" is to understand female movement in American literature written by men in the nineteenth century as an occasion of confrontation with and a mark of contradiction to the gendered relations and restrictions of American culture.

In literature written by women, however, the woman traveler becomes the hero rather than the Other to the text. Her deconstruction of gendered categories of masculine movement and feminine stasis is complemented by her construction of alternative patterns of feminine agency as revealed in studies of the women travelers examined in the following chapters. In the next section, to focus on the travel text in works usually considered from the perspective of traditional genres or period—the captivity narrative, the modernist text, and the slave narrative—is to discover options and attitudes of Mary Rowlandson, Willa Cather, Edith Wharton, and Harriet Jacobs not otherwise apparent.

PART II

Alternative Representations

CHAPTER 2

Moving Targets: The Travel Text in A Narrative of the Captivity and Restauration of Mrs. Mary Rowlandson

On February 20, 1676, Mary White Rowlandson and three of her children were taken captive at her Lancaster, Massachusetts, home during one of the raids of the Native American uprising known as King Philip's War. Her account of that experience, published in Boston in 1682, was the first full-length work of what has come to be known as the Indian captivity narrative, but it is also by nature of its content the first travel book by a woman published in North America. For eighty-two days Rowlandson accompanied her captors—a small band of Wampanoak braves and all of their dependents—on a forced march that traversed and doubled back over a fifty-mile radius of New England between the Connecticut River and Wachusett Mountain. Rowlandson's narrative is really two accounts, the first, the story of spiritual progress signaled by her own title—*The Soveraignty and Goodness of God, Together with the Faithfulness of His Promises Displayed; Being a Narrative of the Captivity and Restauration of Mrs. Mary Rowlandson*—the second, a woman's travel narrative, a peripatetic record which, like the course of her journey, crosses and double-crosses the straight path of her story of salvation, demonstrating that the contradictory trope of the woman traveler may express that which is suppressed in the dominant culture.

Rowlandson presents the objective of her religious account as declaring "the Works of the Lord" that preserved her in the "Wilderness," returned her to safety, and comforted her with scripture during her ordeal (57).[1] It is this Puritan parable of God's providence and salvation, rather than the female travel narrative, that has been read by most critics and scholars. Richard VanDerBeets describes Rowlandson's narrative as "an intense and satisfying expression of profoundly felt religious experience" (*Held*, 42) and makes Rowlandson's religion the basis for generic classification of all seventeenth-century captivity narratives as spiritual instruction (*Indian* 1–9).[2] Even Annette Kolodny, who astutely observes that Rowlandson's popular work presents the first publication of "a white woman's journey" through the wilderness, by concentrating on the typology of spiritual captivity, concludes that Rowlandson represents the captive heroine's anguish in a forbidding landscape rather than the adaptation to new surroundings paramount in the travel narrative.[3] And yet Rowlandson's pious instruction is always grafted on to the main text. For example, after Rowlandson sets forth her "principall ground" quoted above, she again takes up her primary account: "But to Return, We travelled on till night; and in the morning, we must go over the River to Philip's Crew" (57).

This pattern of travel text and religious digression is especially striking in the initial paragraphs, which describe the raid. Just before Rowlandson's captivity, her sister was "struck with a Bullett, and fell down dead over the threshold." Rather than continue her dramatic description of the life-threatening events, Rowlandson pauses to comment on her sister's regeneration, the Puritan realization of personal salvation through the emotional experience of the truth of God's word as revealed in the Bible that served as evidence of election. During her sister's early years, Rowlandson explains, her sister's spirit was often troubled until "it pleased God to make that precious scripture take hold of her heart." Secure in the promise of Grace, her sister was comforted for twenty years, Rowlandson muses. But at this point in her recollection, she again turns her attention to the brutal action taking place around her, the capture and murder of friends and family (44). There is no disputing that Rowlandson's interposition at such a juncture signals the extreme significance and genuine reassurance of her religious faith. That her sister was the recipient of God's grace would allay the suffering of earthly experience through the promise of heavenly reward. Nevertheless, mundane reality dominates Mary's consciousness and cannot be suspended for long.

The basic structure of *A Narrative of the Captivity and Restauration of Mrs. Mary Rowlandson* is the graphic presentation of details of the secular captivity regularly interrupted by religious interpolations and quotations from scripture that predict the ultimate restoration of Rowlandson to her community and her family. Given this split structure, to read the narrative only in the light of its digressions is to miss a significant portion of the text. Of course, Mary Rowlandson's captivity narrative, and captivity narratives in general, have always been read from perspectives other than that of moral instruction. They have provided historians with documents bearing on significant events, supplied ethnologists with details of Native American life, furnished patriots an enemy to contest, lent politicians an excuse for the acquisition of land,

and given ordinary readers a taste of high adventure and a hint of low prurience.[4] But as a narrative of female travel *A Narrative of the Captivity and Restauration* has rarely been considered.[5]

The text, made up of an introduction detailing the initial attack followed by a series of twenty segmented "Removes" determined by the stops and starts of the forced march, is organized around the principle of problematic movement. Although the travel account is a narrative history, it eschews the orderly sequence of diary or chronicle, the available Puritan forms for the organization of private and public experience,[6] for an invented structure dependent on geographical rather than chronological arrangement. As Richard Slotkin observes, "time is marked not in temporal days . . . but in spatial and spiritual movements" (109). The compelling issue is not, however, *how* this text is structured, but *why*. "The central concern is not how narrative as text is constructed," cognitive psychologist Jerome Bruner contends, "but rather how it operates as an instrument of mind in the construction of reality" ("Narrative," 5–6).

What, then, is the effect of *The Captivity*'s unconventional structure? How does the emphasis on travel affect the text as an instrument of perception? First, and most obviously, the structuration of the narrative divides the text in two, leaving the reader to speculate on the relation between the divergent elements. Second, it develops the notion of what I shall call the "haphazard" as an experiential category and a psychological frame literally unthinkable within Puritan epistemology. Third, it allows for the revision and representation of two other unthinkable concepts: the Indian[7] and Mary Rowlandson herself. The effect of the spatial pattern, the shift in emphasis from *when* to *where*, allows her to move outside of the proscriptive narrative of Puritan teleology. Thus a critical focus on textual journey inaugurates a study of the constructive effect of the trope of the woman traveler.

READING DOUBLE

From the traditional religious perspective, the only purpose of the travel subtext in *The Captivity* is to magnify the significance of the religious text. The determination of the structure by Indian movement, in this reading, emphasizes Mary's[8] loss of power and makes the "test" of her faith all the more arduous. Rowlandson's own interpretation along these lines draws on parallels to the Biblical wanderings of the Israelites in the desert and specifically invokes the type of Job in his unbearable afflictions.[9] But contemporary psychological study of the story-making process suggests a critical paradigm[10] for the study of Rowlandson's dual text which would not subjugate the alternative purposes of the travel narrative to the religious text. In "Narrative Thinking as Heuristic Process," cognitive theorists John Robinson and Linda Hawpe maintain that "narrative thinking," or the process of making stories out of raw experience, is a kind of problem solving: "Stories are a means for interpreting or reinterpreting events by constructing a causal pattern which integrates that which is known about an event as well as that which is conjectural but relevant to an interpretation" (112). There are two different causal procedures that may be brought to bear on this explanatory process: the "search for precedents," in which the present is categorized in terms of definitive past models, and the creation of hypotheses "derived from . . . knowledge of human behavior" (117).

Ransomed from her eleven-week captivity, living in temporary quarters in Boston,[11] Mary Rowlandson must "reinterpret" for herself, and ultimately for her readers,[12] the events that deprived her of her six-year-old daughter Sarah and her family home. That is, she tries to combine both what can be "known" and what is "conjectural" about her powerful experience in the recognizable pattern of a public narrative. One explanation for her dramatic adventure, well established in the kind of epistemological precedent Robinson and Hawpe refer to, is near at hand in Puritan doctrine as God's providential intervention in the lives of his saints, the stuff of diaries and histories of the period, which forms the substance of Rowlandson's salvation account. But, as the complete narrative reveals, there are also inconsistencies, "conjectural" elements, with which at some level of consciousness Rowlandson must struggle. To omit the experience that doesn't conform to precedent would be to destroy the causal efficacy of the narrative, yet how can Rowlandson write a story she cannot conceive? Rowlandson's logical quandary, the conflict between Puritan philosophy and existential events, is frequently represented in the text in terms of the motif of ambiguous movement, as an important incident of impeded and indecisive motion suggests.

"The Fifth Remove" recounts the flight of the Indians from an English Army in close pursuit. Despite Rowlandson's loyalties, the Indians emerge for the reader as an enterprising and dedicated group. A small contingent of warriors drops back to delay the English forces,[13] while the rest of their band gets away by traveling rapidly and efficiently. Yet expediency does not overshadow compassion during the desperate escape: "some carried their decrepit mothers, some carried one, and some another." When a group carrying a large Indian on "a Bier" through "a thick Wood" can "make no hast," they take him "upon their backs" (53). Even Mary, because she is wounded, is "somewhat favored in [her] load" (53–54). When the Indians arrive at the

Baquaug River, the company quickly cuts dried trees and fashions rafts for transportation. After burning their wigwams, hundreds of Indians of all ages, some wounded, help one another over the winter-swollen river to safety, while the English troops following at their heels turn back, unwilling to brave the same obstacle, a discrepancy that continues to trouble Rowlandson throughout the narrative. Mary attributes the deficiency of the British troops to God's intervention: "we were not ready for so great a mercy as victory and deliverance; if we had been God would have found out a way (54–55).

Before concluding her narrative with the details of her restoration to her loved ones, Rowlandson interrupts "The Twentieth Remove" to enumerate some of the "remarkable providences" she had observed during her time of affliction. High on her list is the failure of the English Army. "But what shall I say? God seemed to leave his people to themselves and order all things to his holy ends" (81). The episode at the Baquaug River is still especially worrisome. She can only note her rueful wonder at God's preservation of "the heathen for farther affliction to our poor Countrey" (82). Although Rowlandson's religious interpretation of this event as an instance of God's mysterious will certainly adheres to doctrine, it does not sufficiently close the matter the first time so that she does not have to return to it again in a place in the story that signals its rankling significance. Even VanDerBeets considers the incident an instance of a breach of faith and describes Rowlandson's explanation as rationalization (*Indian*, 6).

If appeal to philosophical precedent cannot provide a fully satisfying causal explanation, according to Johnson and Hawpe, circumstances solicit an explanatory appeal to conjecture based on past experience of human behavior: when there "are no socially validated rules which could apply unambiguously to such incidents," a strategy of inferential "hypotheses" provides another option (118). As a twentieth-century reader of Rowlandson's text I cannot accept a providential explanation; I account for the fact that the Indians could get across the river while the English failed by citing the demonstrable skill and determination of the fleeing Indians on this occasion. My own cultural and personal experience equips me with a sense of human behavior upon which to base this hypothesis. But for Rowlandson this explanation is unavailable. She, no doubt, recognizes the concepts of skill and determination. But she cannot recognize Indians within these human categories, because within Puritan ideology the Indian is not human, an issue to which we shall return. Thus the mode of explanation based on human reference is logically unavailable to her.

The narrative of the incidents of the Baquaug River, for example, defines the English in the characterological terms of "courage" and "activity," while the Indians, desperate, loyal, practical though they be, are never described as such. Instead of adjectives, the text provides an account of serial actions through which occluded categories are represented but not designated. Thus by focusing her account on the travel story Rowlandson can present as experience what she cannot articulate as ideological or social concept. According to narrative theory,

> When a person confronts a novel situation for which no ready-made category is available, the occurrence remains unsubstantiated, unclassified, or unassimilated until a class or category is located or invented. The recognition of partial similarity on some dimension or construct provides the basis for analogy, and if linguistic translation is necessary, is expressed as metaphor. (Sarbin 4)

Born of the need to account for experience that outstrips her strategies of causal relation, Rowlandson's travel account is developed as just such metaphor: the inassimilable existential events and psychological responses of Mary's captivity are cast as the incidents of a confusing journey.

COGNITIVE MAPPING

As Ulrich Neisser observes, "perceiving is often most effective during motion" (109). Noting that spatial organization provides an array of metaphors for mental process, he turns to his definition of the "cognitive map" as an "orienting schema," an "active, information-seeking structure" (110–11): "When we go around a corner or through a door, we obtain whole new vistas that were previously hidden. This means that every opaque object—indeed, every occluding edge—defines a region that could be brought into view by some movement" (109). What Neisser discusses as biological and psychological operation, Fredric Jameson applies to social understanding. Extrapolating from Kevin Lynch's discussion of cognitive maps in *The Image of the City*, Jameson posits a postmodern "gap between phenomenological perception and reality" that is comparable to the inability of Lynch's subjects to map a modern city and calls for an "aesthetic of cognitive mapping" to address political problems ("Cognitive Mapping," 353).

Something like cognitive mapping as aesthetic strategy in Jameson's sense and as exploratory schema in Neisser's sense is at work in Rowlandson's travel narrative. Cognitive mapping, as psychologists understand the term, is the mental process of becoming acquainted with a new physical environment, an experimental effort to determine routes and identify landmarks until the area becomes familiar.[12] Mary has been forced by circumstance into radically unknown territory—not the geographical region of New England, which she can identify roughly with reference to the names of rivers and settlements, but an existential space well beyond cultural bounds. In order to survive she must learn to negotiate an alien world. The practices of Indian communal life are areas of experience not easily accessible through Mary's Puritan "maps" of reality. Her reports of geographical movement certainly record her literal journey but also serve as metaphoric commentary on the confusing psychological reorientation necessary to her survival in a new social space.

This shift from literal to psychological report is very apparent in the first sentences of many of the Removes:

> Now away we must go with those Barbarous Creatures, our bodies wounded and bleeding, and our hearts no less than our bodies. ("The First Remove," 45)
>
> We went on our travel. I having got one handfull of Ground-nuts, for my support that day, they gave me my load, and I went along cheerfully (with the thoughts of going homeward) having my burden more on my back than my spirit. ("The Fifteenth Remove," 70)
>
> We took up our packs and along we went, but a wearisome day I had of it. As we went along I saw an Englishman stript naked and lying dead on the ground, but knew not who it was. ("The Eighteenth Remove," 72)

Anger, disappointment, optimism, even curiosity are states of mind linked here to reports of the journey. For Rowlandson, to report on movement is to create the occasion to report on Mary's shifting state of mind. The travel is consistent, but Mary's reactions change constantly in contrast to the doctrine of certainty invoked in the Puritan passages. Such changes of mind are, of course, vital to Mary's survival, which is a result of her ability to adapt to the demands of her surroundings, but they run counter to the static conviction sought through her orthodox faith and the entrenched immobility of imperialist ideology endorsed by her culture. It is no accident that the last sentence of the narrative, after Mary rejoins her religious and social community, reestablishes the cessation of movement. Rowlandson quotes Exodus 14.13: "*Stand still and see the salvation of the Lord*" (90).

HAPHAZARD MOTION

As a result of the conflicting demands of experience and culture, movement is coded paradoxically throughout the text. Despite Rowlandson's familiarity with the region, she can only experience her location through features of landscape and describe routes of travel. She never articulates the achieved order of a new cognitive map, either geographical or psychological. The Indians' journey, in actuality an army's aggressive and evasive movements, is represented from Mary's point of view as erratic motion, an ethnocentric figure also noted by Ivy Schweitzer in Roger William's presentation of the seemingly aimless wandering of Narragansett hunting parties in implicit contrast to the purposive pilgrimages of American Puritans (213–15). If Mary is expecting to go to Albany, her captors unexpectedly remove to another destination (59). If she desires to go "toward the Bay," they arbitrarily change direction and proceed "five or six miles down the River into a mighty Thicket of Brush" (63).

This dominant figure of haphazard movement is well exemplified in a passage from the beginning of "The Eighth Remove." Just as the Indians are about to cross a river into Connecticut, there is a shout of alarm among them which disperses the band:

> and instead of going over the River, I must go four or five miles up the River farther North-ward. Some of the Indians ran one way, and some another. The cause of this rout was, as I thought, their espying some English Scouts who were thereabout. In this travel up the River, about noon the Company made a stop, and sate down; some to eat, and others to rest them. As I sate amongst them, musing of things past, my son Joseph unexpectedly came to me. (56–57)

The Indians' change of plan is fully motivated in the passage by the observation of the English scouts, but the dominant rhetorical impression conveyed by the diction is of senseless activity: "Some of the Indians ran one way, and some another." Mary's perspective of "musing" dignity rooted in her recollection of a meaningful "past" distinguishes her from the apparent helter-skelter motion of her captors. Yet Mary is also a part of the Indian community. She sits "amongst them." Indeed, her reward of an unexpected visit from her son who is the captive of another group suggests the value of haphazard movement, which the rhetoric of Rowlandson's presentation would dismiss as an inferior property of Indian behavior.

Nevertheless, Mary herself practices haphazard movement. In "The Ninth Remove" she obtains permission to visit her son who she has heard is in an encampment about a mile away from her. When she becomes lost, "travelling over Hills and through Swamps," she has to turn back. Upon her return, she asks directions of her "Master," sets out once again, and finally locates Joseph (60). Obviously motion, however disorganized it may appear at first, eventually effects positive results. It is the power to move in order to secure survival that characterizes the Indian in Rowlandson's narrative, but active exploratory movement is also the strategy that Mary adopts for her own survival. When she is not traveling with her captors, she is in constant motion in the camp—visiting the English who come into her vicinity, bartering her needlework for provisions, or going from wigwam to wigwam to obtain food and warmth from whoever will provide them. Even when her "Mistriss" censures her for "begging" and threatens her life, Mary refuses to cease moving about to enlist the aid of anyone who will help her: "I told them, they had as good knock me in the head as starve me to death" (73). On the one occasion when she is confined because the Indians suspect her of plotting escape with an English boy, Mary comments that she would rather be killed for foraging than die of hunger (67). Throughout her captivity, Mary understands that the more dangerous course is stasis and acts accordingly. And even after her release, she makes use of this random pattern of exploratory motion. When, without any exact information about her children's release, Mary and her husband ride eastward without destination to try to discover their whereabouts, they recover both son Joseph and daughter Mary. The trope of haphazard motion implies, however, the cultural contradictions that movement activates, not in Mary, the captive who understands that only movement can secure survival, but in Rowlandson, the author of the text.

In broad terms, movement is the political issue underlying Rowlandson's narrative. According to contemporary accounts collated by Frances Roe Kestler in *The Indian Captivity Narrative: A Woman's View*, there was ample warning of imminent attack. As early as January of 1675, the magistrates of Plymouth had been warned of the large-scale war that broke out that June and did not end until October of 1676. About seventeen thousand Indian warriors, a loose confederation of various tribes, eventually participated in what Ezra Stiles described as the most important of the New England Indian wars. Lancaster, a small frontier settlement on the outskirts of the first skirmishes, fortified itself by building six garrisoned houses, one of them the home of the minister Joseph Rowlandson, to which the whole community could retreat in case of battle. By January of 1676, the governor of Massachusetts had heard rumors of a planned siege of Lancaster, and by the first of February an outlying farm in that area had been burned. Shortly thereafter, the Reverend Rowlandson, Mary's husband, went to Boston to try to secure military assistance, while Rowlandson herself remained with her family. Indeed, troops from Cambridge, having obtained on the eve of the attack intelligence of a raid planned for February 10, marched to Lancaster, but they were too late to protect the company of about forty gathered at the Rowlandson home (7–12).[12]

In typological terms, the arrival in America ended the wandering in the desert by the Chosen People; settlement was the achievement of the

Promised Land. And as evidenced by the reaction of the Lancaster community to intelligence of imminent attack, colonial imperialism demanded entrenched immobility as the correct response to credible threat of war. Domestic occupation was to be fortified rather than abandoned, with women and children serving as entrenched tokens of tenancy. In the politics of Puritan settlement, defense was conceived in terms of stasis, and movement was to be resisted at all cost. This coding is symbolically expressed twice in a passage from the introduction as impeded and indecisive motion. During the bloody carnage of the Indian attack, Mary hesitates, uncertain how to proceed: "Some in our house were fighting for their lives, others wallowing in their blood, the House on fire above our heads, and the bloody Heathen ready to knock us on the head, if we stirred out" (44). However, when she and her sister and their children press forward to escape, their motion is again checked by the rain of bullets against the door. As Rowlandson describes the scene, the domestic space is aflame and can no longer provide a sanctuary to the dying mothers and children forced outside, but advancement also poses a deadly threat, so those engaged in escape are temporarily forced back. Although movement is evidently necessary, it is also marked in narrative presentation by deep ambivalence.

OCCLUDED IDENTITY

To present Indian movement as erratic in the face of English consistency is to falsify the actual events, as the example of Rowlandson's troubling experience at the Baquaug River clearly indicates. But it does more. Within a Puritan philosophy of divine sovereignty and providential intervention, the personal agency implicit in the Indian model is debarred; therefore, the idea of "haphazard" motion establishes a putative Indian Other in contrast to the determinant stasis of Puritan doctrine and the politics of colonial settlement. Such a classification is consistent with other binary definitions that constructed the Indian as the agent of the devil in opposition to the Puritan as the "saint" chosen by God, and the Indian as the Canaanite to be cast out of the Promised Land to make way for the new Israelites of Puritan typology.[13] As Francis Jennings contends, the "constant of Indian inferiority" in all colonial-Native American relations was based on the myth of Indian inhumanity in contrast to European civilization, an imputation that authorized inhumane treatment (59). But with regard to the characterization of the Indian, Rowlandson's travel text tells another story.

While Mary encounters "Heathen" (43), "Barbarous Creatures," "hell-hounds" (45), and "Pagans" (47) in introductory passages, generally her captors bear more the neutral epithet, Indians. As her exposure to the Indian community lengthens, individuals emerge who define themselves through their distinctive actions. Small and significant deeds, especially those of generosity to Mary, are frequently noted, and some few of the Indians briefly emerge as rounded characters. For example, in describing her Master, Quonopin, to whom she was sold by the Narragansett Indian who first captured her, Rowlandson comments on her gladness at his return (73). On this occasion, Quonopin demanded that she be fed, and he fetched water himself so that Mary could wash "and gave me the Glass to see how I lookt" (71).[14]

The Puritans who have financed Mary's release are defined as "tender-hearted and compassionate" (88). Yet despite the life-saving acts of numerous Indian benefactors, Rowlandson withholds similar attribution. Only once does Rowlandson use adjectives to define an Indian. Mary depicts her difficult Indian Mistress as "severe" and "proud" by comparing Wattemore's festive regalia to the toilet of a high-born English woman: "bestowing every day in dressing her self neat as much time as any of the Gentry of the land: powdering her hair, and painting her face, going with Necklaces, with Jewels in her ears, and Bracelets on her arms" (74). But, in effect, the ironic usage rescinds human attribution. In Rowlandson's text, Christians *are*, while Indians only *do*. Restricted to the report of Indian action, the travel account, nevertheless, inscribes, rather than names, the complex humanity of the Indians Mary encounters.[15]

The most significant problem of occluded identity addressed by the travel account is, however, that of the protagonist. Mrs. Mary Rowlandson, the Puritan matron, reinstates her priority at the end of *The Captivity and Restauration* as the author of its concluding platitudes: "The Lord hath shewed me the vanity of these outward things" (90). After her release in May of 1676, Rowlandson spent the following winter in Boston, accompanied her husband to a new pastorate in Wethersfield, Connecticut, in 1677, and was voted a widow's pension by that community the next year. In the absence of definite information, commentators assumed that Rowlandson's own death occurred shortly after that of her husband, but Kestler's recent publication updates the history of a woman fully determined by family relationships throughout her long life. In 1679, Rowlandson married a widower with eight children. After his death in 1691, she made her home with her son Joseph until her own death in 1710 in her seventy-third year (17–18).

Yet in the travel text we glimpse an alternative identity, that of Mary. During "The Third Remove" Mary encounters Goodwife Joslin, a Puritan matron whom the Indians later put to death. Pregnant and terrified, Mrs. Joslin evidently gives way to emotion and vexes her captors "with her importunity" by bemoaning her situation and begging for release. They strip her, dance around her and the child in her arms, kill both of them, and burn their bodies as an example to other captives (52). Joslin's fatal hysteria contrasts Mary's stoic suffering.

During the first days of her captivity, Mary functions in stunned silence. Wounded herself by the same bullet that ultimately kills her child, she nonetheless bears her dying "Babe," a six-year-old daughter, over the winter landscape without nourishment and without complaint for nine days. That the Indians respect her comportment is evident in the fact they put mother and child on one of the horses, eventually bury the child, and take Mary to see the grave (46–49). Mary does not even cry in front of her captors until "The Eighth Remove," whereupon she receives the assurance that none will harm her and is given a "half pint of Pease" and "two spoon-fulls of Meal to comfort me" (58). Whereas Joslin is overburdened by her pregnancy and the child she has with her, Mary is functionally childless during most of her captivity. Joslin behaves like an English woman; by behaving in a reserved manner under duress, which solicits marks of favor by her captors, Mary apparently comports herself in a style the Indian aspires to, an opposition that is not coincidental. It implies that in Mary's circumstances, to retain the role of the Puritan matron of the salvation text would be disastrous. Her survival depends on her ability to conform to Indian values and practices.

Rowlandson, in fact, insinuates circumstantial similarity between Mary and the Indians through the terms of a shared comparison. At the beginning of the narrative Rowlandson describes the Indian marauders through a conventional comparison. The dead Christians look like sheep torn apart by "a company of Wolves" (45). In "The Fifteenth Remove," Rowlandson returns to the central motif of Mary's appetite by making an observation about the "Wolvish" appetite that she shares with other starving people. She was often so hungry that she would willingly burn her mouth on a proffered bit of hot food (70). Both Mary and the Indians behave at times like predatory animals. The condition of starvation that Mary shares with her captors effects an equivalence between them, with the necessary changes in her dietary habits representing a total reorganization of customary values. During her first week of captivity Mary was unable to eat, and although she suffered the pangs of hunger during the second, she still found it hard to swallow their "filthy trash." But by the third week, although she could remember her previous squeamishness, the Indian food became "sweet and savoury to my taste" (54). This significant shift to determination of values and behavior by circumstance rather than by principle is well exemplified by the hospitable meals Mary enjoys with an Indian benefactor although his wigwam contains the "bloody Cloaths with Bullet-holes in them" belonging to the Englishmen her host has recently murdered in the battle at Sudbury (77).

MOVING TARGETS

Of the women captives of Indian unrest during the early period—Mary Rowlandson, Hannah Swart, Hannah Dustan, and Elizabeth Hanson—only Rowlandson had the erudition to write her own story. The educated clergy who transcribed and revised the unlettered women's narratives shaped form and content to support their own beliefs. Even Rowlandson's narrative was framed between a preface, probably written by Increase Mather, and a sermon by her husband (Breitwieser 18–19). Such silence and control was standard by Mary's day. As Patricia Caldwell notes in her study of *The Puritan Conversion Narrative*, although the direct relation of conversion experiences by women did occur in some early New England churches, the dominant pattern was for ministers and elders to report to congregations on behalf of female applicants, a practice becoming more general after Anne Hutchinson was condemned in 1638 for the dangerous expression of heretical views. Mary Maples Dunn reports in her study of women in early colonial churches that by 1660 female silence in relations of conversion was the rule (34).

If Puritan practice imposed female silence, Puritan ideology enjoined feminine passivity. As Ivy Schweitzer demonstrates, the extensive appropriation of the "bride of Christ" imagery to masculine religious experience in sermons and meditations served to restrict Puritan women. As scripted by this gendered figure, conversion was imaged as the passive feminine soul ravished by the active male deity. Its effect was to emphasize an imaginary ideal of feminine submission, leaving actual female activity unimaginable: "Despite the constant appearance . . . of 'woman,' the silence and absence of the concerns of women are conspicuous" (17). Margaret W. Masson's study of Puritan preaching from 1630 to 1730 reveals that the type of feminine submission never included any model for exertion, initiative, or choice (311).

Excepting the reluctant publication of Anne Bradstreet's poetry, Mary Rowlandson's unprecedented account of women's travel is the only conspicuous breach of the Puritan ideology of female public silence and private passivity. Significantly, male-authored Puritan accounts of female captivity omit detailed presentation of the captive's journey. For example, in Cotton Mather's treatment of the ordeal of Hannah Dustan, whose murder of her Indian captors serves as an exemplum in his zealous condemnation of both the pagan Indians and the papist French, a 150-mile trek through the wilderness is disposed of in a single sentence ("A Narrative of Hannah Dustan's Notable Deliverance from Captivity," from *Magnalia Christi Americana* in Vaughn and Clark, 163). Among early captivity narratives, only Rowlandson's text makes important use of the travel structure, and it is only through this structure that her provisional deviations from dogma are presented.

In his comprehensive survey, *Travel Literature and the Evolution of the Novel*, Percy G. Adams declares that most of the travel writers before the eighteenth century were impelled by "secular motives" rather than religious ideology: "they were fascinated by new worlds, new people and customs" (184). John Smith's worldly descriptions of travel to Virginia and New England were widely available to Puritan emigrants. In addition to mapping and describing the geography and features of North America, he often used the encounter with new territory to introduce the adventures of his shrewd and active third-person hero, John Smith, a tendency also at work in the development of Rowlandson's Mary. If Puritan theology insisted that the world was known and determined in advance, the Renaissance travel genre Rowlandson adapts held out hope for an undetermined future in an unknown world in which human choices and activity might effect outcomes. If anything, Rowlandson's adaptation of the travel form, which is structured to emphasize haphazard motion, exaggerates the potential for freedom inherent in the genre.

The male travel literature of the period, Puritan and secular, bespeaks confidence and accomplishment. Both John Smith and William Bradford dare to risk significant breaks with prevailing social opinion, Smith for love of adventure and in pursuit of gain, and Bradford for love of God in pursuit of a New Plantation for his people. *A Narrative of the Captivity and Restauration of Mrs. Mary Rowlandson*, however, unlike the travel texts of male predecessors, intimates rather than claims a new world. Rowlandson sets the radical freedom of the travel tradition against the absolute determination of Puritan faith, sets her experience of Indian life against a socially constructed Indian Other, sets the feisty Mary against the faithful Mrs. Rowlandson. But despite energy and spirit, neither the author nor her protagonist nor the Indians whose actions instigate the narrative are free of control by external circumstances. Rowlandson's denial of Indian sexual impropriety[16] speaks to her obvious recognition of the social pressure of her community. Ann Kibbey argues persuasively that for the New England Puritan orthodoxy the persecution of Anne Hutchinson and the Pequot War established the woman and the Indian as related categories of violent oppression. Mary travels at the whim of the Indians, and they respond to the maneuvers of the English army, both captors and captive ultimately subject to Puritan control. Mary and the Indians are moving targets, a designation I mean to indicate their positions of vulnerability within a system and their assertive motion in response, a tension replicated in the double structure of the narrative.

In spite of the textual inscription of constraint, it is evident, however, that the removes of Mary contradict Mrs. Rowlandson's political role as a static counter in a strategy of imperialist occupation. And the active initiative of the woman traveler of *The Captivity* contrasts the representation of woman as a type of passivity in the drama of conversion as defined by male clergy. Rowlandson's female travel text suggests that the trope of movement may provide a structure through which women may register contradiction to dominant ideology. By introducing an existential account of the "removes" of Mary's experience along with her Puritan interpretation, Rowlandson introduces a rudimentary cognitive map of the way out of a static epistemology that could not contain the complex historical reality of its author. As Rowlandson's narrative demonstrates, alternative identity may be described as action, as paradoxical movement through an unknown region, well before it can be defined as reality. Mary's maiden voyage, then, serves to introduce women's travel as a generic means of indicating alternative possibility.

In the next chapter we turn to the predication of alternatives realized through the trope of travel in modern texts. The gothic journey introduced in *The Professor's House* by Willa Cather and developed in *Summer* by Edith Wharton registers narrative expression of contradictions to gendered ideologies of travel and stasis.

CHAPTER 3

"The Perilous Journey through the Human House": The Gothic Journey in Willa Cather's The Professor's House *and Edith Wharton's* Summer

Whereas seventeenth-century Puritanism restrained expressions of feminine authority and agency, the early years of the twentieth century, when Willa Cather and Edith Wharton came to maturity as writers, witnessed an unprecedented emergence of female opportunity, especially in the period after World War I. If the double structure of Mary Rowlandson's captivity narrative evades restriction, the split allegiances of Cather's and Wharton's fiction communicate a complex response to the increasing freedom of women to define themselves in contrast to proscriptive standards of female decorum and expression. Both of these successful authors, one a divorcee, the other a lesbian, used travel in their own lives to claim traditionally masculine privileges. Wharton's European excursions and residency provided a context for participation in a culture that valued artistic accomplishment, an ambition unacceptable for women within the gendered constraints of her New York upper-class upbringing. In the words of biographer R. W. B. Lewis, her journeys to the continent provided "an alternative vision of the possibilities of life that she could look back upon from the limited horizons" of American proscription (58).[1] According to Sharon O'Brien's biography, Cather's 1902 visit to Europe was a similar attempt to ally herself with empowering masculine literary precedent (245–58). But an implied conflict between female possibility and cultural authority negotiated in their actual uses of travel finds expression in fiction as the more ambiguous relation of domesticity to travel evident in *The Professor's House* (1925) and *Summer* (1917).

Because both of these writers endorse the significance of the domestic interior—Wharton in her early *The Decoration of Houses* and Cather in the extended metaphor of "The Novel Demeublé"[2]—the ambivalence of the meaning of domestic space in *The Professor's House* and *Summer* is striking. The representations of houses in these works express the difficulty of domestic arrangements, and the surprising emergence of the gothic journey in contrast to progressive depictions of travel discloses problems of domestic relationship.[3] The standard gothic journey—conventionally expressed as a traveler's transposition from a familiar home to its alternative represented as a mysterious dwelling—defamiliarizes customary meanings of home and family. The gothic journey converts the member of the home to an alien in the home, and the protagonist enacts this new relation of alterity as a discoverer of the enigma inherent in the gothic house and the motives of its residents. By way of the gothic journey, a protagonist enters the second domestic space (even if is the same structure) from the point of view of an Other. The imaginative alienation created by the motif of the gothic journey is related to projects of estrangement effected by characteristic devices of the traditional gothic genre: the doubling of settings or characters, which suggests the existence of radical alternatives to known relations, and the use of narrative frames, which accentuate the deviation of the story from ordinary circumstances. In addition to opening domesticity to alternative interpretation, the gothic journey establishes the parallel between the female exploration of a set of interior relationships consigned to domestic relations and the male exploration of the exterior world narrated as stories of adventure. The female gothic[4] projects feminine relationships within the home as a journey into the world, an exploration of the interior landscape as a problem of exterior location that configures feminine psychological and cultural limits as spatial experience.

Although the trope of women's movement in the gothic narrative is rarely emphasized by theorists of the form, it is noted in several studies. Juliann E. Fleenor comments provocatively in passing that the female gothic is "essentially formless, except as quest" (15), but Sydney McMillen Conger describes the traditional gothic plot as "fearful periods of pursuit or flight and confinement, persecution, and escape" (92). Irving Malin observes that the heroine's "voyage" may be "horrifying because the movement is usually erratic, circular, violent, or distorted" (106), whereas for the readers in Janice Radway's survey of consumers of the contemporary popular gothic, the Harlequin romance, the detailed journey of the heroine is a valued aspect of plot: "romances are a good substitute for the traveling [readers] would like to do" (110). These opposing evaluations introduce positive and negative effects of figurative travel. In general, tropes of travel address women's struggle to practice the prerogatives of experience, but in the modern novels of Wharton and Cather the use of gothic devices, especially the motif of gothic journey, expresses the problems of women's domestic situation.

CATHER'S PATTERNS OF JOURNEY

The Professor's House tenders three patterns of journey: the heroic journey of male adventure which is the subject of the professor's life work, the denatured journey of acquisition embarked on by his wife, and the voyage of discovery by his protégé Tom Outland that introduces key features of the gothic journey. In his eight-volume history of the *Spanish Adventures in North America*, which elaborates the first pattern of journey, Professor Napoleon Godfrey St. Peter identifies four ideals of heroic conquest that he has sought to replicate in the creation of his masterwork: (1) the challenge of adversity, (2) the pursuit of desire, (3) the necessity of freedom, and (4) the establishment of male peer relations.

Adversity is actually experienced by St. Peter in the form of household irritations—the cramped, poorly lit, dangerously heated attic study; the inadequate plumbing; and the general discomfort of his home—conditions which have apparently contributed to his sense of accomplishment. His retention of the old house despite his wife's construction of a fine new dwelling suggests that the "needless inconveniences he had put up with for so long" (11) heighten the value of the writing he has managed to accomplish despite domestic distractions. This litany of residential complaints affirms what the title, *The Professor's House*, implies: Cather is examining the connection of male journey to issues of domesticity. Despite his identification with the Spanish explorers, Godfrey St. Peter does not light out for any territory; instead, he brings the conditions of the territory into his home. For this reason his achievement is realized as a complex negotiation between contending needs. The "desire" (25) invested in his work represents a sublimation of marital sexuality; the "bachelor" freedom of his garden retreat is purchased by sending his wife and daughters on vacations without him (15); and genuine kinship—with "a few young men, scattered about the United States and England" who appreciate his early work (33)—represents an alternative to his domestic bonds. Through themes of travel *The Professor's House* poses questions about the possibility of combining family attachments and the demands and rewards of work.

Modern travel, according to Eric J. Leed, is marred by "the pervasive feeling that *real* travel—outward-bound, hard, dangerous, and individualizing—is no longer possible" (286), and St. Peter's "delightful excursions and digressions; the two Sabbatical years when he had been in Spain, two summers in the South-west on the trail of his adventurers, another in Old Mexico, dashes to France to see his foster brothers" (25) have all taken place in the past. Cather's first pattern, the idealized male journey, is presented as history, not possibility. Ironically, it is St. Peter who is housebound and static; Mrs. St. Peter has moved on to new relations and new activities. She represents the second pattern of journey: nonidealized acquisition. She has substituted for the lost seductions of her husband the gallantries of her sons-in-law: "*Beaux fils*, apparently, were meant to take the husband's place when husbands had ceased to be lovers" (160). This substitution is signaled by her junket to Paris with her daughter Rosamond and her daughter's husband Louie Marsellus, a journey also meant to signify Lillian St. Peter's materialism and marginality. As the professor's trip with the same couple to buy furniture for their new house has established, the Marselluses embark on derivative voyages of consumption, plundering the heritage of the Old World to furnish the New. In Cather's stereotyped presentation, both the Jew (Marsellus) and the wife (Lillian) are parasitic figures dependent on authentic providers. Lillian St. Peter has built her new home with the money from Godfrey St. Peter's Oxford Prize; Louie Marsellus is constructing his out of Tom Outland's legacy to Rosamond. So although their parvenu journeys can imitate the characteristic acquisition of the male explorer, they lack the epic rigor necessary to male adventure.

Neither Godfrey's nor Lillian's journeys are presented as direct action, but Tom Outland's story, around which Cather constructed the rest of the novel (Stout, *Journey* 87), is fully rendered. Mediating between the masculine journey of past adventure and the feminized journey of modern acquisition, Outland's narrative evolves through several generic identifications to finally install the rudiments of what I define as the gothic journey.[5]

When young Tom Outland meets Roddy Blake, they are both working for the railroad. Tom, an orphan employed as call boy for the community of switchmen, brakemen, firemen, and conductors, appears to be a budding Horatio Alger, and Roddy, tougher and older, is cast as a potential proletarian hero: "one of those fellows with a settled, mature body and a young face, such as you often see among working-men. There was something calm, and sarcastic, and mocking about his expression—that too you often see among working-men" (Cather, 181–82). But for the portrayal of the initial stages of their shared Southwestern adventure, Cather borrows from another popular genre, the narrative of the American cowboy hero. Shortly after Tom's bout with pneumonia, Roddy and Tom literally become cowpunchers in the area of the blue mesa, the enigmatic site which eventually draws them into exploration.

According to John G. Cawelti, the cowboy connects the contrasting values of wilderness and community. The unsettled plains represent the energy of unlawful male freedom and are marked by unimpeded movement, while the community, with its civilizing female relationships and nascent institutions of law, religion, and education, is self-contained and static. The hero is introduced at a point when the savagery of the frontier "is implicitly understood to be on the way out" (63), but lawlessness is still potent enough to "pose a local and momentarily significant challenge" (65). The cowboy hero, whose roots, activities, and relationships link him to the unfettered world of men, must switch his loyalty to the threatened domestic order of the town and come to its defense. Tom seems at first to be a genuine exemplar of the heroic wilderness, yet his allegiance changes in the course of the story. Whereas the western drama of the hero's skillful and violent defense of civilization effectively obscures the unresolved ambiguities of his shift from the license of adventure to the order of domesticity, Cather's work, on the other hand, fully represents the unresolved contradictions of such a conversion. Like the western hero's, Tom's role in the center of the St. Peters' story is to arbitrate between the lost world of male adventure and the ambivalences of the domestic order, but Cather's presentation eschews the violent foreclosure of the western formula narrative. In Tom's narrative the division between wilderness and community, left unresolved in the plot, is mediated through his discovery of a symbolic landscape that introduces aspects of each—the challenge leading to adventure and the domestic order that produces civilization.

During the months that Tom and Roddy tend the Sitwell Company cattle, the mesa, which looms above their winter cabin, "bothered" and "tempted" them (193) until Tom becomes determined to find a trail to the summit and investigate it. When he finally enters the canyon leading to the prehistoric Native American village he discovers on the mesa, his generic identity changes again from that of the cowboy to that of the male explorer. He exhibits curiosity, determination, and mastery in the face of geographical limit, first by systematically exploring the base of the butte to search for paths of entry, then by fording the winter river to gain access to the only route to the top. Roddy Blake, Tom's foil, matches this adventurous spirit throughout the construction of a road and the archaeologic exploration of the "sky village" (202) the next spring. It is Roddy's sale of artifacts from the Indian village the following year that asserts the plunder of an alternative location as the true objective of masculine exploration.

But Tom's Christmas vision of the purity, immortality, and "eternal calmness" of "the little city of stone, asleep" in the "falling snow-flakes" (201–202) inaugurates a different relation. Fascinated by the architecture of the "Cliff City" (203), he is increasingly awed by what it implies about the advanced civilization of its ancient cliff dwellers. In claiming the lost world as the home of the "ancestors" of homeless boys (242), he substitutes a relation of domesticity for one of conquest. Nevertheless, this idyllic interpretation cannot evade the implied destructiveness of the domestic condition. The mummified remains of the female the explorers name "Mother Eve" are thought to prove her to have been the victim of a passionate domestic tragedy; the absence of the cultivated inhabitants of the abandoned village is a mystery that can never be satisfactorily solved; and the man whom Tom thinks of as a brother finally betrays his deepest values. Tom Outland's journey, which begins as the adventurous conquest of the outer world, becomes the ambiguous exploration of inner realities: the search for the meaning of home and the puzzle of family relationships. In Tom's story, however, such mysteries remain forever unresolved. After an acrimonious quarrel about the sale of the archeological treasures, Roddy leaves, never to be found again. Dying in the first World War, Tom never has the opportunity to unravel the domestic enigma through a marriage of his own; and the industrial patent he leaves to his fiancée, Rosamond St. Peter, creates the wealth that complicates all of the domestic relations of the novel.

The thematic imbrication of the orders of adventure and domesticity is first symbolized in the novel by the attic study the professor shares with Augusta, the family sewing-woman. In this setting, St. Peter's history of male adventure corresponds to the dressmaker's record of the evolving "forms" of the St. Peter women. Inside the storage compartment of the box couch they both use, his notes on the Spanish explorers and her "notched charts which followed the changing stature and figures of the Misses St. Peter from early childhood to womanhood" symbolically commingle: "In the middle of the box, patterns and manuscripts interpenetrated" (22). Godfrey's professional specialization is relevant in this regard. Like many contemporary historians, he has shifted his interest from public to private history, from a focus on the broad issues of continental exploration to an overriding concern with the intimate politics of everyday life. The ultimate significance of domestic history is fully realized in the last section of the novel in which the professor is only able to close with the issues of his divided loyalties through a suicidal gesture. When he comes close to asphyxiation in the old study one stormy night and doesn't want to save himself, he is rescued by the unworldly and faithful Augusta, who represents the acceptable symbolic counterpart to the wife with whom he has fallen out of love. Yet the Professor's attempted suicide at the conclusion of the novel registers powerful conflicts inherent in domesticity.

Pierre Macherey's Marxist theory of narrative displacement illuminates the gendered divergences of plot and theme in *The Professor's House*. In his essay "Jules Verne: The Faulty Narrative," Macherey argues that it is not the meaning of a literary work but its "strange power of *internal variation*" that demands consideration (160). For Macherey, the disparity between the initial project of the text and its realization as symbolic structure points up the ideological limits that the writer must work within and the genuine achievement produced by the work in its attempt to overcome them. In the course of the writing, the author's intention is transmuted into a symbolic representation of more genuine issues. Cather's initial theme, as commentators observe,[6] was the encroaching inadequacy of the modern world, represented in this novel by the problem of materialism. This general theme is elaborated at the level of plot by the selling of the domestic treasures of the blue mesa and through the symbol of new houses. Male adventure, as characterized by Roddy Blake, is, Tom learns, corrupted by materialism, but so is the domestic world of St. Peter's acquisitive wife and his jealous daughters. But what Macherey labels the "fable" of the text—in Cather's novel Tom Outland's story of masculine adventure—reverses the implications of a superficial reading of its primary symbols.[7] The reverent return of the orphan hero to the womblike village with its maternal tutelary spirit suggests that the refinements of feminine domestic order may, in fact, be a "cradle of civilization."

The problem of the writer, according to Macherey, is to make use of inherited generic resources to express emerging contemporary insights. The difficulty of this enterprise is represented in *The Professor's House* by the tenuous plot connection between two very different stories: the narrative of the professor's domestic dilemma and Outland's adventure tale. That there is no easy fit between literary resources and contemporary meaning is witnessed by Cather's extensive testing of generic possibilities in Tom Outland's story. For Macherey, the formal solution to the problem of composition, well exemplified by this novel, is to "confront one form with another" (Macherey 199). The expression of conflicting options is, I believe, the basis of Cather's achievement in *The Professor's House.* As Sharon O'Brien's sensitive biography argues, Cather's homosexuality produced a complicated, frequently contradictory, interpretation of gender in her works. Although she clearly wished to ally her own artistic endeavors with the heroic conquest of the male hero,[8] her own homosocial relationships had evidently taught her the value of domestic alliances. *The Professor's House* embodies the discrepant threats and attractions of the gendered orders of masculine movement and feminine stasis Cather was trying to negotiate. Through her struggle to give her initial theme generic expression, Cather expresses the conflicting problems and advantages of gendered feminine and masculine modes.

The description of the interruption of St. Peter's scholarly concentration by some domestic emergency as "that perilous journey through the human house" (27) provides an excellent thumbnail definition of the gothic project of *The Professor's House*: to present the domestic situation in terms of its both attractive and dangerous complexity. To this end, Cather's modern novel makes use of several traditional gothic devices.[9] Its central episode, Outland's narrative, is elaborately framed, and its domestic roles are decidedly doubled.[10] There are the duplicate mothers and wives—Lillian and Augusta—the light and dark sisters—Kathleen and Rosamond—and the multiple imaginary sons—the idealized figure of Outland; the literary progeny, "your splendid Spanish adventurer sons" (165) as Louie puts it; and the actual deficient sons-in-law, Louie and Scott. These variant sons represent possibilities and deficiencies of St. Peter himself, a motif also reinforced when St. Peter bemoans the loss of an alternative identity, the Kansas "boy" he had left behind in pursuit of his European adventure (263–64). Further, Tom even takes on the character of the gothic heroine. After he hears the story of Roddy's sale of the Indian artifacts, he grows as weak kneed as the female protagonist in a popular melodrama: "I remember I sat down on the sofa in Hook's office because I couldn't stand up any longer, and the smell of horse blankets began to make me deathly sick. In a minute I went over, like a girl in a novel" (238).

Most important, the novel is suffused with variants of the principal gothic setting: the enigmatic house.[11] The central concerns of characters' lives are represented as questions of housing. Will St. Peter occupy the empty house of the past in which his study is located? Or will he move into his wife's new house, which signals all that the professor finds objectionable in their changed relation? Will the envious Kathleen and her embittered husband, Scott, find some way to accommodate to the middle-class limitations of their residence? Will they accept Louie's generous offer of his own castoff furniture? Will the Marselluses find some way to temper the ostentation of their new home? Will the Cranes find a way out of the extraordinarily straitened circumstances represented by their thoroughly uncomfortable house? Can the idealized domestic world of the cliff village ever be realized in the modern world? Is domesticity doomed to failure because of the avariciousness of the human character or can it function properly as the source of gracious culture? What is the meaning of and form for human community? Is there a space in which the needs for freedom and connection can be resolved? These are the issues raised, but left unresolved, by the evolution of the gothic journey from adventure to an uneasy approach to conflicting meanings of the home in *The Professor's House*.[12]

Finally, the characteristic reversal of perspective that opens the domestic order to alternative interpretation through the trope of gothic journey is exemplified by Tom Outland's change of attitude in the course of his exploration of the cliff village. It culminates in the professor's story. Whereas Tom's "outland" adventure unexpectedly introduces the interior values of domestic order, the house-obsessed professor's attempted suicide bears witness to an opposing vision of domesticity: the home as a place of dangerous, possibly unbearable, ambiguity. The professor's self-destructive impulse in reaction to questions of housing is an expression of the strain between the competing models of experience represented as masculine adventure and feminine domesticity; it does not, however, suggest the means of their integration. The gothic journey in the novel is a figure through which uncomfortable oppositions are realized rather than resolved. Conflicts between security and adventure, authenticity and corruption, the past and the present, restriction and opportunity suggested by the adaptation of this figure in *The Professor's House* are even more fully expressed in Edith Wharton's *Summer*, in which the gothic journey of the surprising ending reverses the confident project of woman's travel with which the book begins.

WOMEN'S TRAVEL VERSUS THE GOTHIC JOURNEY

Drawing on Laura Mulvey's "Visual Pleasure in Narrative Cinema," Susan Wolstenholme emphasizes the stasis of the woman in gothic literature as constructed by the male gaze. The characteristic "fetishized image of the woman" (8), which interrupts narrative flow in gothic texts, genders female characters as objects of masculine control. This feature is exemplified for Wolstenholme by the *tableau vivant* in which protagonist Lily Bart participates in Edith Wharton's 1905 *House of Mirth* (Wolstenholme, 134–35). As an "art object" Lily is "powerless and appropriable" (Wolstenholme 135).[13] Significantly, Wharton reverses this gendered convention in *Summer*, published twelve years later, in an early scene in which Charity Royall hides outside the bedroom window of her soon-to-be-lover Lucius Harney and makes him the object of her own amatory gaze. Watching as he removes his jacket and vest and unbuttons his shirt collar, Charity sees "the vigorous lines of his young throat, and the root of muscles where they joined the chest" (103).

Initially, Charity appears to be a character fully capable of overturning restrictions of female power, an implication developed through the trope of women's travel. The presentation of the female body in motion constitutes a radical alternative to the domination of the male gaze. The woman traveler is not defined through her relationship with a controlling perspective. At issue in the act of travel is the constant modification of the traveler's own perspective toward what she encounters. In effect, the trope of the woman traveler replaces the male-objectified woman with the self-creating woman: it replaces the female body as object with the female body as agent.

In most of *Summer* Charity's travels manifest her genuine potential. Her frequent flights into the natural setting signify an invigorating vitality that contrasts the confining interior space of The Honorius Hatchard Memorial Library where she is employed in a "prison-house" (14) of decaying books. In expeditions about the countryside with Harney, it is Charity who drives the buggy, a sign of her mastery. Their Fourth of July trip from the tiny hamlet of North Dormer to the larger community of Nettleton is planned to satisfy Charity's desire for experience in the greater world. Even her journey to the Mountain in the penultimate episode of the novel is a necessary step in Charity's pursuit of the terms of her own identity. Only the wedding journey at the end of the novel, which Mr. Royall, Charity's guardian/husband, defines, arranges, and executes, undermines Charity's extraordinary agency; and it is this journey which marks *Summer* as a gothic text.[14]

According to Irving Malin, a central characteristic of the gothic form is the alternation of images of motion with spatial constriction, and Charity's movement in the novel is contradicted by her occupation of a series of restricting domestic spaces. The conventional gothic location, the confining and dangerous house, is presented by Wharton in terms of male control. The novel is framed by incidents of Charity's retreat into Royall's house. In the opening scene, startled by the appearance of a bold young man who turns out to be Lucius Harney, Charity "draw[s] back into the house" (8). This prescient withdrawal predicts her implicit action in the last words of the novel: "Late that evening, in the cold autumn moonlight, they drove up to the door of the red house" (291). Two other houses entered by Charity—the abandoned house and the brown house—are also homes dominated by men. The most significant male domestic space is the "deserted house" (202) Charity and Lucius inhabit as a love nest. The insufficiency of its shelter, implied by the provisional quality of the temporary appointments provided by Harney, is indicated directly by Royall's challenge to his young rival: "Is this the home you propose to bring her to when you get married?" (206). The "brown house under Porcupine" (77) visited by the young couple is occupied by a marginal family from the Mountain, and the effect of the beauty of its classic architecture is diminished by the deficiency and subjugation of its occupants. When Charity and Lucius are forced to shelter in that "bare and miserable" place during a sudden rainstorm, they observe a senile grandmother and a wife and children who are evidently very frightened of what may happen when the "sodden and bestial" husband awakens from his drunken stupor (83). Although Royall's home is clearly preferable to these deficient domiciles, the danger of the domestic space is an important pattern of the novel. The gothic houses of Edith Wharton's *Summer* are habitations outside the traditional nineteenth-century "woman's sphere" of influence. Controlled by men, they are inadequate, restrictive, and even threatening spaces for their female residents.

Masculine control of domestic space in the novel is a result of male cultural power. It is significant that Harney is an architect who has a publisher's contract to convert houses into text, and it is revealing that Royall's stature at the ceremonial celebration of "Old Home Week" is secured by his powers of rhetoric. Although it is actually social class that separates Charity from Harney, that separation is experienced as a failure of language. Just as Charity cannot understand the French words Lucius is able to speak in the Nettleton restaurant, she abdicates control of their relationship by her incapacity to communicate with her lover in the written words of a letter, although he has been able to summon her easily with a written note. In fact, he has upbraided her inability to handle language—for losing a packet of letters from him when she first attempts to return to the Mountain. It is also important that Verena, the old woman whom Royall appoints as "another woman in the house" (30), is a figure of powerlessness precisely because she is too deaf to participate in the household exchanges conducted through language. The library is the primary symbol for the conversion of feminine space into a region subject to the control of masculine culture. Charity is supposed to be in charge of the local library, but she experiences the "queer little brick temple" (13), an "old vault" (39) constructed to house unread books and the memory of one man's minor achievement, as both a locus of confinement and a means to power. As a masculine social institution, its atmosphere of stale constraint is presented in contrast to her female relation to the natural world of the "swallow's nest above one of the [library] windows" she checks for eggs on her way in (14).

The figuration of the gothic house in Wharton's novel as a preserve of masculine authority afforded by language prefigures Jacques Lacan's interpretation of Freud's oedipal complex as the point of entry into the patriarchal system he calls "symbolic." According to Lacan, at the conclusion of the oedipal period the maturing girl enters the social system of language and culture, a phallocentric order that secures masculine predominance through binary opposition to feminine powerlessness. In *Summer*, the confident female person represented by the trope of the woman traveler is converted, through her entry into the symbolic order, into a disempowered Lacanian female "subject." Charity's marriage to her "father" suggests the Freudian nature of her transition, and the wedding trip, the gothic journey at the conclusion of the novel, symbolizes her Lacanian diminishment.

The gothic doubling of paternal and maternal figures in *Summer* structures the sexual politics of Charity's transition. Her actual father, a criminal whom Royall had prosecuted, had entreated the lawyer to rescue his infant daughter from the outlaw community residing in the area known as the Mountain. Royall had done so, giving her the name Charity as an expression of her resulting dependence on his protection and the name Royall as an indication of paternal relation. Like any child, Charity had viewed him in the private context of a parent-child relationship. When she considered him at all, Charity had thought of Mr. Royall "as someone hateful and obstructive, but whom she could outwit and dominate when she chose to make the effort." But on the occasion of his Old Home Week address, hearing bits and pieces of his speech she had "caught a glimpse of another being, a being so different from the dull-witted enemy with whom she had supposed herself to be living that even through the burning mist of her own dreams he had stood out with startling distinctness" (275).

Royall embodies two kinds of father—the private man, often insensitive to his proud and headstrong daughter, with whom Charity has struggled through her adolescence—and a second figure—Lawyer Royall, whose words convey what Lacan designates as "the law of the Father." Lawyer Royall embodies authority supported by language and culture, features of identification that elude Charity. This alternative public father, like the obscure and threatening adult male of gothic convention, stands for what Lacan defines as the *paternal metaphor*, which denotes patriarchal power, the social authority of men created by the symbolic order.

It is within this order that Charity has been named by Royall and within this order that she has functioned as an object of exchange between two powerful men, the criminal who has challenged the law and the prosecutor who has successfully defended it. For Lacan, it is the tragedy of womanhood that an individual female is reduced to a counter as the result of her entry into the dubious status of social adulthood:

> That the woman should be inscribed in an order of exchange of which she is the object, is what makes for the fundamentally conflictual, and I would say, insoluble, character of her position: the symbolic order literally submits her, it transcends her. . . . There is for her something unacceptable, in the fact of being placed as an object in a symbolic order. (Lacan qtd. by Rose, 45)

In *Summer* this subjection is enacted through the marriage ceremony. After the minister opened the Bible and signalled to the couple to draw near, Charity followed after Mr. Royall almost unwittingly:

> She had the feeling if she ceased to keep close to him, and do what he told her to do, the world would slip away from beneath her feet. . . .
>
> "I require and charge you both, as ye will answer at the dreadful day of judgement when the secrets of all hearts shall be disclosed, that

> if either of you know any impediment whereby ye may not be lawfully joined together. . . ."
>
> Charity raised her eyes and met Mr. Royall's. They were still looking at her kindly and steadily. "I will!" she heard him say a moment later, after another interval of words that she had failed to catch. She was so busy trying to understand the gestures of the clergyman that she no longer heard what was being said. After another interval the lady on the bench stood up, and taking her hand put it in Mr. Royall's. It lay enclosed in his strong palm and she felt a ring that was too big for her being slipped onto her finger. She understood then that she was married. (277–78)

The legalistic authority of the word in this passage, as established by the institution of religion; the official position of the clergyman; and the prestige of the ceremony are contrasted to Charity's growing lack of personal authority, indicated by her failure to comprehend first the words, then the gestures of the procedures that are in effect redefining her. Even her own verbal assent is suppressed in the account. Her physical positioning—following Mr. Royall out of fear—reiterates her social positioning as Lacan theorizes it. Outside of the symbolic order of authorizing patriarchal language there is no existence, but existence within it is purchased at the loss of the self, a process which Lacan calls *aphanisis*, a "lethal" division defined as "the *fading* of the subject" (qtd. by Mitchell, 16) that this passage stages. It is no wonder that the words of the marriage ceremony remind Charity of her mother's funeral service.

Given the inevitable reality of adult self-loss, according to Lacan the pursuit of the chimera of feminine identity is doomed. Such is the meaning of Charity's fruitless pursuit of the mystery of her mother. As in Cather's novel, the place of the mother looms in the distance as a location of promise or retreat. The approach to finding the mother is initially presented as an adventurous quest, but it is no accident that the primary mother figures of both novels are dead and the secondary maternal characters are inadequate. Mrs. Royall, Charity's long-deceased adoptive mother, has faded into unreality by the commencement of the story, although Charity does invoke her memory to protect herself from Royall's first sexual advances. The mother's inability to protect is reiterated in the genteel obfuscations of old Miss Hatchard, whom Charity realizes "had no help to give her" (31) at this crisis, and in the inefficacy of Verena, whose presence lends a sham token of respectability to whatever may occur in Royall's suggestively tinged "red house" (291). Charity herself, of course, eventually willingly submits to Royall's phallic will.

When Charity, pregnant and alone, finally travels up the Mountain to the place of her own birth, she is just in time to witness the crude disposal of her mother's body. The coarse condition of the corpse bears witness to the impotence of adult women and obviates any hope of succor derived from adult female identity. The death of the mothers in *Summer* represents their social debility. Although highly influential in the stage Lacan designates "imaginary," mothers are ultimately powerless, just as the wedding ceremony proves Charity to be, within the symbolic order. The funeral of Charity's mother, "the best scene in the book, and one of the most powerful Wharton ever wrote," according to R. W. B. Lewis (397), contrasts the deficiencies of the maternal imaginary with the proficiencies of the paternal symbolic. The scene is scored in contrapuntal voices: the minister's reading of the burial service interrupted by an argument about who should inherit the dead woman's stove. The power, beauty, and promise of transfiguration of the religious language points up the degradation of the greedy squabble:

> "For man walketh in a vain shadow, and disquieteth himself in vain; he heapeth up riches and cannot tell who shall gather them. . . ."
>
> "Well, it *are* his," a woman in the background interjected in a frightened whine.
>
> The tall youth staggered to his feet. "If you don't hold your mouths I'll turn you all out of here, the whole lot of you," he cried with many oaths. "G'wan minister . . . don't let 'em faze you." (252)

In "a voice of authority that Charity had never heard," Mr. Miles intones, "Our Father which art in Heaven" (256). The poverty, greed, and anarchy of the mother's world is depicted as childish competition, inappropriate behavior, and debased expression.[15] Within the Freudian economy, woman is characterized by what she lacks. In this scene, the maternal lack of the order of paternal culture is exhibited. Without a social system inscribed in language to provide stable definition, the maternal imaginary order is characterized by emotional instability—a constant fluctuation "between the extremes of love and hate towards objects which undergo corresponding shifts in value" (Silverman 158). The funeral scene demonstrates the deficiency of the imaginary order that makes Charity's capitulation to her father's symbolic authority inevitable.[16]

Summer enacts the change from girl to woman.[17] Although the movement of the plot is circular—Charity returns to the same home at the end of the novel that she tried to leave at the beginning—she comes back a different person. This change effects a revision of the meaning of Royall's house. No longer a personal limit that the daughter struggles to overcome, it has become a site of cultural restriction in which the wife must accept a protected place.[18] When Mrs. Royall returns as a willing bride to the house of her stepfather, Wharton invokes the powerful gothic figure of incest, a scandalous allusion that revokes the possibility of recuperation within the terms of domestic ideology and rescinds the auspicious movement and exploration of Miss Royall's initial empowering travel. The violation of the cultural taboo with which Wharton's novel concludes, like the attempt at self-destruction at the end of Cather's, marks the male-dominated family "home" as a location of dread.[19]

In my view, Lacan's account of female transition does not represent an irreversible situation. It is valuable precisely because it provides an historical description of the process of feminine restriction within patriarchal society in which culture and language are prominent institutions of socialization, precisely the kind of society ambivalently inhabited by Edith Wharton. Charity's gothic journey registers the horror of the inscription of a worthy woman within the radically closed space of the symbolic order, a secret Wharton knew well. Although the trope of the woman traveler signals a woman's ability to replace or displace the situations that confine her, the gothic journey symbolizes socially constructed constriction she may not be able to evade.

Through the figure of the gothic journey, Willa Cather and Edith Wharton represent rather than resolve the problem of feminine confinement in the mysterious, dangerous "house" of domestic experience in patriarchal culture. As the discouraging underside of the aspiration expressed by the trope of women's travel, the motif of gothic journey structures an alternative vision of the operation and power of domestic restriction. A Machereyan analysis of *The Profesor's House* and a Lacanian analysis of *Summer* suggest that the employment of the motif of gothic journey by these writers presents the complex problem of women's role in male-dominated culture. Biographers of both Cather and Wharton have interpreted their subjects' ambiguous treatments of gender issues as features of psychological conflicts,[20] but to analyze the gothic journey in both of these texts argues, as well, for their expression of social and cultural discord. The trope of the woman traveler in Mary Rowlandson's captivity narrative and its shadow in the gothic journey of Willa Cather's and Edith Wharton's modern texts reveal conditions and potentialities unresolvable within the authors' experiences or cultures. By contrast, Harriet Jacobs's *Incidents in the Life of a Slave Girl*, a woman's record of enforced enslavement and deliberate escape, is a record of constructive solution. In the next chapter the stops and starts in the journey of a female slave are assertions of prerogatives and objectives excluded by Southern slavery and Northern racial prejudice.

CHAPTER 4

A Woman's Place: The Politics of Space in Harriet Jacobs's Incidents in the Life of a Slave Girl

If Mary Rowlandson's captivity narrative is double-voiced, then the nineteenth-century slave narrative is polyvocal. As with the captivity narrative, the typical accompanying prefaces and postscripts by white men intend its appropriation. And, with roots in the seventeenth-century captivity genre, the eighteenth-century autobiography, and nineteenth-century sentimental fiction, the slave narrative itself also expresses complex affiliations. Henry Louis Gates, Jr., observes that its characteristic "florid asides, stilted rhetoric, severe piety, melodramatic conversation, destruction of the family unit, abuse of innocence, punishment of assertion, and the rags-to-riches success story"—conventions adapted from sentimental fiction ("Binary Oppositions," 215)—embrace ideologies of the white middle-class reading public, even as it models black freedom. Richard Slotkin argues that the black slave "undergoes a classic captivity" marked by the "inborn meekness" that leads to Christian redemption (441), whereas Robert Stepto counters the thesis of black humility. The fully achieved slave narrative he defines is a "figurative account of action, landscape, and self-transformation" (179). His language suggests that the central project of the black narrator may be understood through the generic lens of male heroic quest, while Gates compares the slave narrator to the picaresque hero ("Binary Oppositions," 214).

This emphasis on itinerant action is significant. Despite its many generic influences, the slave narrative is, in fact, a dramatic instance of the travel text. It begins by defining its endpoint as freedom to be realized in a new location, it proceeds by organizing a sequence of actions that connect the achievement of the goal to a journey to a new vicinity, and it concludes with an arrival that claims provisional attainment of the alteration desired. Reading the slave narrative as a travel text inevitably foregrounds issues of progress and process, as reflected by the black male's quest for freedom and autonomy in the autobiographical *Life of Frederick Douglass* (1845). The differing situation of the black female slave may also be perceived through attention to figurative movement in her story. Harriet Jacobs's *Incidents in the Life of a Slave Girl* (1861) is usually interpreted as an uneasy alliance between the slave narrative and the sentimental novel: a story that yokes the hazards of virtue in one genre to the project of liberation in the other.[1] But to translate this hybrid into travel literature[2] produces an account of the contradictions a female slave must negotiate, presented through the pattern of obstruction and an enactment of the conditions of liberation as process—a project distinct in object and expression from that of the male slave narrative as well as the white female text.

For *The Life of Frederick Douglass* and for subsequent slave narratives following Douglass's example, according to Gates, the achievement of freedom is predicated on the protagonist's ability to reverse his initial situation (Introduction xiii). The characteristic *chiasmus* of the slave narrative is the reversal of the institutional opposition of man to animal[3] which differentiates between slave owners and slaves on the basis of the "inhumanity" of the latter. For Douglass the means of this reversal is the performance of acts that assert the claims of manhood: the practice of aggression, the acquisition of literacy, the connection to a male group, the ability to define the conditions of his labor, and the arrival in a free territory. The gender differentiation of Jacobs's title, *Incidents in the Life of a Slave Girl*, signals important alterations in the means modeled by Douglass's masculine text.[4] Although both male and female protagonists acknowledge literacy as important, in Jacobs's text it neither identifies a self nor serves to write a "pass" north[5] as it does for Douglass. In fact, her ability to read provides yet another avenue of access for her indefatigable seducers.[6] And whereas Douglass's bond to an idealized male group is a direct source of self-worth, the connection of Jacobs's protagonist to an actual family is much more complex. Nor does physical aggression operate as a means of liberation in the female slave/travel text. Not only does her body not provide a way to freedom, it is problematized as an occupied territory. It is, instead, the protagonist's deployment of tactics of stasis and movement that negotiates necessary reversal when *woman* rather than *man* is one of the principal terms of the slave narrative chiasmus.

PLACE AND SPACE

In order to understand the complexity of Jacobs's renegotiations, we turn to Michel de Certeau's theories of revolutionary praxis. "Stories," he proclaims in *The Practice of Everyday Life*, "carry out a labor that constantly transforms spaces into places and places into spaces" (118). A *place* is, for de Certeau, a concrete realization of a political order; it is a defined location that designates stability or predictable placement within a social system. *Space*, on the other hand, "is composed of the intersections of mobile elements" which are "actuated by the ensemble of movements employed within it. Space occurs as the effect produced by the operations that orient it, situate it, temporize it, and make it function in a polyvalent unity of conflictual programs or contractual proximities" (117). The relationship between the two terms is that of dynamic contradiction: stories may perform acts of displacement against the predominant order by founding alternative spaces within the shadow of established places. Within this conceptual frame, the *travel narrative* constitutes the movement—or stasis—necessary to put this challenge of place by space into operation.

The slave/travel narrative provides a focal occasion for this kind of confrontation, and the female travel text of Harriet Jacobs demonstrates the complicated indirection such a challenge may take. Chattel slavery provides an extreme case of the colonization of place in de Certeau's sense. All locations within *Incidents in the Life of a Slave Girl* are controlled by the slave owners—the slave owner's properties, certainly, but also the homes of the slaves. Even the house of the "free" grandmother is subject to uncontrollable incursions by all whites. Dr. Flint, the slave owner, and members of his family visit without invitation on many occasions and the chapter "Fear of Insurrection" recounts destructive raids by white "rabble" (396) on all the black dwellings of the neighborhood. Yet in spite of institutionalized emplacement, the trope of women's travel in *Incidents* operates as an instance of spatial insurrection.

Douglass can claim his own body as a source of freedom through participation in masculine violence: "The battle with Mr. Covey was the turning point in my career as a slave. It rekindled the few expiring embers of freedom, and revived within me a sense of my own manhood" (298), whereas for Linda Brent, Jacobs's pseudonymous protagonist, the body becomes the locus of her most intense colonization. Her master, Dr. Flint, forty years her senior, first violates Linda's ears with "foul words" when she is fourteen: "He told me that I was his property; that I must be subject to his will in all things" (361). Slavery is for women, Jacobs explains in her appeal to principled white women of the North, a situation of "all-pervading corruption" (360), "a cage of obscene birds" (383):

> The slave girl is reared in an atmosphere of licentiousness and fear. The lash and the foul talk of her master and his sons are her teachers. When she is fourteen or fifteen, her owner, or his sons, or the overseer, or perhaps all of them, begin to bribe her with presents. If these fail to accomplish their purpose, she is whipped or starved into submission. . . . resistance is hopeless. (382)

As a sign of the impossibility of physical resistance by female slaves, slave narratives frequently present the female body in terms of torture and submission. In contradiction to Douglass's own emergent spiritual resurrection through physical violence, he presents the abjection of a slave woman through beating in the very first chapter of his autobiography:

> I have often been awakened at the dawn of the day by the most heart-rending shrieks of an old aunt of mine whom [an overseer named Plummer] used to tie up to a joist, and whip upon her naked back till she was literally covered with blood. No words, no tears, no prayers, from his gory victim, seemed to move his iron heart from its bloody purpose. The louder she screamed, the harder he whipped; and where the blood ran fastest, there he would whip the longest. He would whip her to make her scream, and whip her to make her hush; and not until overcome with fatigue, would he cease to swing the blood-clotted cowskin. (258)

It is Linda's desire to resist the sexual colonization of her body that generates the central conflict in her story. Given the nature of this conflict—social codes of external ownership set against the protagonist's refusal of internal occupation—Linda's spatial tactics in the plot of the story acquire symbolic significance. Instead of Douglass's direct action and movement—he is inspired to fight Mr. Covey and run away to the North by observing the unimpeded motion of sailboats on Chesapeake Bay—Linda must begin her tactical insurgency by employing the much more convoluted strategies of stasis.

It is notable that unlike the path of Douglass, who achieves freedom through direct flight, Linda's progress toward freedom is initially marked by important episodes in which movement is checked. Having decided to escape the strictures of slavery, she is first secreted in the home of a friend, then immured in a lumber room and then a cramped cellar of a female slave owner's dwelling, and subsequently confined for six years and eleven months in a crawl space, three feet at its greatest height, under the pent roof of her grandmother's storage shed. These confinements are described in terms of gravelike restriction. "In my narrow bed [of the cellar hole]," Linda explains, "I had but just room enough to bring my hands to my face to keep the dust out of my eyes" (428). In her garret, there is broiling heat in summer, freezing cold in winter, inadequate space for exercise, oppressive darkness, and insufficient air in all seasons.

Houston L. Baker, Jr., astutely observes that the "confined space of movement," a definitive difference between masculine slave narratives and Jacobs's feminine text (50), has tactical value: "the slave girl's total retreat from the scenes of daily life, her interiorization and enclosure that are equivalent to being buried alive" are effective limitations to the slave owner's external control (53). Valerie Smith observes that the real differences in mobility between male and female slaves provides a practical basis for the differences in their autobiographical configurations of self,[7] and she also discovers in Linda's account of the manipulation of her immobility stratagems of liberation: "confining spaces are at once prisons and exits" (xxxv). The serial confinements, according to Smith, are genuine choices that constitute paradoxical acts of empowerment.

Linda's own evaluation of her situation suggests limited political triumph: "there was no place, where slavery existed, that could have afforded me so good a place of concealment" (440). De Certeau's concept of revolutionary location theorizes the basis of her equivocal victory. Within the system of slavery, there exists no site of self-definition or control for the female slave; nevertheless, Linda, like the postmodern subjects de Certeau endorses, has created and occupied a zone of personal determination, however constricted. When Linda employs the subterfuge of sending letters to Dr. Flint that are mailed from northern locations, he travels in an attempt to secure her captivity. In this significant inversion, his mobility functions as a kind of imprisonment, whereas her immobility allows a measure of genuine control. Thus her attic functions as the spatial metaphor for a guerilla victory over slavery: it is contingent, temporary, achieved at great personal cost, but it creates a space that fashions her own agency in a social geography where that volition is absolutely debarred. A "polyvalent unity of conflictual programs" and "contractual proximities," it demonstrates the complex politics of an extraordinary achievement: the establishment of power where none existed.

Where Douglass inscribes confident reversal, Jacobs recounts provisional resistance. "You have seen how a man was made a slave; you shall see how a slave was made a man," he exclaims (294). Linda Brent's parallel declaration implies her gendered difficulties: "I would be virtuous though I was a slave" (387). The contradictions of Linda's plight are produced by the conflicting demands of the ideologies of femininity in which she participates as well as by the "patriarchal institution" (403) which she resists. As a female slave, Linda is publicly designated a kept woman whose sexuality is controlled by her owner. Privately, however, she aspires to the sexual purity a free white woman may choose as an avenue to virtue, the definitive moral choice of the northern Christian women whom Jacobs addresses in her narrative.[8] For a female slave to pursue virtue is to attempt personal instead of institutional definition. Further, Linda's role as mobile heroine of a slave/travel text conflicts with her role as a stationary mother whose primary loyalties confine her to home and family. Therefore, Linda's abortive journey may reflect a rejection of conventional options of both masculine and feminine definitions. Her prolonged stasis is a response to her unacceptable public condition as a slave as well as an expression of her unresolved personal predicament as a woman. The narrative of Linda's equally enabling and confining relationship with her grandmother represents the contingent balance of clashing constructions.

THE GOOD/BAD GRANDMOTHER

Joanne M. Braxton characterizes the grandmother unambiguously as the heroic mother who supports, shelters, and defends Linda at the same time that she provides a positive role model: Aunt Martha, who teaches the principles of "sacrifice and survival," is "the bearer of a system of values as well as the carrier of the female version of the black heroic archetype" (30). Hazel V. Carby explicates *Incidents* as a text structured between opposite portrayals of motherhood—the grandmother's honor, strength, and love counterpoised by the ignominy, weakness, and vituperation of Mrs. Flint, the slave mistress (56–57). But Jacobs's portrayal is even more complicated. As William L. Andrews notes, the grandmother plays a "complex part in Jacobs's memory as both protector and censurer, defender and judge" (*To Tell*, 249).

For example, the most painful consequence of Linda's sexual action that effectively blocks Mr. Flint's determined advances is her grandmother's abandonment on the occasion of Linda's first pregnancy. Although Linda's affair with Mr. Sands is a strategic choice that empowers her—she chooses her white lover as an act of defiance of her owner and in hopes of her purchase and future manumission—the grandmother symbolically excludes her from the female community of the family by stripping the granddaughter of her dead mother's legacy, a wedding band and a thimble, and banishing Linda from the household. Whereas Linda is inspired by her grandmother's apparently impossible achievement—feminine virtue in the face of slavery—Aunt Martha's constant councils of hopefulness, faith, and submission are always presented in the plot of *Incidents* as detrimental choices. More like her father, uncle, and brother in their stance of rebellion, Linda shares their basic impulse to actively resist Mr. Flint's demands.

The grandmother functions in the text to translate gender differences into spatial options. When Aunt Martha's son Benjamin responds to the provocation of slavery by planning and executing an escape to the North, Linda articulates on the grandmother's behalf the feminine prerogative of a stasis that stands for family connection in opposition to masculine flight. When Ben confides the reasons for his escape, she responds ambivalently, "He was right; but it was hard to give him up. 'Go,' said I, 'and break your mother's heart" (355). These passive-aggressive terms are spelled out by the grandmother herself when Linda attempts to pursue the same desperate option: "Linda, do you want to kill your old grandmother? Do you mean to kill your little, helpless children. . . . Stand by your own children, and suffer with them till death. Nobody respects a mother who forsakes her children; and if you leave them, you will never have a happy moment" (417). Even after Linda has spent her seven years in crippling confinement in the grandmother's home, Aunt Martha continues to characterize "escaping" as "forsaking": "Whenever I alluded to the subject, she would groan out, 'O, don't think of it, child. You'll break my heart'" (468). Both Linda's initial and final attempts to flee are delayed in response to the grandmother's powerful influence.

Cited by Andrews as presenting the realization of Carroll Smith-Rosenberg's homosocial female community, *Incidents in the Life of a Slave Girl* (*To Tell*, 254), in my view, more accurately expresses the complexity of African American female familial relationships. For one year, previous to his escape, Douglass reports that he lived in a perfect community of fellow slaves: "We were linked and inter-linked with each other. . . . We never moved separately. We were one" (305). At the heart of this idealized community is a band of brave young men with whom Douglass makes his confident plans. His greatest fear, realized by their capture, is the "separation" of the group (310). By contrast, Linda's halts and starts may represent the connection-separation dialectic Nancy Chodorow defined as the main feature of the mother-daughter bond in contemporary father-absent families. For Chodorow the mother's overidentification with her female child results in lifelong issues for the daughter in an ambiguous process of imperfect "individuation." And complicating this conflict is the fact that in the slave family, according to Deborah Gray White, the mother-daughter bond was historically the source of security most likely to be maintained.

Certainly, Linda's attenuated concealment in the womblike hiding place in her grandmother's home may connote a daughter's dilemma like that Chodorow describes. Unlike her "good grandmother," who represents absolute commitment to static womanhood, Linda embodies the conflict between masculine movement and feminine sessility, a contradiction expressed in the metaphor of serial confinements as a prolonged agony of suspended motion.

The symbolic register of this pattern is most explicitly realized in the episode of Linda's concealment in "Snaky Swamp." Just before Linda enters the appropriately entitled "Loophole of Retreat" in her grandmother's house, she is hidden for two days in a location that repulses her. Assisted by Peter, who had been a companion of Linda's father, she is dressed in sailor's clothing for her escape from the storeroom of her slave-owner benefactress. So disguised, she is able to move through the town with impunity to take up residence on a vessel that can shelter her only at night. During the day she must hide in a swamp that functions symbolically in the text as a kind of Negro free zone. When, later, she finally does begin her voyage North, the kindly captain observes as they pass the area of the swamp, "There is a slave territory that defies all the laws" (476). For the woman slave, however, such defiance is played out within a semiotics of female stasis that sharply contrasts the heady movement authorized by the disguise of the male traveler she adopted in the episode just preceding this new situation:

> Peter landed first, and with a large knife cut a path through bamboos and briers of all descriptions. He came back, took me in his arms and carried me to a seat among the bamboos. Before we reached it, we were covered with hundreds of mosquitoes. In an hour's time they had so poisoned my flesh that I was a pitiful sight to behold. As the light increased, I saw snake after snake crawling around us. (436)

What is most striking about this description is Linda's literal positioning as the passive recipient of the benefits and detriments of the chivalrous actions of knife-bearing Peter and the ravaging attacks of the phallic-aggressive fauna. The snakes themselves are, of course, over-determined symbols in a bad Eden, where, bigger and more plentiful than in her ordinary life, they may remind Linda of Eve's original sin against prescriptive boundaries. Within the text, snakes also signal the ubiquitous sexual threat of the slave owners and the complicity of the institutions that support them. "O, the serpent of Slavery has many and poisonous fangs!" Jacobs expostulates (392). It is doubly significant, then, that Linda almost dies from the bite of a reptile during her escape from the plantation and that her daughter Ellen, whom she is unable to care for adequately when they are brought to the plantation to be "broke in," has been wandering unsupervised in the dangerous vicinity of a large poisonous snake that had "crept from under the house" (413). Damned both if she does and does not escape, Linda experiences snakes as a contradictory representation of her slave/woman dilemma.

Just as we may read Jacobs's repeated references to snakes as conventional symbols, we should also interpret the pattern of Linda's stops and starts as part of a complex symbolic field. In *Tristes Tropiques*, that quintessential book of modern travel, Claude Lévi-Strauss discovers in the asymmetrical facial decorations of the Caduveo Indian women the expression of the basic contradictions of their societal experience: "since they could not live it out in reality, they began to dream about it . . . in their art" (196–97).[9] More than a report on her own experience, Jacobs's autobiography is art that represents the play of contradictions within which the woman traveler under slavery must struggle. Its spatial vocabulary of cessation and progression obsessively enacts the social, gender, and psychological contradictions Jacobs lived. The attenuated stasis, especially Linda's extended residence in the "little dismal hole" (467), the recurrent pattern Jacobs imposes on the varied "incidents in the life of a slave girl" in the first section of the text, may be understood as necessary Freudian dream work[10] that prepares the protagonist for action in the second section.

The obsessive repetition of restricted movement and constricted space in Jacobs's story eventually results in Linda's ability to adopt in her life and in her text the alternate pattern of productive motion with which the narrative concludes. Contemporary cultural theorist John Fiske contends that the semiotic "excess" of exaggerated presentation is a kind of parody of dominant meaning that allows for disengagement (192). In writing her autobiography twenty years after the events occurred, Jacobs imposed a hyperbolic pattern of extraordinary stasis, an exaggerated physical experience embodying the contradictions of female "virtue" she had to fully explore before she could replace this ideal with the practice of active black motherhood realized as metaphoric movement in the latter half of the text.

THE MEANING OF MOTION

In the last section of *Incidents* the pattern of recurrent stasis is replaced by a pattern of repeated movement. Unlike the voluntary excursions of some upper-class white women of the period, Linda's journeys, like her initial escape, continue to be responses to the conditions caused by Southern slavery and Northern prejudice; nevertheless they are expressions of her growing personal and political assertion of African American dignity. The serial confinements of Linda's Southern experience are replaced by her serial journeys in the North: the initial voyage to Philadelphia; the conveyance from the station; the railroad trip to New York; various excursions with her employers, including a visit to England; and several dramatic flights to New England to escape continued threats of captivity by the Flint family. This pattern of motion, like the pattern of stasis, reveals the contradictions that affect Linda, but the journeys, unlike the confinements, serve as opportunities for direct confrontation of restriction.

Her initial voyage over Chesapeake Bay on the kind of sailing vessel that so inspired Douglass, while it signifies health-bestowing freedom also recalls the omnipresent power of men and slave owners. Jacobs notes that sunshine and salt water massages almost restore the movement of her damaged limbs, but she also observes that she is "so completely" in the sailors' "power, that if they were bad men, our situation would be dreadful. . . . slavery had made me suspicious of everybody" (476). When she and her female companion are taken advantage of in negotiations for the conveyance of her luggage in Philadelphia, an observant gentleman comes to her assistance. In subsequent journeys, however, Linda herself makes use of the difficulties of travel as occasions to protest conditions that restrict her independence and disparage her value. On her railroad journey to New York she learns that being in the North does not guarantee her equality because blacks are denied first-class accommodation. Later, Linda observes and protests her restriction to second-class status on steamboats and trains, the conveyances she uses on summer trips with her employer. In one hotel she refuses petty degradation with positive results: "finding I was resolved to stand up for my rights, they resolved to treat me well. Let every colored man and woman do this and eventually we shall cease to be trampled under foot by our oppressors" (492). And the courage and self-assertiveness Linda employs in casual travels stands her in good stead in her necessary flights. On one such escape to Boston when Mr. Flint is imminent in New York, Linda locates her brother and sends for her son. On another occasion she is accompanied by her daughter Ellen, thus removing the child from bondage to relatives of the unreliable Mr. Sands.

On her return from her last flight, Linda discovers that her employer has purchased her emancipation. Although she is grateful to be removed from danger, she rails at the implications of a contract that underwrites imprisonment within the dominant system: "So I was *sold* at last! A human being *sold* in the free city of New York! The bill of sale [proves] that women were articles of traffic in New York late in the nineteenth century of the Christian religion" (512). In her final sentences Jacobs claims the "freedom" required as the conclusion of the slave narrative rather than the "marriage" expected as the culmination of the sentimental novel (513). Nevertheless it is a false liberation that satisfies the public conditions of the Fugitive Slave Law rather than the requirements of self-respect and personal agency enacted in the travel text, a condition which she meets with appropriate protest. Where Douglass's masculine travel narrative equates freedom with his arrival in New Bedford, Jacobs's feminine version presents it as a continuing process of complicated negotiation by a black woman traveler with a hostile world. Whereas Douglass's escape assumes the form of the solitary male's adventurous quest, Jacobs's journey is constantly modified by her relationships with family members and is, therefore, as much a vehicle for the exploration of issues of community as a symbol of autonomy.

A focus on the journey of the woman slave in Harriet Jacobs's *Incidents in the Life of a Slave Girl* reveals personal and political contradictions unknown to white women travelers. The trope of travel in *Incidents in the Life of a Slave Girl* delineates potentialities and purposes also unavailable in the male slave narrative and demonstrates how stasis and movement, the basic operations of the female journey, may produce subversive determination and enact the experiential articulation of engagement and change even within the complex political restriction of the female slave. The themes of stasis and movement also express contradictions within the female role and Jacobs's redefinition of it. In the course of the narrative, Jacobs abandons the unrealizable passive "virtue" inspired by white Christian women; she struggles instead toward the achievement of black motherhood that combines loving stability with the assertive activity symbolized by the woman traveler. The political objectives of the female slave narrative—to create out of the woman slave's experience and capacity the possibility for a free black family—introduce those works in the next section which fashion alternative social patterns out of female family relationships. Sarah Orne Jewett's *The Country of the Pointed Firs* and Marilynne Robinson's *Housekeeping* exploit the oppositions between masculine and feminine travel narratives to develop active and supportive female communities defined through women's journeys.

PART III

Travel as Social Reconstruction

CHAPTER 5

The Genteel Picara: The Ethical Imperative in Sarah Orne Jewett's The Country of the Pointed Firs

Standard literary handbooks define the designation *local color* in surprisingly dismissive terms. Karl Beckson and Alfred Ganz's *Reader's Guide to Literary Terms* (1960) stresses its lack of "crucial importance to the plot or for an understanding of motivation." When "the relationship of region to action" is achieved, the result is renamed "regional literature" (112). Even the latest imprint (1996) of the William Harmon and C. Hugh Holmon *Handbook to Literature* continues to stipulate that "*local color writing* lacked the basic seriousness of true realism; largely it was content to be entertainingly informative about the surface of special regions. It emphasized verisimilitude of detail without being much concerned about the truth of the larger aspects of life" (295). Although Josephine Donovan's 1983 feminist study *New England Local Color Literature* adroitly redeploys this terminology to describe a "woman's tradition" of realist aesthetics, to read Sarah Orne Jewett's greatest work in terms of its trope of travel rather than its rootedness in a locale is a better way to put into relief the special nature of her serious concern "about the truth of the larger aspects of life." Jewett's reconstitution of the travel sketch in *The Country of the Pointed Firs* is a formal means of realizing the cooperation within a female community to contrast the male travel text, which for her symbolizes isolation within commercial adventure.

"In the light of Sarah Orne Jewett's expressed affection for the rural villagers of Maine, it might seem inconsistent that she so often uses flight imagery" (36), observes Marilyn E. Mobley. Although it does celebrate the intensely local, *The Country of the Pointed Firs* is dominated by the formal and thematic trope of travel. This figure does not signal an impulse to escape, however; instead, an episodic account of female travel structures for Jewett an ethic that can blend the public and private experience of women through the exercise of mature maternal relation. What is remarkable about all the "dear old women" in all the "dear old houses"[1] of *The Country of the Pointed Firs* is their refusal to relinquish the dynamic community beyond the home. While honoring the codes and arrangements of domesticity of the local color genre, each is also significantly defined by travel.[2] Jewett's "Angels in the House" simply do not stay put!

In the 1896 version of the work, the "old women" associated with the occupation of a domestic setting include Mrs. Todd, Mrs. Blackett, and Joanna Todd. The later stories, which make use of the same characters and locale, add Mrs. Martin and Mrs. Tolland, and Mrs. Hight.[3] Of these, only Mrs. Hight, because of a crippling stroke, is immobile. Yet, significantly, Mrs. Hight's inspiriting conversation with the narrator is described in a vocabulary of travel: "between us we had pretty nearly circumnavigated the globe and reached Dunnet Landing from an opposite direction to that in which we had started" (168).

Mrs. Todd is associated with the snug cottage that serves as a kind of hermitage to the narrator, but in addition to her own frequent marches about the garden and into the countryside for herbs, she also serves as a "captain" of the narrator's excursions to Green Island and the Bowden family reunion. Further, as a young woman on the trip with the minister to Joanna's "Shell-Heap Island," it was Mrs. Todd who took over the tiller and managed the sail. Mrs. Blackett, Mrs. Todd's mother, who occupies the central domestic shrine of the work, makes the ceremonial "expedition" over land and sea to the reunion. And even "Poor Joanna," who retreated from the disappointments of the community to the isolation of her island, "took a poor old boat that had been her father's, and lo'ded in a few things, and off she put all alone, with a good land breeze right out to sea" (98). Mrs. Tolland is a "foreigner" brought back by a local sailor on a voyage to Jamaica, and Mrs. Abby Martin, poor, isolated, even deranged, managed in her youth an extraordinary journey of self-fulfillment. Convinced that the great gift of her life was a spiritual bond with Queen Victoria, who was born on her birthday and also had a husband named Albert, the "Queen's Twin" voyaged to England on her brother-in-law's vessel as a cook for the crew and managed to see her heroine review her troops in London.

Travel is the central defining quality of Jewett's characters, and it is travel which promotes an ethical perspective of involvement with the larger community. As the narrator explains, shipping was so prominent in the Maine of former years that

> among the older men and women one still finds a surprising proportion of travelers. Each seaward-stretching headland with its high-set houses, each

> island of a single farm, has sent its spies to view many a land of Eschol; one may see plain, contented old faces at the window, whose eyes have looked at far-away ports and known the splendors of the Eastern world.

These ordinary adventurers, among the "last of the Northmen's children" to follow a life of travel, put later tourists to shame, she explains. Not only did they brave high seas, but they "brought up their hardy boys and girls on narrow decks. "More than this, " she declares, "one cannot give to a young State for its enlightenment; the sea captains and the captain's wives of Maine knew something of the wide world, and never mistook their native parishes for the whole" ("The Queen's Twin," 201).[4]

Yet the celebratory rhetoric of the voyage of exploration is modified in this passage by constant contradiction. The islanded farms contrast the unbounded ocean, the old are set against the young, and the working sailors of former times oppose the modern tourist. The primary juxtaposition is that of female domesticity and male adventure. Such terms as *spies*, may betray the unacknowledged anomaly of mothers and children on board for the heroic male journey. But, in fact, Jewett's contradictory passage serves to redefine the purpose of such adventuring. Instead of the fruits of the male voyage of discovery—wealth, freedom, excitement—Jewett endorses contentment and *enlightenment*, a term that for the author denotes the perspective gained through the active practice of inclusivity. The vocabulary of a male topos has been modified here by Jewett's insistent female ethic. At the heart of this remarkable passage is the insistence on the value of a world view through which both men and women can locate themselves and come to terms with that location. The object of that view is what I am defining as the ethical imperative of Jewett's mature fiction.

The trope of the journey as Jewett constructs it combines inner requirements with outer possibilities. It provides a bridge between the house and the world, which all her women traverse. That traversal fashions an ethic combining empowerment with care in the communal vision that is the theme of Jewett's text. A semiotics of travel, with its rudimentary requirement of a traveler, a journey, and a territory, insists on the active engagement of the needs of the self with the exigencies of the world. A traveling woman, then, must inevitably encounter along the way the social facts of her subjective reality, and the adventure and moral benefit of such an encounter are addressed by the travel structure of *The Country of the Pointed Firs*.

THE GENTEEL PICARA

Jewett's earliest education in literature reflects the tastes of both her parents. Her mother introduced her to Jane Austen, and throughout her life

Jewett was happy to note the parallels between Austen's fiction and certain interludes in the social life of South Berwick.[5] Her mother also shared with her daughter her interest in American female writers of the period, and Jewett's encounter with Harriet Beecher Stowe's *The Pearl of Orr's Island* (1862) in early adolescence was a watershed moment that allowed her to "to follow eagerly the old shore paths from one gray, weather-beaten house to another" (quoted by Cary, *Deephaven*, Introduction, 11). Although commentators generally assume that the series of sketches that comprise *The Country of the Pointed Firs* imitate the local color writing she grew up on,[6] there may be another source for its peripatetic structure. As Josephine Donovan observes, "One cannot overestimate the influence of her father in the formulation of Sarah Orne Jewett's literary standards" (*Sarah Orne Jewett* 4), and his endorsement of tempered realism was based on the travel texts of Cervantes' *Don Quixote* and Sterne's *A Sentimental Journey*.[7] While Jewett indicates that she was in her youth unable to appreciate these narratives of episodic wanderings, there is no reason to assume that Dr. Jewett's recommended reading, like his literary advice, did not influence her maturity.

In his comments on the generic status of *The Country of the Pointed Firs*, Paul D. Voelker observes that it "could always be related to the picaresque form" (238), and about the time she was writing it, William Dean Howells, whose opinions she respected, was suggesting that the picaresque was a fitting structure for the depiction of American experience (Wicks 14). Although Jewett was no student of the classic genre, her adaptation of the picaresque mode in *The Country of the Pointed Firs* allows her to foreground the dynamic process of moral construction evolving from a chain of visits. In formal terms, Jewett may be understood to be writing what Claudio Guillen defines as a picaresque myth: "an essential situation or significant structure" derived from the historical genre (qtd. by Wicks 38). The picaresque structure minimally includes (1) a first-person narrator, the picaro, who is an outsider in the society through which he travels, (2) an episodic plot based on the journey of the picaro through a social world, (3) a realistic vocabulary and setting, and (4) a satiric perspective. Jewett's work may be seen to adapt these key features.

It is the necessity for the division of subject and object, the separation of the picaro and the world he experiences, that accounts for what might otherwise appear to be the condescension of Jewett's narrator in the first short chapter, which describes her return to Dunnet Landing, a place, as she describes it, of "elaborate conventionalities" and "childish certainty of being the centre of the universe" (47). The unnamed narrator, having first glimpsed the locale from the deck of a yacht, is an outsider, but unlike the picaro, she is not a social inferior. The issue raised by her difference is the question of the genuine source of worth. From the perspective of wealth and social position, a writer from the wider world has a distinct advantage, but from the point of view of moral education, the narrator's status is fluid. In the rented schoolhouse where she goes to write, her actions mimic those of "the great authority" of the teacher even as she shares the expectant humility of the "small scholar" (53). Further, the initial outside status of the narrator introduces the central theme of the book: the necessity of establishing social contact.

In an important article, which explores Jewett's novel as the geographical expression of Carol Gilligan's care ethic, Elizabeth Ammons describes the moral imperative of the text as a home-seeking journey. But the 1896 text ends with the departure of the narrator at the end of her vacation, and although she sets off from Mrs. Todd's house and apparently returns to it after each excursion into the wider community, the emphasis in the text is on the expedition rather than the return. The home-seeking journey results in the establishment of a static safe haven, while the episodic plot of the picaresque journey as Jewett constructs it emphasizes the experiential encounter as ethics in action.

In "The Origin of Morality in Early Childhood Relationships," Carol Gilligan and Grant Wiggins define ethical development as a constructive and cumulative practice.[8] They explain that the adolescent girl, whose maturation makes it apparent that she is no longer a dependent child, must fashion a synthesis between issues of self-empowerment and attachment. Wishing "to be able to disagree, to be different without losing contact with others, leads outward in girls' experience from family relationships to relationships with the world" (120). The girl, according to Gilligan, is seeking "to affirm truths about herself by joining those truths to her mother's experience" in order to validate her own perceptions through connection ("Exit-Voice," 155). Gilligan's postoedipal girl, in both method and motive, is very much like Jewett's narrator, who is also attempting an integration of self and world through mature maternal relations. Gilligan emphasizes ethics as an integrative process, an emphasis captured in Jewett's metaphor of a chain that links the people along the route to the Bowden family reunion.

As the narrator travels with Mrs. Blackett, she observes in the older woman's responsive welcome at various houses along the way evidence of "the constant interest and intercourse that had linked the far island and these scattered farms into a golden chain of love and dependence" (118). One stop implies the moral operation of all the others the three travelers make at various homesteads on their route. Observing that one of the old farmhouses is occupied by a new family, Mrs. Todd pauses to water the horse and readjust the checkrein. The "thin, anxious mistress" of the farm emerges to greet her visitors "with wistful sympathy to hear what news" they bring. When Mrs. Blackett gently suggests that they may be intruding, their hostess brings out a plate of freshly baked doughnuts as a gesture of hospitality. Mrs. Todd observes that although it has been apparent that all the women of the region are baking doughnuts, "you're the first that has treated us," while the farmer's wife "flushes with pleasure." Before their departure, the visitors, upon learning that the woman will also be attending the reunion, have invited her to sit with them at the gathering. On their way they deliberate her kinship and consider the possibilities of her incorporation into their own complex network (119). Soon afterward Mrs. Todd extends similar solicitude on a visit to a favorite ash tree. The last time she was in this neighborhood, the tree was "kind of drooping and discouraged," she remarks. "Grown trees act that way sometimes, same's folks; then they'll put right to it and strike their roots into new ground and start all over again with real good courage" (120).

All the visits in the book operate on the several key principles observable in these two examples: that life is hard and imposes painful isolation, that growth and courage are required, and that these qualities can be supported through the conscious and tactful establishment of mutual bonds of human appreciation and empathy. The reiteration of visits and the important arrangements for travel that make them possible underscore the significance of the moral principles they demonstrate and the narrator's requirement of a process for assimilating them. Each visit seeks to perceive the individual needs of the host—as Mrs. Blackett understands the farm woman's need to establish some claim of intimacy by sharing her doughnuts—and to respond supportively. Thus, independence and connection are both honored. The narrator learns again and again what the girls in Gilligan's study sought to internalize: that individuality does not preclude sympathy, and that mothers and daughters can cooperate to construct a social ethic that works in the world as well as in the home.

A second metaphoric device of the episodic travel narrative employed by Jewett is the use of the promontory description. In *Imperial Eyes: Travel Writing and Transculturation*, Mary Louise Pratt exposes this common Romantic and Victorian device as a vicious form of co-option. In her analysis, a European explorer looking down from a great height describes a panoramic native landscape in a rhetorical strategy she labels "the-monarch-of-all-I-survey genre" (202). His object is to incorporate the local into the European by recasting the landscape in terms of his own discourse. Specifically, the view is "estheticized" to appeal in terms of landscape painting to European sensibilities; his semantic descriptions reconstitute the unknown in terms of the "explorer's home culture"; and his painterly depiction is meant to establish a relation of mastery of the scene: if he does not have the "power to possess" the new world he encounters, he does claim the prerogative of its evaluation (204–205). An excerpt from Richard Burton's rendition of his first sight of Lake Tanganyika in *The Lake Regions of Central Africa: A Picture of Exploration* (1860) provides an example:

> To the south, and opposite the long, low point, behind which the Malagarzi River discharges the red loam suspended in its violent stream, lie the bluff headlands and capes of Ugahha, and as the eye dilates, it falls upon a cluster of outlying islets, speckling a sea horizon. Villages, cultivated lands, the frequent canoes of the fishermen on the waters, and on nearer approach the murmurs of the waves breaking upon the shore, give a something of variety, of movement, of life to the landscape, which like the fairest prospects in these regions, wants but a little of the neatness and finish of art—mosques and kiosks, palaces and villas, gardens and orchards—contrasting with the profuse lavishness and magnificence of nature, and diversifying the unbroken coup d'oeil of excessive vegetation to rival, if not to excel, the most admired scenery of the classic regions. (qtd. by Pratt 203)

Moving from the world to the self, Burton dominates the landscape, judges it inferior to his own ideal view of what it should be, and proposes its corrective modification by adding a few graceful touches from his own culture—"palaces and villas, gardens and orchards"—to improve it.

Jewett's travel narrative makes frequent use of the promontory perspective. For example, the narrator looks at the funeral from the elevated perspective of the schoolhouse at the beginning of the novel and ends with a view from the same site; there are two vista views in the Green Island sequence, and the Bowden family reunion is introduced through a panoramic view, but her rhetorical strategy provides a marked contrast to that which Pratt describes. The description of the scene that unfolds on the way to the reunion, like Burton's a water view, is typical. The narrator describes emerging from the shade of the forest road to suddenly glimpse a "wonderful great view" of cultivated fields and glittering bay below, which stretched toward "distant shores like another country" and contained much activity: a schooner sailing away from a shore village and many "flitting sailboats." "It was a noble landscape," the narrator observes, and with vision dimmed by the forest road, she "could hardly take it in."

Mrs. Todd identifies the scene as the "upper bay": "Those farms 'way over there are all in Fessenden. Mother used to have a sister that lived up that shore." If the family set out as early as possible on a summer morning, they couldn't reach the sister's place until late in the afternoon, "even with a fair, steady breeze, and you had to strike the time just right so as to fetch up 'long o' the tide and land near the flood. 'Twas a ticklish business."

Mrs. Blackett explains wistfully that she and her "dear sister" had been separated by marriage, each with her own family and her own cares, but they were "always lookin' forward to the time we could see each other more." Once in a while the sister could visit Mrs. Blackett's island for several days while her husband fished; and one time she came with her two children "and made him some flakes right there and cured all his fish for winter. We did have a beautiful time together, sister an' me; she used to look back to it long's she lived" (120–21).

The contrast to Burton is remarkable. First, although Jewett is evidently aware of her participation in a shared artistic tradition—indeed, her diction acknowledges depiction of a "noble landscape"—she deliberately abdicates the powerful control Burton insists upon. At the end of the first paragraph, despite her authorship of the visual description, the narrator insists that she can hardly "take it in," a rhetorical gesture meant to situate the locus of authority in the scene itself. The narrator in fact resists incorporation of the view by insisting that it is "another country."

Further, the response to the landscape is not rendered as the exclusive property of the narrator, but serves as the basis of a shared view developed out of three differing perspectives. Mrs. Todd assigns a personal meaning to the scene based on her geographical and nautical experience and her participation in family life. Mrs. Blackett responds to the scene as an emotional symbol. Although both Jewett and Burton make use of the landscape painter's device of miniaturization to signal the observer's controlling point of view, it is significant that the narrator's esthetic perspective, unlike Burton's, does not dominate but, instead, opens the scene to alternative readings. The tripartite scene moves, as does Burton's description, from the foreign to the domestic, but Jewett's multivalent presentation does not insist on the superiority of this favored position. The depiction of panoramic landscape, a staple of Jewett's travel structure, as this example demonstrates, reinforces the necessary interplay between the world and the self as a means of establishing an ethic of cooperation.

THE PICARESQUE ALTERNATIVE

The main task of the picaresque narrative, according to Barbara A. Babcock, is to speak the truth about society from an "inverse perspective" (95). For Josephine Donovan the parodic function of the picaresque form is an important influence in local color writing, which she understands as a realistic alternative to women's sentimental writing. She points specifically to "the satire of the 'female-quixote' figure in the women's tradition" (*Local Color* 11)[9] as a critique of the romance plot of the sentimentalist bourgeois novel whose heroine is an economically and socially powerless woman.[10] For Donovan the antirealism of Jewett's local color literature contrasts an "alienated world of real experience" to the "transcending vision of a supportive, fulfilling community" (*Local Color*, 99). The positive community of *The Country of the Pointed Firs* is, however, in Donovan's view, an elegiac recreation of a lost "matriarchal world" of the "foremothers" of Jewett's generation "and their longing to reconnect with it" (*Local Color* 113). A similar sense of preoedipal loss has intrigued feminist scholars of nineteenth-century fiction by women and influenced studies of Jewett's fiction.[11]

Basing her findings on the theories of object-relations psychologists, Sally McNall discovers in the painful persistence of the preoedipal relationship the basis of nineteenth-century women's fiction: "Unable to accept the loss of the 'good' mother, [the girl child] searches endlessly to project the image onto another, and to recreate it in herself. Unable to believe that she can separate from the 'bad' mother, she tries endlessly to propitiate or make reparations to projections of this image" (120–21). Influenced by Nancy Chodorow's theory of a lifelong bond between mothers and daughters that retains important features of their earliest attachment, Sarah Way Sherman argues in her 1989 *Sarah Orne Jewett: An American Persephone* that the principal concern of Jewett's fiction is the reestablishment of the bond with a lost and idealized mother. But while mother figures and daughter figures are central to *The Country of the Pointed Firs*, their relation is that of engagement with individuals rather than imaginary replication of lost projections. Instead of recreating the uncomfortable cycle described by McNall, *The Country of the Pointed Firs* is a corrective to earlier women's genres. In Jewett's work the narrator and Mrs. Todd do not take on the qualities of the distant figures of childhood obsession. Adult women, they are engaged in a cooperative enterprise to construct the ethical arrangements of social experience.

The form and value of these new arrangements are indicated through contradictory male and female travel narratives included in Jewett's text, with the "chain of visits" ethic a corrective to the masculine journey. The normative version of the travel narrative is portrayed satirically in Captain Littlepage's sea story, "The Waiting Place." Although the narrator is compassionate, the old captain's name—which hints at the deprecation of his literary product—and his apparent senility frame his narrative for a satiric reading. The gender role reversal at work in the depictions of all the men in the novel further erodes the authority of his tale.[12] Captain Littlepage is, indeed, cast as a male version of the female antiquixote figure who, like her, has "overset his mind with too much reading" (22). The captain's story, like Edgar Allan Poe's *The Narrative of A. Gordon Pym of Nantucket*, tells of a fantastic journey beyond the charted regions. After his own ship was wrecked, Captain Littlepage spent a dreary winter with a Scotchman, old Gafflett, who had "shipped on a voyage of discovery" (63–64) only to wind up in "the next world to this," a spectral region "neither living nor dead" (64), inhabited by "fog-shaped men" who finally attack Gafflett's fellow seamen like "incessant armies." Littlepage, at Gafflett's behest, and to the detriment of his own career, sought to convince the scientific community of the actual existence of this "waiting-place between this world and the next" (65).

Littlepage has served as an emblem for traditional critics of the decay of the shipping industry, the devastation of the male population in New England as a result of the Civil War, and the development of the factory system, which robbed the region of its youthful population. Warner Berthoff, for instance, in 1959 termed the description of the waiting place as "in some ways the boldest and most decisive passage in the book, for it secures that reference to the life of male action and encounter without which the narrator's sympathy for backwater Dunnet would seem myopic, sentimental" (153). For Berthoff, the male journey, even in its decay, supplies the standard. In his reading, the vitality of the women of the novel is a "sacrifice required for survival . . . to give up a woman's proper life and cover the default of the men" (149–50). Francis Fike, on the other hand, countering Berthoff's emphasis on dissolution with a celebration of the universal and "natural resources of human character" he discovered in the novel, at the same time resuscitates the spent Captain as the misunderstood prophet of "a myth of immortality" (175).

But it is the response of the narrator to Littlepage that supplies the best index to a genuinely critical reception of his tale. The narrator resents his interruption and responds with tact rather than interest during most of his recitation. She appears to disapprove of his complaints about his crew and the conditions of the voyage, and she is actually engaged only during Gafflett's mysterious tale within the tale. Littlepage is depicted as unaware of the narrator's needs and generally oblivious to the world around him. He is, for example, totally unconscious of a swallow that enters the schoolroom and beats its wings against the walls before escaping while he is talking.[13] Littlepage is presented as a product of the mercantile world of shipping, a world that generates metaphoric encounters of militancy and death. He is described as characteristically "pathetic, scholarly" rather than "alert" and engaged (66), and Gafflett, whose cause he identifies with, is "crippled," "brooding," and distrustful (63). Littlepage appears palpably isolated, even among the group of mourners in which the narrator first observes him, and he accounts for his habit of reading as a result of the customary nautical requirement keeping the ship's captain from the fellowship of the crew. In the absence of human connection, he has turned to books for company. Yet despite his profession he strikes the narrator as a particularly inept traveler, as if "he was meant to hop along the road of life rather than to walk" (58). It is significant that the antisocial journey described by Littlepage leads to the stasis of the "waiting place" in contrast to the movement of the narrator's serial excursions into social engagement.

The masculine journey of life, as represented by Littlepage, suggests constriction and isolation even to the point of death. Unlike the feminine journeys of "enlightenment," which include the wives of sea captains and lead to enlarged perspective and contentment, the male journey of Gafflett's tale leads to a dark and disturbing place. Unlike the evolving community of feminine sympathy the narrator discovers in her travels, Littlepage experiences Gafflett's paranoid suspicion and the hostile rejection of the learned societies with whom he shares Gafflett's account, and his own general attitude of narcissistic self-absorption is directly opposed to the striking inclusivity of the feminine journeys. The narrator, working alone on her own writing in the schoolhouse at the beginning of the novel, must recognize an uncomfortable similarity to her scholarlike and lonely guest. She experiences in Littlepage's narrative a parodic version of attitudes she herself has absorbed from the world outside of Dunnet Landing and to which her travels in the text are meant as corrective alternatives. Captain Littlepage's journey, which is introduced within the context of a funeral, condemns a conventional ethics of success without community, knowledge without human use, and power as personal entitlement rather than mutual benefit.

Unlike the male picaro the narrator does not signal a constant counterpoint to the community through which she travels. Instead, she learns to substitute for the myth of male journey, which is her initial orientation, a new paradigm of female travel, indigenous to the maternal teachers whom she encounters on her way. That journey is neither the universal entitlement Fike suggested nor a simple stopgap in the face of the failure of male heroic enterprise as Berthoff defined it. It is an incremental structure for the development of a moral system of mutual support and connection that contradicts dominant practice. As feminist historians have pointed out, periods of confusion in male history—such as the decline of New England in Sarah Orne Jewett's lifetime—have frequently opened the way for the participation of women in the construction of civilization.[14] The ethical imperative of the genteel picara of *The Country of the Pointed Firs* is an example of such a project.

MATURE DEPENDENCE

Just as unwitting masculinist bias may read the decrepitude of setting as the sign of irredeemable loss rather than radical opportunity, feminist inclination has led to a view of the aging mothers of Jewett's work as preoedipal projections rather than postoedipal partners. But Nancy Chodorow's influential work may also support the latter view. In her 1974 essay on "Family Structure and Feminine Personality," she contrasts the exclusive mother-daughter relation of the Western middle classes to the communal bond of matrifocal societies defined as "mature dependence."[15] Whereas the offspring of contemporary families vacillate between the unacceptable polarities of "infantile dependence" and "forced independence," daughters in matrifocal societies develop identities separate from those of their mothers but nonetheless embedded in an ongoing connection with mothers and other adult women, their societal functions, kinship relationships, and social status (62).

The necessary shift from the exclusive mother-daughter relation to that of the daughter within a maternal community is outlined in Jewett's text by the visit of Mrs. Fosdick to the narrator and Mrs. Todd. The imagery of the account designates Mrs. Fosdick metonymically as "a strange sail on the far horizon" who enters the snug harbor of the intimate relation of the narrator and her hostess, an intimacy presented in imagery suggestive of the child in the womb: "I had been living in the quaint little house with as much comfort and unconsciousness as if it were a larger body, or a double shell, in whose simple convolutions Mrs. Todd and I had secreted ourselves" (89). Mrs. Todd uses the presence of Mrs. Fosdick to tactfully foster a "sincere" friendship that includes both her new friend and her old in an enlarged community of sympathetic and active visitors (56) that defines the postoedipal maternal relations of Jewett's text. The diction of the account casts the narrator as the girl child awaiting with some anxiety the acknowledgment and approval of the guest. Mrs. Fosdick functions as a postoedipal mother[16] who, significantly, has outlived "a large family of sons and daughters" to become a "woman of the world" and an "entertaining pilgrim" who welcomes the narrator as a fellow traveler, an equal participant in the triadic community forged by the three women for the interval of the visit. The postoedipal mother is defined by her facilitation of communal cooperation instead of preoedipal dependence. Combining the virtues of home and voyage, she is Jewett's most emblematic genteel picara, a syncretic figure whose serial embarkations and arrivals serve to fashion an inclusive ethic in which domestic fidelity is enriched by the "enlightenment" (92) of the engaged journey.

Just as the women travelers of Sarah Orne Jewett's *The Country of the Pointed Firs* fashion a female community out of the revision of the mother-daughter relation as an ethical pattern, Marilynne Robinson's *Housekeeping* uses the trope of women's travel to examine and redefine the mother-daughter relationship and to revise women's roles and expectations. But unlike Sarah Orne Jewett's women travelers who can combine the stability of the home place with the mobility of journey in an ethics of renewable female community, the protagonists of Marilynne Robinson's 1981 novel must reject stationary domesticity to establish supportive female relationship beyond the control of masculine social regulation. Extending the topos of the story of the itinerant wanderer to include the female, *Housekeeping* expounds transience as a formal and narrative trope.

CHAPTER 6

Sisters of the Road: Transience as Theme and Form in Marilynne Robinson's Housekeeping

Just as the seventeenth-century captive and the nineteenth-century escapee of previous chapters have transgressed the ideologies of feminine stasis and masculine movement to enact alternative priorities, the female vagrants of Marilynne Robinson's 1981 novel *Housekeeping* adapt the outcast situation of the historical male hobo to challenge contemporary gendered values vested in the meaning of maternity, the stability of the domestic setting, and the sanctity of domestic order. Paradoxically, *Housekeeping* demonstrates that the woman traveler can reinvigorate the domestic promise of authentic female relationship and realizable feminine options only by leaving behind what home has come to represent.

Tramps, bums, hoboes, vagrants, migrant workers[1]—the army of itinerant laborers created by economic upheavals in the first several decades of the American twentieth century—for all their unprecedented homelessness and experiential poverty did little to alter the basic tenets of a bourgeois cult of domesticity retained from the previous century. The vaunted wanderlust and celebrated freedom of the vagrant lifestyle is countered by actual domestic investment—both in terms of sentimental attachment and/or economic support of home and family—a pattern dominant in male hobo culture, and, more surprising, evident even in the autobiography of the famous female vagabond known as Box-Car Bertha.

Woodie Guthrie's exemplary ballad "Hard Travellin'" outlines the standard features of male itinerant labor: constant movement in search of masculine employment and the idealization of a feminine world of home and sexuality. "Hard Travellin'" begins with a lively description of the most popular means of conveyance, riding the rails:

> I've been ridin' those fast rattlers. I thought you knowed.
> I been ridin' them flat wheelers, way down the road.
> I've been ridin' those dead enders, blind passengers,
> kickin' up cinders.

The rest of the song recounts an assortment of jobs undertaken in various locations: running a "pressure drill" "muckin'" "six feet of mud"; "workin' at Pittsburgh Steel" "dumpin' red-hot slag," "blastin'," "firin'," "pourin'"; "harvestin'" hay from North Dakota to Kansas for "a dollar a day." Despite the transience necessary to give him access to employment, Guthrie's protagonist is like most men of his era. He enters the world of work in order to make a living, and his primary identity is derived from his activity in that world, but although the necessity of finding employment takes him far from feminine domestic comfort, he evidently values it: "Heavy load and a worried mind, / Lookin' for a woman that's hard to find" (qtd. in Allsop vii).[3] In fact, one of the likely sources for the derivation of the term *hobo* is "home-bound."[4]

Even the existence of increasing numbers of women travelers did little to annul the ideological implications of masculine movement and feminine sessility. According to Nels Anderson's 1923 sociological study *The Hobo*, itinerant women were at that time extremely rare: "Tramping is a man's game," he explained, because women were prevented from traveling by the "conventions" of the society as well as the "inconveniences and hazards" of the road (137). Nevertheless, in *Sister of the Road: The Autobiography of Box-Car Bertha*, as told to Ben Reitman, published in 1937, her memoir of fifteen years as a female hobo, Bertha Thompson recalls two transient women she met during her childhood whose pride, freedom, unconventionality, and facility in hopping a freight left a lasting impression: "The world was easy, like that," Bertha observes on the basis of their example. "Even to women. It had never occurred to me before" (14). By fifteen, she herself had joined a growing sisterhood of radicals, anarchists, and other traveling women for whom actual female movement provided alternative feminine options. Fifteen years later, she estimates their number at about 13,600 (9).

Bertha's own experience as hobo, hitchhiker, socialist, free lover, commune member, unwed mother, shoplifter, prostitute, and social researcher certainly challenges domestic ideals, yet much in her account indicates the perseverance of traditional gender ideology. For example, although many found ways of refusing, Bertha points out that women "on the bum," unlike men, were generally expected to pay their way with sexual favors, and the ideology of sexual and domestic feminine roles affects her own behavior in significant ways. In recounting the story of how she became a prostitute, independent Bertha explains her decision in the discordant terms of romantic melodrama. When a manipulative pimp named Bill approached her for a date, he had already declared his intention to put her in his "stable." Even knowing this, she dreamily pressed "his roses to my breast," praying, "it must not be." She "tingles" at his look, is "magnetized" by his touch, and willingly goes to work in a Chicago brothel at his instigation (164–66).

The sentimental feminine helplessness in the face of exploitative "love" here, so strikingly different from Bertha's usual attitude of proud agency, is matched by the maudlin return to motherhood imagined as spiritual salvation which concludes the book:

> "Oh, darling, I'm going home," I said eagerly. "I'm going home to my baby. It sounds silly, but I feel as though I'm going home for the first time in my life!"
>
> "Bless you, dear," he said, and kissed me. . . .
>
> Crazily I found one of the Home Colony hymns going through my head: "I'm saved, I am. I know I am. I don't give a damn 'cause I know I am" (279).[5]

Bertha's actual experience, of course, also provides an alternative "hymn" to the adventure and freedom of female travel:

> I went on hitch-hiking east [in 1934], purposely stopping at shelters, and I found that a great army of women had taken to the road, young women mostly, gay, gallant, sure that their sex would win them a way about, far too discontented to settle down in any one place. Their stories were very much the same—no work, a whole family on relief, no prospects of marriage, the need for a lark, the need for freedom of sex and living, and the great urge to know what other women were doing. (251–52)

Nonetheless, her rhetoric in crucial instances witnesses a continuing confusion about the meaning and value of female domestic stability. The exposure of the limitations of a destructive domestic ideology so deeply embedded in women's psyches that even a Box-Car Bertha must endorse it and the replacement of that ideology with a praxis of female travel is the purpose of Marilynne Robinson's *Housekeeping*. By introducing the possibility of female transience as narrative subject and method, the novel deconstructs the cultural concepts that delimit women's place and enacts the construction of an alternative psychology of female agency in a revised feminine family.

FREUD'S GRANDDAUGHTER

Housekeeping centers on what Nancy Chodorow's influential argument in *The Reproduction of Mothering* posits as the central issue of female development: the daughter's separation from the mother and the terms of her own individuation. Through obsessive reconstruction of the motif of maternal abandonment, the novel represents the primal event of preoedipal psychoanalytic theory, the infant's loss of the projection of the fully satisfying "good" mother described by object relations psychology.

In terms of the plot, Helen, the mother of Ruthie and Lucille, has inexplicably borrowed her neighbor's car, driven from her residence to her mother's home in Fingerbone, left the little girls on her mother's porch with a box of Graham crackers to entertain them until the grandmother's return from church, and driven on to plunge into the deep and deadly waters of the lake that is the chief landmark of the town. After their mother's suicide, the children reside with their grandmother until her own death. The maiden aunts to whom they are next entrusted summon, by means of classified ads in newspapers across the nation, Helen's transient sister, Sylvie, and with evident relief consign Helen's adolescent daughters to her care in the grandmother's residence. Despite her love for her charges, Sylvie is ill-suited to the domestic vocations of motherhood and housekeeping as they are conceived by the town of Fingerbone, and the meanings of her failures and adaptations comprise the theme of the book: the reconstruction of female relations.

Those meanings are both psychological and cultural. At one level, the book is an exercise in grief work that differs significantly from the Freudian depiction of the same issues. In *Beyond the Pleasure Principle*, Freud observed that his three-year-old grandson responded to the temporary absence of his mother by inventing a game with a reel to control her abandonment by rehearsing her departure and her return. Throwing out the spindle, the little boy would shout "Fort!" (away) and "Da!" (here) as he pulled it back again, a representation that grants him imagined power to control his mother's comings and goings. Freud's exposition of this event suggests a masculine economy of control comparable to the intolerable regulation experienced by the characters of *Housekeeping* through the threatening interventions of the local sheriff who enforces the social regulations of Fingerbone. Maternal abandonment is the initiatory event of Freud's parable and Robinson's novel, but instead of the terms of closure Freud's grandson imposes, *Housekeeping* is styled as a radically open text, a dream-layered novel of painful circumstances expressed rather than foreclosed.

French feminist theory addresses the need for a pattern of development with important differences from that which Freud theorized. In "Toward an Ethic of Mothering: Luce Irigaray on Mothering and Power," Eleanor H. Kuykendall evaluates Irigaray's credo of the mother-daughter relationship as a source of "transformative power and mutuality" (263) unavailable through the Freudian psychosocial structure. Although Kuykendall faults Irigaray for her essentialist bias and her failure to offer a concrete political basis for her recommendations, Irigaray, Kuykendall acknowledges, does mythologize the principles for "a feminist ethic of nurturance" (264) that evades "the psychic separation between mother and daughter required by patriarchy" (267):

> The first [principle] is that the power exercised toward the nurtured (as by a mother toward a child) be not merely dominant or controlling but primarily healing, creative, and transformative. The second principle, which complements the first, is that the relationship between the nurturer and the nurtured be not merely symmetrical, but at least potentially mutual and reciprocal. (264)

For Irigaray this kind of relationship is not created through the oedipalization of the male child Freud defines, but may be approached through the relational structure of mother/daughter preoedipal experience. "The Otherness of the infant is wounding to both [males and females], according to Irigaray, who writes that our irreparable wound is the cutting of the umbilical cord, and not, as Freud had fantasized, castration."[6]

Freud, of course, did not live to fully examine the significance of the preoedipal wound, but *Housekeeping* is a mythic expression of its formative significance. The central characters, memorable as personalities, are primarily expressions of psychological positions in a preoedipal drama. Helen symbolizes the absent ideal mother. Her abandonment expresses the impossibility of an infant's total satisfaction. Sylvie the "drifter" (31) represents the inevitably inadequate mother of actual experience. Her itinerancy embodies a mother's unavoidable unavailability to the narcissistic demands of infancy. The daughter's prerogatives are similarly split. Lucille signifies the retention of the ideal through rejection of actuality. She abandons the contingent conditions of her chaotic household for the invented conventional order of life with her home economics teacher. An imaginative ability to relate to the imperfect mother available to her is enacted by Ruthie through her growing connection to Sylvie. The trope of women's travel, which ultimately unites them, structures their rejection of idealized restriction and fashions the enactment of the terms of the transformative, healing, reciprocal ethic Irigaray defines. Although I am not arguing that *Housekeeping* is a novel written to illustrate the theoretical positions of the philosophy known as French Feminism, it is productively approached through the terminology and psychopolitics of that movement.[7] Encountered from the perspective of Irigarayan principles, Ruthie is the granddaughter Freud never had!

The structural doubling of the novel—two opposing sets of "mothers" and "daughters"—exemplifies the characteristic splitting of preoedipal object relations. Further evidence of this psychological stage is the virtual excription of postoedipal male-female roles and relationships in the novel.[8] Object-relations theorists focus on the influential emotional patterns emerging from the earliest experience of childhood. During the first months, an infant feels only blissful symbiosis with an undifferentiated mother, but as a realization of the mother's separateness develops, contrary images are born. The "good" mother is that being who is perpetually available for the complete satisfaction of all needs, while the "bad" mother stands for the experience of the mother's unavailability or her inability to fully meet all the infant's requirements. She is the omnipresent "missing" mother Mickey Pearlman identifies as the most striking characteristic of contemporary women's fiction (1–8) and the constant feature of American female fiction of the past three centuries, according to Sally McNall. All popular women's fiction in America from the seventeenth century to the 1980s, McNall asserts sweepingly, has been an expression of the unsolved problem of the preoedipal mother-daughter relationship:

> These stories, from early to late, are about the fear of doing without, of being without, one exclusive love, and about the anger that accompanies this fear. In these stories, possibility after possibility is sacrificed, to prevent the realization of that fear. . . . I have traced the terror and rage reflected in women's fictions to its origins in the girl child's inability to fully relinquish her unintegrated fantasy images of her earliest love, her mother. (120)

In the contemporary women's literature McNall studied, the daughter, "like every heroine of popular fiction, suffered a loss with which she cannot come to terms. So she commences a journey which she expects will explain her inner emptiness, reveal to her the secrets of her inner world." In women's romances, this quest fails, McNall explains, because the heroine replaces her desire for lost perfection with spurious images borrowed from popular culture: "a 'normal family' as defined by infantile wishes, television and the experts" (124). *Housekeeping*—with its focus on maternal loss and its formal emphasis on the female journey—retains comparable concerns and methods, but instead of the unexamined propitiation of the good/bad fantasy projections of mothers in McNall's texts, it challenges the cultural uses to which the psychologically loaded concepts of motherhood are put. Robinson adapts the formula of the immature romantic heroine to allow her protagonist to develop beyond the bounds of the preoedipal Lacanian *imaginary* that limits her generic predecessors.

THE MOTHER TONGUE

In the tradition of Sarah Orne Jewett's *The Country of the Pointed Firs*, instead of pursuing the infinite regression of preoedipal experience, *Housekeeping* transforms female relationship through a redemptive recreation of "figuration" of the "literal" (Homans 4, 5) through transient practice. In *Bearing the Word*, Margaret Homans develops Irigaray's argument that Western culture depends on the mother's absence to authorize masculine symbolic expression.[9] In Lacanian psychoanalytic theory the *symbolic* order of culture replaces phenomenal experience in the actual world with representation through language. Since that phenomenal experience is ideologically associated with the prelinguistic feminine order of Nature, the Mother as the sign of Nature and all the literal experience associated with the physical perception of the natural world must be suppressed in order for masculine figuration (which is the symbolic replacement of experience) to take place, according to Homans. As noted in the discussion of Edith Wharton's *Summer*, in Lacanian terms the masculine symbolic order must replace the feminine imaginary; thus the extinction of the "Mother" and all she represents is imperative to the masculine generation of culture. In feminine texts, then, the mother's absence may signal cultural predicament as well as psychological problem. A woman's text, while making use of masculine symbolic figuration, may find ways to inscribe literal evocations of phenomenal nature, which has been excribed along with the Mother, and such refiguration constitutes a radical challenge: "That we must have access to some original ground of meaning is the necessary illusion that empowers the acts of figuration that constitute literature," Homans declares. "At the same time, literal meaning would hypothetically destroy any text it entered by making superfluous those very figures—and even, some would argue, all language acts—just as the presence of the mother's body would make all language unnecessary" (4).

Such is the case in *Housekeeping*. The repeated abandonment of the daughters by almost every maternal presence—the mother, the grandmother, the two maiden aunts—is an excess that parodies the necessary elimination of the Mother in the masculinist text, while the persistent presence of the imperfect mother, Sylvie, whose name suggests her affinity with the natural world, negotiates a new relation that replaces the patriarchal construct of motherhood and executes a reinscription of the textual feminine through the inclusion of phenomenal nature. The gendered character of this challenge is apparent in the contrasting masculine and feminine landscapes that begin the novel. According to Homans, masculine culture replaces more direct depiction of literal experience with figurative accounts, a circumstance evidenced in *Housekeeping* by Grandfather Foster's paintings of mountains. All of his depictions are crude and fantastic copies of a magazine picture of Mount Fujiyama. One has careful trees painted at right angles to the mountain, like plush fibers on stiff cloth, each tree replete with vivid birds and fruit hung parallel to the earth. Each landscape is bordered with legions of large galloping beasts with colorful markings, fanciful creatures contrived out of "ignorance" or imagination (4).

When the grandfather emigrates in search of the fanciful mountains of his art, he experiences what, the narrating granddaughter believes, may have been a "malign joke." The actual landscape of Fingerbone exceeds the capacity of masculine figuration—the stylized copy of a stylized copy—to refine or contain: Fingerbone has countless mountains, and where there are no mountains "there are hills" (4). In addition to the superfluity which exceeds symbolic bounds, the landscape also escapes figuration in its characteristic indeterminacy: the boundaries between discrete features of landscape become indeterminate. So in the spring lost lakes may return to flood the cellars of human habitations and engulf the very earth until it brims over with muddy water (4–5).

In *Housekeeping*, the capacity of culture to modify nature is parodied and rescinded, while the repressed power of nature to change social contrivances is supported by such images as the return of the lake. In the initial passages, the figuration of landscape, gendered as masculine, is deposed by the literalization of landscape, gendered as feminine. Further, the very features of the stable world are redefined as fluxional, introducing the theme of transience, which finds expression in all aspects of the novel.

TRANSFORMATIVE JOURNEYS

The thematic transiency of the setting is reinforced in characterization, symbolism, and formal method. Sylvie, of course, is the central instance, and her history as a hobo accounts for the singular habits that unsettle her nieces. She wanders about town in an ill-fitting man's overcoat, she talks to the vagrant population of the area, and sometimes sleeps on the lawn; she collects old papers from the railroad station, prefers sequined ballet slippers to practical oxfords for children's footwear, and knows nothing about housekeeping. Ruthie and Lucille decide that Sylvie is "not a stable person" (82), an ironic understatement, and they are mortified when they come across her sleeping on a bench in the town park under a tented newspaper in the middle of the day. In addition to disturbing their assumptions about proper maternal appearance and deportment, Sylvie challenges their comforting beliefs about the nature of reality with the alternative values of "hobohemia"[10] through stories of the women travelers she has encountered. Through Marie's story, Sylvie exemplifies the inevitability of human loneliness and shocks the children by admitting that key features of her narrative may not even be reliable (65–66). Through the story of Edith, "who came to her rest crossing the mountains in a boxcar" (87), she propounds the inevitability of death, and in offering hospitality to the "lady who had ridden the rods from South Dakota to see her brother hanged" (103–104), she makes a case for human acceptance that contrasts Lucille's social intolerance: Sylvie is apparently unaware that it is wrong "to make friends with people who fly on their backs a thousand miles, twelve inches from the ground" (104).

On the day she arrived, the girls fashioned a snow-woman that could not be made to retain its proper form in the bright sunshine (61). This is the symbol for Sylvie. Everything she is or does or encounters becomes a sign of the value of contingency or the means of metamorphosis. Wind, fire, and especially water are her elements,[11] and all are employed in the novel as central images in rich symbol systems of inevitable transfiguration. An insistence on thematic transformation also informs the primary formal device of the novel: the motif of journey. There are three transformative journeys in *Housekeeping*, one undertaken by Ruthie and Lucille and two more by Ruth and Sylvie. The first begins as a fishing expedition by the two girls during the summer before Lucille leaves home. Engrossed in their adventure, they fail to keep track of the time and have to spend the night in the woods because they are afraid to negotiate the difficult terrain in the dark. The dominant natural feature they encounter is the lake, which is described in extensive detail.

"Clear" and "ordinary," the "modest" body of water is full of life, and its "calm" persistent response to all it is touched by is a reminder that it is also "vast and in league with the moon." Lined with "smooth stones and simple mud," it shows the subtle variegations of "jet, and white, and hazel." At sunset when the girls see it, the shoreline is a "long, slow curve, outward to a point beyond which [lie] three long islands of diminishing size," and the land sweeps "toward the depths of the lake, tentatively, like an ellipsis." The high rocky point beyond the lake is footed by a "narrow margin of brown sand abstracted . . . into one pure curve of calligraphic delicacy." It is at this place the sisters have "crossed" and climbed down a slope to a place where perch are biting. A quarter of a mile beyond the barricade of a great peninsula the open expanse of the lake is shining. But set "apart from the drifts and tides and lucifications of the open water, the surface of the bay seemed almost viscous, membranous, and here things massed and accumulated, as they do in cobwebs or in the eaves and unswept corners of a house. It was a place of distinctly domestic disorder, warm and replete" (112–13).

This description functions as a kind of travel writing, a precise depiction of a natural landscape encountered on a journey—stones so accurately envisioned underwater that they are the indeterminate "hazel" of a human eye—and, like the rest of the novel, it works on both the psychological and cultural levels. As travel writing it is especially striking in its humility, as indicated by the absence of an imperialist perspective. Unlike the male imperialist traveler described by Mary Louise Pratt, whose account also opposes Jewett's scenic observation, the narrator in *Housekeeping* does not assume the elevated perspective of the promontory vista (72–74). She is not above the lake looking down but at the same level, thus establishing a rhetorical relation of contiguity rather than superiority. Nor does she attempt to incorporate the scene by reducing it to the terms of her own experience. Until the last sentences, she resists the domestication of the spectacle in favor of allowing it to manifest a dialectic between the small and the vast (a little pond that covers "half the world" (112)), the ordinary and the sublime ("a simple puddle in league with the moon" (112)), the intimate and the distant ("cobwebs in "corners" and the "lucifications" of faraway water), and the masculine and the feminine. The vastness, power, and sublimity conventionally associated with conquest in masculine travel is matched by the evocation of the conventionally feminine domestic protective space in the last sentence. Every evocation of grandeur and distance is followed by a reduction of scale and a suggestion of intimacy; the open water, for example, is framed by the bay. Perhaps the most effective dialectic device in the passage is the alternation of tactile with visual imagery. The persistent maternal touch of the water lapping the stones near the shore complements the "abstracted," "sweeping" (112) paternal features seen nearer the horizon.

In this passage Robinson repeats the strategy of contrasting presentations of masculine and feminine landscape noted above. At issue is the regendering of nature and writing. The allusions to the masculine practice of "figuration" ("abstracted," "calligraphic") are subsumed by the "literal" depiction of the natural world. The effect of the passage is to introduce a Nature that functions in its plenitude to obviate binary categories that structure conventional systems of definition; in addition to those mentioned, the language introduces white/dark, cold/warm, crude/delicate, rank/pure, and barricade/shelter. The rhetorical strategy is to suggest the appeal of unresolved contradiction that we have already observed in Whittier's deconstructive representation of Harriet Livermore. Of a magnitude that compels energetic struggle—the girls must "climb" the point—the scene also requires the extraordinary delicacy necessary to part a membrane, oppositely gendered intensities that are each appropriate. The setting invites *both* or *all* or *any* or *neither*, a symbolic location of open possibility that may serve as a conduit to transformation. It is appropriate that the most significant human action provoked by a landscape so conceived is a "crossing."

For Ruthie this symbolic journey is indeed the occasion of a significant crossing or conversion.[12] In the deep dark of the forest, insecure in a flimsy lean-to, she sleeps, sensing the motion of the natural life around her: "accepting that our human boundaries were overrun" (115). The temporary shelter in the woods, like the landscape of the lake, retains some of the protective qualities of the domestic—but it is a "disordered domesticity" which induces an open perspective that allows Ruth to begin to come to terms with the consuming problem of her mother's loss. Instead of erecting defensive barriers between herself and her fears, she is able to "simply let the darkness in the sky become coextensive with the darkness in my skull and bowels and bones" (116). "So this is all death is," she concludes (118).

The woman traveler in *Housekeeping* journeys from obstruction to openness in her encounter with a literalized nature that fosters psychological development in place of the psychic stasis of the conventional heroine described by McNall. The representation of nature also operates culturally to reinscribe a vital, transformative, powerful, unsentimental revisionary feminine operating through associative rather than logical process, as theorized by French Feminism. These are the same qualities that define the relationship Sylvie develops with Ruthie.

The children are inevitably surprised when Sylvie greets their deviations with sympathy rather than remonstrance. She is unalarmed by their truancy from school, and even the night spent in the woods without permission elicits cocoa and comfort rather than punishment. "Sylvie will kill us," Lucille announces wistfully on that occasion, apparently hoping that her aunt will resort to the strict discipline of a conventional mother. But while Lucille is upset by Sylvie's tolerance, Ruthie comes to recognize the difficult freedom it conveys: "I waited for Sylvie to say, 'You're like me.' I thought she might say, 'You're like your mother.' I feared and suspected that Sylvie and I were of a kind, and waited for her to claim me, but she would not" (106).

Eleanor H. Kuykendall's definition of Irigaray's "spiritual vision of mothering" (272) as the evocation of a mother-child relationship that is not "dominant or controlling but primarily healing, creative, and transformative"—a relationship that contains the potential for reciprocity—is the kind of relationship Sylvie's abdication of coercive "claims" introduces. The first journey Ruth and Sylvie take together enacts this vision. On the Monday morning following Lucille's departure, Sylvie steals a rowboat from a fisherman and takes Ruth to an isolated region on the far side of the Fingerbone lake. If the imagery of Ruth and Lucille's journey suggested natural transformation, Ruth's journey with Sylvie concentrates on psychological rebirth and cultural redefinition. Ruthie has already realized that she is "now in Sylvie's dream with her" (110), and the trip they take together is a dream replication of the primal issue of the mother's abandonment, with important differences. In this version

Sylvie does indeed leave Ruth, but she returns to comfort her after Ruthie has gained important insight into the loss issues that preoccupy her.[13]

Telling Ruth to watch for the "ghost children" who inhabit the cold and lonely region, Sylvie disappears, leaving Ruthie to wait out the day in the ruins of an abandoned house. In this location Ruth senses the ghostly presences of abandoned children and comes to recognize them as projections of her own psychic condition. "I had been, so to speak, turned out of house." And so there was no definitive distance between her own body and the projections of loss which seem to reach out of the haunted landscape to touch her hair (154). Ruth finally realizes that the derelict homestead and its lost children are more than a regional phenomenon; they represent a universal condition. If you sit alone in a bus station long enough, she observes, people will inevitably confide "long lies about numerous children who are all gone now, and mothers who were beautiful and cruel" (157). The way out of the haunting impasse of the loss of the "good" mother, according to McNall, "is a complete and completed process of mourning for our earliest love, the mother of our child-minds and emotions whom we must relinquish as we attempt to acquire adult minds and emotions" (9). At the end of Ruthie's meditation, she realizes that her own mother has become "a music I no longer heard, that rang in my mind, itself and nothing else, lost to all sense, but not perished" (160). Ruth has managed what McNall's desperate protagonists could not: she has accepted her actual mother's death and mourned the loss of the ideal Helen represents. It is at this point that Sylvie returns to tender an alternative maternal relation: "She opened her coat and closed it around me, bundling me awkwardly against her so that my cheekbone pillowed on her breastbone" (160).

The beginning of this journey is marked by images of birth. Ruth is aware that in mimicking Sylvie's stride across the morning landscape, "[w]e are the same. She could as well be my mother. I crouched and slept in her shape like an unborn child" (145). In the boat on the trip to the far shore, as they change seats: Ruth "crawled under" Sylvie's "body and out between her legs" (145). On the return trip, the implications of this process are questioned. In the boat, Ruthie feels "like a seed in a husk" with the "immense water of the lake" thudding beneath her. Imagine, she demands, that this water overwhelms and fills her to the point of bursting: "Then, presumably, would come parturition in some form, though my first birth had hardly deserved that name, and why should I hope for more from the second?" (162).

In *The Varieties of Religious Experience*, William James describes the "second-born" as those who have, like Ruthie, been "born" into the realization that "[b]ack of everything is the great spectre of universal death, the all encompassing blackness" (122): "mankind is in a position similar to that of a set of people living on a frozen lake, surrounded by cliffs over which there is no escape, yet knowing that little by little the ice is melting, and the inevitable day drawing near when the last of the film of it will disappear, and to be drowned ignominiously will be the human creature's only portion" (125). But for James the realization of such "radical pessimism" (expressed in metaphoric terms so similar to those of *Housekeeping*) may usher in a positive psychic reorganization, as is also the case of Ruth's conversion to Sylvie's philosophy of transience.

Having comprehended contingency through psychic immersion in the meaning of maternal nature, Ruth must learn the power it affords, an insight presented as the next stage of the visionary journey. On their way home, Sylvie rows Ruth to a position just beneath the huge railroad bridge that spans the lake, from which Grandfather Foster aboard the Fireball Express had plunged to his death years before. As a train passes above them, there is light like the flashing of a meteor, the physical shock of loud noise, and a "trembling" which passes through them (167). After this phenomenal sensation of the force and agency of the practice of movement, Ruthie herself is empowered to take a turn at the oars. As dawn rises, the sad daughter and her errant aunt return to shore and, for the first time, hop a freight together for the trip back to town.

THE CONTRADICTIONS OF MOTHERHOOD / THE REJECTION OF HOUSEKEEPING

According to Sara Ruddick, maternal practice is defined by three competing interests: the necessities to preserve the child, to foster her growth, and to make her acceptable to the community (215–16). It is the conflict between the claims of protection and acceptability that makes maternity an impossible condition in Robinson's novel. Sylvie's maternal practice provides security and encourages development, but it cannot foster the replication of the community's dictates of propriety. Housekeeping, like motherhood, is split between the concerns of caretaking and conformity. The home is the preserve of the domestic bonds of family in which the development of its members may be secured through the provision of physical and emotional support, but it is also the location through which community standards of feminine deportment are imposed.

According to Ann Romines in *The Home Plot: Women, Writing and Domestic Ritual*, for many American woman writers housekeeping operates as "the center and vehicle of a culture invented by women, a complex and continuing process of female, domestic art" (14). Similarly, Sylvie's homemaking asserts the value of female enterprise, albeit through a radical insistence on alternative values in place of traditional domestic arts; her home opens a pastoral feminine space in a masculine world. A place of natural rather than artificial light, an inside world opened to outer nature, a "house . . . attuned to the orchard and the particularities of weather" (85), Sylvie's home turns into a renovated maternal environment, but the intervention of the sheriff in that home indicates that patriarchal law continues to dictate the terms of the domestic setting.[14] The necessity for an even more radical challenge than Sylvie's innovative housekeeping is signaled in the novel by frequent allusions to Henry David Thoreau.

Like Thoreau in *Walden*, Robinson is engaged in the revolutionary redefinition of the domestic. The symbolic settings in *Housekeeping*—water as a scene of transfiguration, the omnipresence of the railroad, the inimical village nearby, the house as a metaphor of redefinition—are often reminiscent of *Walden*.[15] The cellar holes and lilacs of the lost inhabitants of the winter landscape of Ruth and Sylvie's journey recall Thoreau's description of "Former Inhabitants; and Winter Visitors." Echoing Thoreau's famous declaration, Ruth declares that Lucille "went to the woods . . . to escape observation. . . . She had gone to the woods "for the woods' own sake" (99). Thoreau dreamed of a commodious house in "a golden age" where "the weary traveller may wash, and eat, and converse, and sleep without further journey; such a shelter as you would be glad to reach in a tempestuous night, containing all the essentials of a house, and nothing for housekeeping" (1381). Sylvie's own priorities would appear to be similar, and, like Thoreau's, Sylvie's unorthodox housekeeping in the service of an alternative vision defies dominant standards. But whereas Thoreau's masculine eccentricity can be excused by a supportive community, Sylvie's feminine deviance cannot.

The allusions to Thoreau also suggest that the issues of housekeeping are matters of communal norms, something Ruthie and Sylvie learn after they come home in a freight train and the community expresses its disapproval of Sylvie's "unredeemed" (177) transience through threats to remove the child from the home. Because of her love for Ruthie, Sylvie attempts to conform to communal standards by throwing out the accumulation of old cans, bottles, magazines, and newspapers that have taken over the parlor and by sweeping out the "wings and feet and heads" of her cats' prey that startle the neighbor ladies who begin to visit (181). She fusses over Ruthie's appearance and worries about her attendance at school, but nothing works. Thoreau defines a "*community*" as "a league for mutual defence" (1337), and Ruthie interprets Fingerbone's disapproval as necessary fortification against its own "terrifying" instability: wanderers must be met by fierce rejection, because moral repulsion is a "check" on powerful temptation (178).

As Ruth has learned through her journeys, "sorrow" is the natural condition of everyone "put out of house" (179), but what she must learn in the conclusion to the novel is that female sacrifice to the ideological illusion of stability is intolerable. Throughout *Housekeeping* the supposed stability of the domestic order is regularly overturned by natural forces. In an early chapter, for example, the springtime flooding of the nearby lake fills the first floor of the house with water so the "house flowed around us" (63–64). Thus it is that the reinscribed ideal of feminine movement displaces the ideology of feminine stasis. Although Grandfather Foster, the patriarchal builder of the house, had assumed its permanence (47), Ruth discerns "that if the house were not to founder, it had to float" (125). After the sheriff's second visit, when it becomes apparent that Sylvie will lose Ruthie in the civil hearing on her competence as a caretaker, the two of them attempt to burn the house itself. This action signals their rejection of the restrictive function of domesticity in a system of patriarchal control and their adoption of the redemptive transience of their second journey: "cast out to wander," they recognize "an end to housekeeping" (209). They escape over the railroad bridge in darkness and high wind and hop a freight to another life. Becoming the "drifters"(213) the community fears, they allow Fingerbone to assume them drowned, like so many others, in the waters of its deadly lake.

Like most secret journeys, this one operates as contradiction, a move beyond what can be imagined or tolerated within the home community the woman traveler rejects or redefines as she executes her own transformation. "Crossing . . . the bridge . . . changed me finally," Ruthie confides. "Something happened" so radical that everything that existed previously seems "diminished" (215). Maternal loss and female rebirth are the thematic sources of a productive process that rejects the feminine compromise of domestic collusion. *Housekeeping* presents, through the philosophical model of transience as an acceptance of human contingency and through the narrative enactment of the female journey as the assumption of the power afforded by movement, a realizable pattern for ideological reorganization. Similarly, in the next section, which concentrates on defining modalities of change, Eudora Welty's short fiction uses the trope of the woman traveler to redefine the woman's options within the complex interrelations of psychological, social, and literary patterns, and Elizabeth Bishop's poetry revises the trope of the gendered traveler to effect epistemological transformation.

PART IV

Modes of Transformation

CHAPTER 7

The Developmental Journey: Narrative, Psychological, and Social Transformation in Eudora Welty's Short Fiction

In her essay "Place in Fiction" (1956) Eudora Welty emphasizes the significance of stable location. It provides the basis for a writer's "goodness" by supplying the "raw material" that supports both the verisimilitude and the ethical "validity" of the fiction, and it is the source of the writer's personal "worth": "place is where he has his roots, place is where he stands; in his experience out of which he writes, it provides the base of reference" (*The Eye of the Story*, 117). Yet "the traveller," according to Anne M. Masserand, "appears as a constant figure in Eudora Welty's work" (40). Concerning everything from brief walks through town to extended ocean voyages, almost all of the forty-one of the *Collected Stories* (1980) are about some form of journey, and all but a handful use travel as the formal narrative pattern through which action is presented.[1] In her autobiographical *One Writer's Beginnings* (1983), Welty observes, "I never resisted it when, in almost every story I ever wrote, some parade or procession, impromptu or ceremonious, comic or funereal, has risen to mark some stage of the story's unfolding" (37). Although Eudora Welty is committed to the authority of "place" in fiction, travel predominates in her short stories as both subject and formal arrangement. This seeming paradox is resolved in that, unlike the more conventional traveler who may leave a destructive environment in order to secure a self, Welty's traveler retains the nurturing world by restructuring his or her relationship to it or by restructuring the social relationships of that world. Both of these readjustments are negotiated through the narrative trope of women's travel. The stability of place in Welty's stories is maintained by a female community that defines and conserves the purpose of human endeavor through social relations and ritual; the male traveler frequently embodies the spurious lure of rootlessness; while the woman traveler or her representatives enact journeys that mediate between the "place" and the world—tradition and innovation—the necessary poles of literary, social, and psychological transformation dramatized through theme and form in Welty's short fiction.

In "The Wanderers," from *The Golden Apples* (1959), for example, the funeral of Mrs. Rainey exemplifies the conservative value of the female community. With food, ceremony, and rigid adherence to proprieties, the women—who come to lay out the dead, decorate the parlor, wash the curtains, cook the food, gossip among themselves, discipline the errant men and children, and advise the surviving daughter—create the supportive and predictable relation of individuals to their social and natural surroundings that Virgie Rainey, the protagonist, recognizes as the "overworked, inherited . . . personal pattern" (431). But whereas the repeated parties, funerals, meetings, and marriages that structure Welty's works celebrate the importance of female community, she also includes the contrapuntal impulse threading her life as well as her fiction.[2] In her stories, men succumb to their seemingly natural impulse to wander from the ties of community. Their going introduces the traditional gendered opposition of masculine freedom to feminine domesticity, but the value of unencumbered independence is discounted.[3] Although King MacClain of *The Golden Apples* is initially portrayed as a mythic adventurer, his true stature is finally established in "The Wanderers." Having returned to his wife after years of absence, he is shown to be a senile old man perpetually hungry for the bountiful provision of the female community.

The status of the woman traveler, however, is always more ambiguous than that of the traveling man. In Welty's first collection, *A Curtain of Green* (1941), Clytie, in the story of that title, performs a daily pilgrimage—a hectic walk through village streets—in search of a familiar face. Her own psychotic family fails to supply her with the recognizable stability generally provided by the female community. However, by characterizing Clytie's ritual journey as humorously demented, Welty suggests it may be impossible for her to find a necessary order anywhere else.[4] The celebrated comic tone of Welty's first collection in such stories as "Lily Daw and the Three Ladies," "A Piece of News," and "Why I Lived at the P.O." denigrates the women who risk moving beyond the restrictions of their intimate worlds to try to attain something they do not have yet sense may be secured in another location. But Welty's emerging sympathy with the dilemma posed by the divergence of place and travel colors the more compassionate portrayal of subsequent women travelers in "Moon Lake," "June Recital," and "The Wanderers" from *The Golden Apples*; "No Place for You, My Love" from *The Bride of Innisfallen* (1955); and the feminine journey of the community in "The Wide Net" from Welty's 1943 collection of that title. These stories exemplify the processes of narrative, personal, and communal transformation as theorized by Mark Freeman, Eric J. Leed, and Victor Turner, respectively, realized through the developmental journeys of Welty's short fiction. Instead of the contradictions to social constraint organized by the trope of travel in previous chapters, in Welty's short fiction the woman's journey is a means to the integration of contradictions through personal and social development enacted as narrative.

DEVELOPMENTAL NARRATIVES

The gendered and complex relationship among male travelers, the female community, and the woman traveler is apparent in the cycle of stories of *The Golden Apples*. In "Moon Lake," Easter's narrative inscribes the advantages and the risks of feminine motion, while Loch Morrison represents the contrasting situation of the traveling man, and the chorus of children and adults clarifies the privileges and detriments of rootedness in the social order. In the story, the little girls of Morgana go to camp at Moon Lake, eight miles from town, accompanied by two counselors; Loch, the boy scout who serves as bugler and lifeguard; and a retinue of Negro servants. Easter, the protagonist, an orphan from the local asylum, is the dominant force among the campers because of her adventurous spirit and her freedom from the restrictions impeding the town girls. Her leadership results from frequent episodes of movement that encourage growth through exploratory experience. Nina Carmichael, from one of the local families, the central consciousness of the story, is inspired by Easter's aptitude for motion. For it is her group of "orphans" who are most adept at unhampered movement. Without watching where they are going, they streak to the spring heedless of the "thorns and stickers" and "slick" pine needles of the rocky and uneven path that apparently hinder the more cautious town girls (345–46). The orphan children, especially Easter, have access to a phenomenal vitality characterized as movement that the socially circumscribed children, represented by Nina, cannot achieve.

At one point Easter leads Nina on an unknown path to the lake where they get into an old rowboat and play at journey. For Nina, the significance of this adventure isn't that the children were able to drift, but that the "world drifted, forgot," the "dreamed-about" changing "places with the dreamer" (360). Through reverse identification with the unfettered Easter, Nina confronts an alternative self and the possibility of alternative roles:[5] "secret ways . . . to slip into them all—to change . . . for a moment into Gertrude, into Mrs. Gruenwald, into Twosie—into a boy. To *have been* an orphan" (361).

Before Nina turns into the woman traveler Easter represents, however, the story contains that impulse through a graphic presentation of its dangers. Easter's rootlessness gains her freedom, but does not secure her protection. One afternoon, the orphan girl, who cannot swim, climbs onto the diving board. Struck by a meddlesome black boy with a willow switch, she plummets into the deep water and comes very near to drowning. She recovers only because of the heroic efforts of Loch Morrison, the life-saver, whose manipulations of her body in the act of rescusitation are so intimate and suggestive that they appall the watching town women.[6]

The adult world of "Moon Lake" is evidently both perilous and gendered, and the female community erects culture as necessary protection against the overt threats of society and nature and the covert threat of male sexuality. The characteristic distance between protection and potential for the would-be woman traveler is doubly marked throughout Welty's short fiction, symbolically, as in "Moon Lake," with both the promise of vitality and the reminder of danger. The ambivalence of travel is also directly expressed in *One Writer's Beginnings* as Welty reminiscences about family journeys:

> Taking trips tore all of us up inside, for they seemed, each journey away from home, something that would test us, or something that had better be momentous, to justify such a leap in the dark. The torment of having a loved one go, the guilt of being the loved one gone—comes into my fiction as it did and does into my life. And most of all the guilt then was because it was true: I had left to arrive at some secret joy, what was unknown. (94)

The fictive equivalent of these mixed emotions in *The Golden Apples* is Virgie Rainey's story, begun in "June Recital" and taken up again in "The Wanderers." A talented and impetuous girl from a poor family who, in her seventeenth year, hops a freight with a sailor-lover only to return to support her aging mother, Virgie vacillates between male wandering and female stability in both youth and maturity to become a true woman traveler only after the death of her mother allows her finally to leave home for good. In the first story her genuine musical talent has secured the favor of a German piano teacher, whose example and instruction induct Virgie into both the torment of exile and the reward of aesthetic release. "Miss Eckhart and Virgie," muses Cassie, who provides the interpretation for the events in the story, "as if all along they had been making a trip" (330).

The structural device of a third perspective which mediates the actions of others evident in "Moon Lake" and "June Recital" represents Welty's own participation in the narrative testing of alternative possibilities. In her autobiography Welty claims identification with the internal core of the "strange" and intense Miss Eckhart, who personifies the artist (103). Virgie, the protégé, described as "[p]assionate, recalcitrant, stubbornly undefeated by failure or hurt or disgrace or bereavement," who "knows to the last that there is a world that remains out there, a world living and mysterious, and that she is of it, . . . might," Welty acknowledges, "have always been my subject" (101–102). The subject Virgie represents is the development of a personality that can bridge the competing claims of the home place and the living world realized through the theme of travel.

Virgie's story of dislocation, death, and the initiation of journey is the realization of all the stages of narrative self-development defined by Mark Freeman in *Rewriting the Self: History, Memory, Narrative.*Employing a progressional schema adapted from Paul Ricoeur, Freeman sketches phases in the narrative creation of self. The initial stage of *recognition* identifies the "disjunction" in the life of the protagonist between experience and possibility. The narrative task at this point is "to recollect who and what we are and have been, toward identifying the source of our alienation" (44). Virgie's transportation to the alternative order afforded by music initiates the "recognition" that endorses alternative. The second stage, *distantiation*, is a negative process of realized "differentiation, a separation of self from self, such that the text of one's experience becomes transformed into an object of interpretation" (45). Virgie's repeated acts of independence serve to differentiate an alternative "self." By playing the piano for the local movie theater, Virgie distances herself from Miss Eckhart's prohibitive aesthetic aspirations, and by displaying her joyful illicit union with the sailor in tableau for the Morrison children, Virgie differentiates her person from the restrictive morality of the female community. During the final stage of *appropriation* there is "articulation," which gives "form," clarifies, and defines "the direction" in which the self must proceed (40–41).

The achievement of "appropriation"—the articulation of a new pattern of being—is enacted in a stunning scene of ritual journey. On the evening after her mother's death, Virgie takes a swim in the river "forcing it gently, as she would wish gentleness to her body. Her breasts around which she felt the water closing were as sensitive at that moment as the tips of wings must feel to birds, or antennae to insects." She feels the sand "and the many dark ribbons of grass and mud touch her and leave her, like the suggestions and withdrawals of some bondage that might have been dear, now dismembering and losing itself." Like a floating cloud, she is "aware but only of the nebulous edges of her feeling and the vanishing opacity of her will, the carelessness for the water of the river through which her body had already passed as well as for what was ahead." The shore and the river blended. "Memory . . . not darkening her for more than an instant. . . . If she trembled it was at the smoothness of a fish or snake that crossed her knees." Suspended in "the middle of the river, whose downstream or upstream could not be told by a current . . ." Virgie "had reached the point where, in the next moment she might turn into something without feeling it shock her" (440).

The possibility of transformation implied at the conclusion of this scene is realized through the resolution and refiguration of gendered oppositions. The dominating figure of this complicated trope is of a sexual union in which the swimmer phallically "forcing" the female body of water is herself enclosed, her own body encircled with maternal gentleness. Thus her action converts the aggression attributed to movement into the achievement of union. This redistribution of masculine and feminine qualities is repeated in the comparison of her breasts to the wings of birds and the antennae of insects. In these roles the breasts configure the movement and exploration attributed to men, yet they retain a woman's sexual sensitivity. In effect, this scene replaces masculine with feminine agency, as the breast, retaining its female qualities, is substituted for the phallus. And this exchange is suggested for a third time, when the traditionally masculine touch of the snake and fish is converted into a smooth caress. This extraordinary resolution of symbolic gender polarities produces the dissolution of other binding oppositions. There is no longer any prescribed or proscribed direction. The swimmer reaches a middle where the difference between upstream and downstream is irrelevant, the distinction between backward and forward is obliterated, memory loses its power to darken, and the "bondage" of what was once "dear" is loosed. In sensuous contact with the world she traverses, the woman traveler reaches a point of balance between masculine force and feminine solicitude that enables transfiguration. The deconstruction of gendered opposites effected by the trope of the woman traveler in Whittier's *Snow-Bound* and Robinson's *Housekeeping* is elaborated here as a constructive means of turning "into something."

For Freeman the process of narrative, like Virgie's river crossing, is a "fundamentally metaphorical one: a new relationship is being created between the past and the present, a new poetic configuration, designed to give greater freedom to one's previous—and present experience" (30). Although "the ends we pursue" are, "irrevocably tied to extant conceptions of the good, the true, and the right," nevertheless, "there is a fair amount of play and difference" out of which to fashion metaphorical alternatives. The "unique constellation of experiences that have characterized a given life" may "yield a vast multiplicity of stories of development" (Freeman 49). For Freeman, the self emerging from narrative process is the realization of a progressive project: to create out of past experience a trope which embodies aspirations for development. Welty's fictions of journey are figures of such transformation. The dissolution of opposed categories in Virgie's river-crossing scene, which joins feminine constraint to masculine freedom, makes possible the connection between a communal past and a personal future, options polarized in Welty's nonfiction as "place" and "travel."

THE PSYCHOLOGICAL JOURNEY

The journey motif in Welty's fiction, a figure of narrative transformation as defined by Freeman, also stages the developmental psychological and social processes theorized by Eric J. Leed and Victor Turner. In Leed's *The Mind of the Traveler*, the phases of the journey script the psychological changes we may observe in Welty's intriguing "No Place for You, My Love" from *The Bride of the Innisfallen*. The first stage, *departure*, is a process of disengagement from defining social orders effected as a change in place and experienced as an engagement with the unfamiliar. In the story, a Northern man meets a Northern woman in a New Orleans restaurant. Together they embark on a motor trip "south of New Orleans," a destination that does not exist within the cognitive limits of either of them (466).

The modern departure, according to Leed, leaves behind "a settled, articulated world—a fully elaborated, if onerous civility" (41). By moving into an alternative space, the traveler enters an unrestricted order of being that contrasts the "internalized prohibitions" (Leed 43) associated with home. This initial liberation is expressed as the connotative content of the physical landscape the couple encounters in Welty's story. On the road below New Orleans, a "universe" (468) of "raging" insects is making "discordant" music like competing "marching bands." "[N]aked" children, "darker and younger" girls proliferate (467), and "crayfish and other shell creatures" litter the pavement in an atmosphere of alien and "primeval" profusion (468) different from their Northern experiences. The sense of divergence from the known world intimated by the imagery is intensified in two specific observations: all the other wayfarers they meet seem to be rushing in the other direction, and the man and woman even enter briefly "a sort of dead man's land where nobody came" (468). In the process of journey the bounded world and settled identity is replaced by the sensational experience of an "array of . . . artifacts and exemplars whose meaning is mysterious to the outsider and must be decoded from appearances" (Leed 45).

The effects of this decoding are the purpose of *passage*, Leed's second psychological stage, in which "motion across boundaries and through space" becomes a "medium of perception" (56): "Motion connects the traveler to the world but also distances one from it. In overcoming this distancing, the serious traveler must develop techniques of reading from the surfaces of things and people to discover their interiors, relationships, functions and meanings" (62). Thus the second stage inaugurates the process of creating new meaning out of new experience. The passage stage in "No Place for You, My Love" occurs in three sequential episodes: when the couple crosses the river by ferry, resumes the road, and then drives through a cemetery. The ferry crossing reiterates acts of interpretation from the point of view of distanced otherness. From the bridge above the main deck, the rest of the passengers—sharing beer and local gossip—appear to the solitary woman as "amateur travelers" because of their active engagement in a social context. She, by contrast, is alienated and characterized by extreme openness to experience, rather than by agency. "[B]elonging to no one," she describes herself and imagines that it must be apparent "that with her entire self all she did was wait." To her companion, who observes her from below, the woman traveler is distinguished by her ability to establish a "set" "distance" from the activities of the crowd and to maintain a "measuring coolness," a condition he finds desirable. During the crossing, he is startled by an alligator the little boys have captured and brought on board, pulling it around the crowded boat "like a toy—a hide that could walk" (470). The observing man asserts his detachment from this juvenile display of masculine prowess. The detachment experienced by both the woman and the man during this stage permits original interpretation inconsistent with predominating perspectives.

On the farther side of the Mississippi, alienating motion continues to provoke necessary interpretation, as in a passage in which the stimulation of internal evaluation by external phenomena is strikingly evident. The intense heat seems to meld the unaccustomed highway to the "unseen river," dead "snakes" stretching "across the concrete like markers." "It's never anything like this in Syracuse," he observes. "Or in Toledo either," she agrees. In the "greater waste" of this alien world, even the certainty of land is lost: there is "water under everything. Even where a screen of jungle had been left to stand, splashes could be heard from under the trees." With her "eyes overcome with brightness and size," she feels a sudden "panic" engulf her. "Just how far below questions and answers, concealment and revelation, they were running now" was the powerful question: "How dear—how costly—would this ride be?" (471–72).

Snakes, unnatural heat, and underlying water, objective phenomena of the journey, perform, respectively, as cultural and subjective symbols of moral transgression, intense experience, and latent meaning, which provoke the woman's questions. The sense of danger and extremity, converted to emotional content here, is expressed as landscape in the next sequence, a surreal drive between the rows of tombs in a churchyard that bring the travelers eye level with the names of the dead. At this point, the woman, who has intuited something of the ultimacy underlying the impulsive expedition, gives voice to the man's repressed concern. When she asks what his wife is like, his hand comes up in a protective gesture that the reader learns at the conclusion of the story is a blow that bruises her face.[7] This mark of alienation suggests that a lover's communion is not the means or object of the transformative effect of the journey. After this event the couple receives the information that they have come to the "jumping off place" (474) where their path meets the sea. There they begin the final stage of the journey, which Leed designates "arrival."

If departure dissolves former stabilities, and the motion of passage generates new perception out of the experience of continuous change, arrival is the occasion for a reintegration of the traveler into a social world on new terms. In this process there are two significant components: *incorporation*—in which the traveler reenters a domestic order—which occurs in Welty's story when the man and woman visit "Baba's Place," a bar at the "end of the road," and *identification*—a redefinition of the self and its relations—which is implied through the narrative of the return drive to New Orleans.

Travel, in Leed's view, erodes the "more recent sedimentation" of personal requirements to uncover primal needs: "Departures evoke the earliest separations of childhood; passage, those experiences of flight and physical freedom; arrivals, the magic of a return to beginnings and an achievement of coherence with others" (129). At Baba's, where a community gathers to gossip, gamble, eat, drink, and celebrate, and a place is made for the two wanderers at a table provided by Baba and his mother, the return to the nourishment and pleasure of homecoming occurs. The man and woman share cold beer and "good solid ham" sandwiches (475). And after their refreshment, they dance to the tantalizing "music you heard out of the distance at night. . . . This seemed a homey place" (478). The music suggests the appeal of recognition at the same time it expresses the attraction of strangeness. Like travel, the dance itself, the climax of the story, provides a shared movement that allows the achievement of connection within the possibility of separation. The dance satisfies the need of even those "immune" from the world for the comfort of another. With their arms circling each other as they turn about the floor in "impervious motion," they believe they have found exactly what they have "desired" (478). The dance, an experiential realization of tenuous, passionate, graceful balance between freedom and necessity, familiarity and newness, the individual and the Other, represents the alteration of identity sought in travel as psychological process. In the presentation of the ride back to the city, these qualities are rearticulated in the symbolic sensations provoked by "wordless" passage through the night world: a Southern "strange" and "amphibious" land (479), which nevertheless fills the Northern driver with a powerful "recognition" of the "extremity of this place." Despite the absence of familiar landmarks it feels like "snow had suddenly started to fall" (479).

Before the end of the journey, he stops the car to kiss the woman traveler who has been sleeping beside him. Despite the kiss, however, this is no conventional love story, unless "love" means sharing the active capacity to reimagine some other way of being and trying to integrate that insight into one's life, which I take to be the project of "No Place for You, My Love" as a travel narrative. The bruise is a corporeal sign of their failure to come together in a moment of compassionate alliance. The unidentified man and the woman never even call each other by name, and the conclusion reveals that their bond is finally a sympathy that precludes intimacy. At the end she "forgives" him, but does not awaken in time "to tell him her story" (480). But even if the real story of the woman traveler remains obscure, her symbolic function may be analyzed. Her secret and separate journey is a trope for alternative desire and experience. Her companionship seems to enable her fellow traveler to experience the dislocation, contradiction, and freedom that may contribute to his own development. Her sexual presence, to which the man responds in his invitation, the dance, and the kiss, appears to warrant a fully sensuous perception of the world presented through the sequenced experience of the journey. Finally, because her own life is, according to his interpretation, apparently structured by flux, her presence provides a positive model for the value of contingency. In "No Place for You, My Love," Welty rejects traditional feminine stability to establish the moving woman as a symbolic source of inspiration for radical personal change.

THE NARRATIVE AS SOCIAL PROCESS

The travel structure in Welty's "The Wide Net" organizes a process of readjustment that extends beyond the issues of personal change to ensure the continuity of the community. Anthropologist Victor Turner theorizes that a ceremonial action undertaken by a group becomes ritual when it has the power to transform. The dramatic enactment through the transformative journey of the male community in "The Wide Net" recreates the necessary alliance between men and women upon which society rests.

As Leed observes, in the gendered world of travel "the journeys of women are secret, necessitated or accomplished through the agency of men" (221), but "The Wide Net" is the only instance I know of in which a profoundly female journey is ritually enacted by a community of men, who drag the river for the body of one of its members. The plot undercuts the profundity of this performance, however, by reducing it to the resolution of a comic[8] spat between ordinary lovers. William Wallace Jamieson, the young husband, is becoming increasingly estranged from his young, pregnant wife, Hazel, a situation he doesn't comprehend. When he comes home one fine morning after a night out with the boys, he discovers his wife's histrionic message: she would not tolerate his mistreatment and was "going to drown herself" (169). The comic tone is initiated through a logical question that rises even through William Wallace's panic and chagrin: how could Hazel drown herself if she's mortally afraid of the water? The answer is supplied by his drinking buddy of the night before: "Jumped backwards," says Virgil. "Didn't look" (171).

That the journey is ultimately controlled by female need is not only evident at the level of motivation but is implied by two internal interpreters of the text. "It's a woman's trick," declares the satirically named Virgil, whose common-sense observations always reduce the epic to the everyday (171). Old Doc, the Polonious-priest of the adventure (and owner of the necessary net), elaborates, "Girls don't just haul off and go jumping in the river to get back at their husbands. They got other ways" (186). Old Doc is right in one respect; the problem at issue exceeds petty vengeance. The humorous tone of stereotypical marital manipulation does not obviate the deeper division literally enacted in the symbolic structure of the story: the satirically presented practical procedural world of the band of men who operate the net, which contrasts the phenomenal implications of experience. In "The Wide Net" the plot and form of symbolic journey dramatize masculine and feminine difference and bring them to transformative resolution.

For Turner, ceremonial action undertaken by a community becomes ritual when it can effect change. Such transformative ritual, which may take the form of literary narrative, is to be understood as "a spontaneous unit of social process," a dramatic enactment that occurs in four phases: "breach, crisis, redress, and *either* reintegration and recognition *or* recognition of schism" (145). The drama is initiated by the *breach* of some rule of etiquette or normative value that is "seen as the expression of a deeper division of interests and loyalties than appears on the surface" (146). When William Wallace does not come back to Hazel because he is with his friends, his action changes the covert contradictions of masculine and feminine priorities into an overt conflict that the drama attempts to resolve. These differences are predicated as feminine connection opposed to masculine separation and masculine procedural logic opposed to feminine phenomenal emotion. The first of these polarities is addressed by plot. The breach issue is that the young husband has failed to accede to the limits of connection/separation implicit in the marital contract. His failure to return home during the night abrogates the minimal connection of the couple and forces his wife to an action that seeks to redefine this aspect of their relationship; therefore Hazel instigates William Wallace's experiential encounter with the implications of separation and connection to redefine his gendered perspective on these central issues. The form of the story, which pits procedure against emotion as an effect of the ritual journey, addresses the second set of divergent terms.

The primary purpose of the *crisis* phase is to reveal fully the divisions suggested by the action of the breach, but it also serves to expose the "more durable, but nevertheless gradually changing social structure, made up of relations that are relatively constant and consistent" (Turner 147). These two different purposes define Welty's employment of the ritual journey in "The Wide Net." The journey of a representative party of men of the community—children, adolescents, and adults, both white and black—proceeds dialectically in three movements. The first, during which the party is gathered and the river is approached, juxtaposes the practical and hierarchical arrangements of male adventure with visionary perspective. William Wallace not only chooses who will participate in the expedition to find Hazel's body, but he asserts his own preeminence over the numerous and overpowering Malones. They would have to be careful, he explains, because it is his "day with the net" (172). Yet the competitive young man forgets the engaging issues of leadership when the group comes to the brink of the river. The party pauses as the dark path through the forest opens onto light, and Doc's comments on the scene stress beauty and transience. In the fall October sunlight, the sky and trees and river look as if they were made of gold. The recent bridegroom thinking of his golden bride while observing the "shining" willows and the net, "strung and tied" with "threads" of gold enters a different relation with his environment: associative and vital. What's the "name of this river?" he demands to know, shocking his quotidian companions who think he's lost his mind not to recognize the river he's been fishing in his whole life (176).

The next movement deepens this division. The masculine activity on the surface of the river—swimming to arrange the net, hauling ropes and buckets, running across the sandbars, floating in the rowboat—is contrasted to an experience of depth. William Wallace has been diving under the water, and his resultant silence contradicts the busy volubility of the rest of his group. In the climactic moment of the story the words of the others are set against his intuitive vision. Throughout the day William Wallace dives deep down into the dark water where nothing stirs. In those quiet depths he begins to guess a secret: the "real, the true trouble Hazel had fallen into, about which words in a letter could not speak" (180).

The paradoxical meaning of this "secret" is symbolized through the third movement in which William Wallace perceives that Hazel had entered into the terrifying and universal "elation" which "comes of great hopes and changes" (180). The company stops on a wide sandbar to feast on the bounty of the river, the fish they have collected in their seine. Their elation during this festival of fulfillment is expressed by William Wallace in a "dance so crazy that he would die next." The ritual dance shifts the narrative from the ordinary register of the group to the mythic register of William Wallace's experience. As if in response, the legendary "King of the Snakes" appears, displaying his "old hoary head" the looping undulations of a "long dark body" (181). Following this apotheosis of phallic power, a terrifying storm rages. The garrulous black children express their passionate hope that there will be "no balls of fire come" to "fry up all the fishes with they scales on." Immediately afterwards, a great gust of wind covers the frightened group with wet green leaves. Now they have scales, wails one of the children: "Us is the fishes" (183).

Through pregnancy, Hazel has entered a zone of power like that experienced by the men on the sandbar. She can realize all the joy of a vital, bountiful world even more powerfully than they because she can reproduce life itself, rather than merely arrange or take life as they do; but she must also confront something of the terrible contingency and absolute vulnerability such joy also implies. It is this perception, which the storm demonstrates to the men, that accounts for her agitation, misunderstood by William Wallace at the beginning of the story but perceived through the three movements of actual journey.

For Turner the operation of *redress* symbolically acknowledges differences and attempts to negotiate a corrective relation on the basis of consistencies. Through the progressive movements of the journey in "The Wide Net," Welty articulates different styles of agency in separate masculine and feminine spheres that lead to the kind of breach this story proceeds from, but she also claims that William Wallace, by employing feminine modes of perception—associative and phenomenal rather than procedural and hierarchical—may discover the deeper commonality that unites men and women in abundant and threatening nature. In the final phase of the processual structure of social drama, the elements of dissent are either reintegrated, "though the scope and arrangement of its relational field will have altered," or there will be an acknowledgment of irreparable dissension sometimes expressed as "spatial separation" (Turner 147). In this story of return, the husband discovers his young wife waiting with supper at home, but it is clear that a new politics of connection and separation in their relationship is emerging. Not only has he experienced the meaning of her loss, but the last scene shows the couple playfully negotiating the intimate terms of their renewed alliance.

WELTY'S WOMAN TRAVELER

"The Worn Path," perhaps Welty's most popular story, was inspired by her observation of a solitary female making slow progress across the land: "her going was the first thing, her persisting in her landscape was the real thing, and the first and the real were what I wanted and worked at to keep" (*The Eye of the Story* 161). The woman whose symbolic journey joins endurance to progress is the principal emblem of the short fiction. This convergence is realized as a conversion consisting of three stages: (1) the initial motion that provides the experiential equivalent for a loss of the familiar, (2) an engagement with the implications of difference, and (3) a realignment of oppositions within the possibilities created by an altered position. For Eudora Welty, what is good emerges out of a past identified with a locatable place, but what is possible emerges out of movement into a tentative future. Welty's woman traveler or her representatives figuratively enact the constructive psychological and social project of the narrative realization of alteration as stages in a phenomenal journey of extraordinary emotional power. The differing journeys in her short stories are not the quests associated with male wanderers, who inevitably come back home without the "golden apples" of traditional adventure. They are phased processes of the experience of difference that lead to reorganization of existing conditions of personality and community. The feminine journey in Welty's fiction mediates between the past and the future, between the nurturing home and beckoning distance, to model a ceremonial assertion of the possibility of change that incorporates the stability of location and the renewal of motion.

Both Eudora Welty and Elizabeth Bishop use the trope of travel to model processes of transformation. But whereas Welty's short fiction makes travel a conservative means of integrative development, Bishop's poetry, to which we turn in the next chapter, treats travel as a postmodern mode of radical revision.

CHAPTER 8

The Postmodern Journey: Elizabeth Bishop's Trope of Travel

Edith Wharton excepted, Elizabeth Bishop is the most avid actual traveler we have considered, and the trope of travel is the central thematic preoccupation and formal strategy of her works. In key poems and prose, her poetics of movement and journey both deconstructs previous cultural forms and political uses of gendered travel genres and reconstructs a vital encounter with a changing world. A biographical sketch to which Bishop contributed foregrounds the importance of travel throughout her own life from "a walking trip in Newfoundland in 1932 or '33" to visits to England, the Greek Islands, and Yugoslavia during the months preceding her death in 1979. Excursions to Morocco, Ireland, Cuba, Haiti, Nova Scotia, and extensive travels in South America, as well as extended stays in Paris, Mexico, Italy, England, and Brazil are noted as principal events. "My mother's family," she observed, "had a taste for wandering" (Goldensohn xvii–xvix). Barbara Page, who studied Bishop's personal journals, argues that the "vagrancy" of her actual journeys and periodic relocations also deeply informs her poetic practice (197). Placing herself as "a traveler at the perceptual center of her poems," Bishop becomes, for Betsy Erkkila, an "American alien who ultimately leaves the land, refusing allegiance to all master narratives—national, ideological, religious, or metaphysical" (120).

Certainly a thematics of travel predominates in Bishop's poetry, and the experience of journey provides the narrative center and the rhetorical form of her oeuvre. But Bishop's poetry does more than recount her journeys or reject master narratives. It constructs an alternative trope of travel through two parallel strategies: the replacement of the genres of both female and male travel writing with a postmodern poetics and the dissolution of all geographical placement into process. For Bishop the essence of travel is the constant displacement of static perception through particularized sensation, an emotional and intellectual process that forms the basis for what she defines as knowledge. Her transformation of the gendered traveler into an ungendered central consciousness in her poems of travel is a refusal of the politicized failures recorded by previous male and female travel writers—the imperialist aggrandizement of masculine adventure and the uncertain abdications to feminine domesticity. Rejecting both colonial acquisitiveness and social restriction, Elizabeth Bishop develops a postmodern epistemology through the trope of travel as active engagement with a mutable environment.

REWRITING THE GENDERED JOURNEY

Whatever the ostensible reasons for travel from the Enlightenment to the present day—"exploration, conquest, colonization, diplomacy, emigration, forced exile, and trade to religious or political pilgrimage, aesthetic education, anthropological inquiry, and the pursuit of a bronzer body or a bigger wave"—Dennis Porter proposes two basic motives for male journeys: the aggrandizement and replication of the self and the escape from social restriction through the pursuit of desire in the non-European world (10–11). And whatever the motives, "the will to represent the world" in masculine travel writing "masks the effort to control it" (Porter 20).

Several of Bishop's most interesting poems reject the premodern and modern priorities of male travel. "Brazil, January 1, 1502" (91–92)[1] is the most explicit. Ostensibly the description of a "tapestried landscape" depicting the fourteenth-century Brazil that must have greeted Portuguese explorers, it quickly becomes instead a representation of vital process: "every square inch filling with foliage— / big leaves, little leaves, giant leaves." This revision replaces masculine priorities of plot with alternative interpretation of form. A politics of masculine invasion of this landscape is specified in the last stanza, which describes the arrival of "Christians hard as nails, / tiny as nails" who have come to Brazil in their "creaking armor" to find it all "not unfamiliar." Despite the absence of a familiar landscape of "lover's walks" and "bowers" and "lute music," the explorers discover a region "corresponding, nevertheless, / to an old dream of wealth and luxury." The imputed correspondence of the home country to the new world here is the mark of imperialist appropriation. The alignment of indigenous features with the familiar "dream of wealth" sanctions the invaders' economic dominance. Subject to the obvious force (and the implied limitations) of the "tiny" armed men of the last stanza, the native abundance depicted in the first two stanzas is converted into European "luxury."

If, as Porter argues, the male traveler dreams of reproducing the economic system of the home country for his own benefit, he also imagines evading the sexual regulation of European society. Such is the effect of the final lines in which the conquistadors, fresh from "Mass, humming perhaps / *L'Homme armé* or some such tune" seek "a brand-new pleasure":

> They ripped away into the hanging fabric,
> each out to catch an Indian for himself—
> those maddening little women who kept calling,
> calling to each other (or had the birds waked up?)
> and retreating, always retreating behind it.

Brazil is portrayed here as the colonial stereotype of the feminized Other to male greed and male lust. The acquisition of the land is equated with the rape of women and also with the destruction of a feminine artifact: "They ripped away into the hanging fabric."

Rapacious imperial invasion is the story the poem tells about the male journey, but the poem also introduces an imaginary women's record. A specifically feminine artifact, the tapestry of "Brazil" worked with a Portuguese motto represents an alternative encounter with a new world from the perspective of a fictitious female observer, a vision almost obliterated by the dominance of the male. That this alternative presentation is also a European projection is indicated by "the five sooty dragons" as symbols of Catholic "Sin," a motif that confirms the shared heritage of the male and female perspectives. Nevertheless, the depiction of verdant abundance and the representation of the sexual power of the female lizard[2] suggests the artist's metaphoric identification with the feminized Otherness of Brazil, which contrasts the male travel narrative of sexualized control. Although no woman traveler could have been historically present, her invented perspective contests the imperial account of triumphant "discovery." This present-absent feminine observer whose gender is defined only though its rejection of the masculine paradigm provides a good example of the tropic traveler at the center of all Bishop's work.

The limitations of the specifically male journey can be noted in Bishop's revision of the archetypal *Robinson Crusoe* in "Crusoe in England." Defoe's *The Life and Strange Surprising Adventures of Robinson Crusoe*, published in 1719, introduced a travel narrative that simultaneously escapes and endorses the structures and strictures of home. The desert island where Crusoe is shipwrecked is an exotic site that he laboriously endows with the culture and technology of Europe; thus, according to Pierre Macherey, his story is the history of an "appropriation": "From an initial absolute poverty, Crusoe becomes a 'king in his kingdom,' and he comes to speak of it as 'my estate'" (243). Defoe's Crusoe, like the conquistadors of "Brazil," transforms an alien world into a

European system of value and domination. According to Kay Schaffer, the "assumption that the masculine (man, Empire, Civilization) has the unquestioned God-given right to subdue or cultivate the feminine (woman, Earth, Nature) and appropriate feminine to masculine is a constant structuring principle of Western discourse" (*Women and the Bush: Forces of Desire in Australian Cultural Tradition* 82, qtd. by Mills 45). Told as autobiography, *Robinson Crusoe*—the record of the victory of the prerogatives of self over the hindrances of the world—is an authorizing myth that helped to inaugurate the colonial discourse Schaffer critiques. In Bishop's rendition, however, the adventurer chides himself for self-importance. In a scene that satirizes vaunting pride, Crusoe, mounted atop the highest of his diminutive dead volcanoes, imagines that if it were the proper size, "then I had become a giant." Despite his ingenuity and his tools—the knife, for example, that, in Bishop's version of Defoe's omitted account, "reeked of meaning, like a crucifix"—Crusoe portrays his attempts to impose his will upon the basic conditions of his island as absurd failures. Because eventually he became bored with "the very colors" of his island, he "dyed a baby goat bright red" with the juice of some berries in order to experience a difference from the monotony of his limited environment. The change he introduced was unfortunate, however, for the baby's mother "wouldn't recognize him." As Bishop redeploys Crusoe's experience, neither masculine aggrandizement nor strategies of control are effective. In fact, through the mother and baby, she introduces a feminine perspective to confute the sketch of masculine desire for control of nature. And Crusoe himself mocks his own imperialist impulses. By deflating one of the founding fathers of the male travel narrative, Bishop derides the imperial enterprise of male travel.

In *The Witness and the Other World: Exotic European Travel Writing, 400–1600* Mary B. Campbell describes "travel literature as we know it today" as "fully narrative, fully inhabited by its narrator . . ." (5–6), a paradigm of masculine control Bishop revises in "Crusoe in England." In the chronological succession of mainly male texts Campbell examines, the modern convention of the powerful narrator replaced the older tradition of an indistinct narrator's desultory presentation of marvels and wonders. The problem with the modern voice, according to Paul Carter in *Botany Bay: An Exploration of Landscape and History*, is its equation with "imperial history," in which the "primary object is not to understand or to interpret: it is to legitimate" (xvi). And the evolution of the male travel narrative as a legitimating structure is implicated, as Campbell observes, in the European destruction of native populations she calls "the American holocaust": "When Europe found the Other World for which it had sought throughout the East, that 'earthly

Paradise' became the scene of the hugest genocide the world had ever known" (7).[3]

Evading the questionable tactics of male travel writing is not, however, the only accomplishment of Bishop's practice. She also avoided the domestic investment of the female travel writing analyzed by Sara Mills. As Mills notes, although there were "many hundreds" of British or colonial female travel writers in the late nineteenth and twentieth centuries, their writing was generally not only ignored or dismissed, it was widely assumed not to exist (1–2), and when read at all, its authors were presumed to be at best anomalous, at worst "improper" (32). This problem of feminine propriety in reception also affected the production of women's travel texts. The traveling women Mills describes felt the need to negotiate a contradiction. Since the aggressive adventure of male travel was considered improper for women, the female travel writer had to invent a way to represent her movement without sacrificing her respectability. Although discursive solutions varied in the body of literature she studied, Mills observed that content which denoted conventional femininity was often prominent: "a concern with relationships, domestic description, a concern with Christianity and morality" operated as a counterbalance to the "unfeminine actions" of the travel account (98). According to Mills, a style of writing that conforms to feminine confessional fiction rather than the scientific descriptive style characteristic of masculine travel writing of the period was the preferred mode (104).[4]

Bishop's rejection of the decorous compromises of her female predecessors is especially apparent in her treatment of the theme of houses, those primary symbols of female rootedness. The tone of "Filling Station" (127–128), for example, caricatures domestic order and comfort and deprecates the feminine impulses evident in such arrangements:

> Somebody embroidered the doily.
> Somebody waters the plant,
> or oils it, maybe. Somebody
> arranges the rows of cans
> so that they so softly say:
> Esso—so—so—so
>
> to high strung automobiles.
> Somebody loves us all.

In "The End of March" (178–180) the narrator humorously introduces her attraction to her "crypto-dream-house," a "crooked box / set on pilings, shingled green, / a sort of artichoke of a house" she sees on a walk on the beach only to literally turn her back and walk away. Helen Vendler frames Bishop's poetry in the interplay between the domestic and the exotic that celebrates the process through which an unknown terrain is humanized by "love" (105). Yet by omitting from consideration the political reality that such humanizing lovers are expected to be women, Vendler gives short shrift to the crucial evasion of the domestic enacted by Bishop's traveler. *"Should we have stayed at home, / wherever that may be?"* (94), the question at the conclusion of "Questions of Travel," is rhetorical. The answer is an emphatic *No*. In "Sestina," "First Death in Nova Scotia," "One Art," "The Waiting Room," as well as "Crusoe in England," the home place is the setting for pain, loss, and death.[5]

Since the 3,000 volumes of Bishop's personal library included a substantial number of works on travel (Goldensohn 61), she was, no doubt, aware of the conventions and limitations of the genre, and she apparently chose to identify with neither masculine adventure and self-aggrandizement nor feminine domesticity and equivocation. Whether consciously or not, Bishop shaped her own narrator in resistance to the gendered deficiencies of imposed male and female roles.[6] In "Santarem" (185–187) Bishop gently rebukes the male traveler, "Mr. Swan / Dutch, the retiring head of Phillips Electric, / really a very nice old man, / who wanted to see the Amazon before he died." The self-glorifying ambition of the heroic journey—exploring the Amazon—apparently blinds him to the genuine enlargement available on the way. As Birgitta Maria Ingemanson observes, "Intensely goal-oriented, male travelers tended to charge ahead toward their destination, interested primarily in conquering land and getting there" (15). However, at the "conflux of two great rivers," the speaker of the poem enacts another kind of practice by observing with extraordinary attention the ordinary details of a scene literally in motion: "Two rivers full of crazy shipping—people / all apparently changing their minds, embarking / disembarking, rowing clumsy dories." There are about a dozen "white-habited nuns" waving "gaily from an old sternwheeler / getting up steam, already hung with hammocks." And in one of the "countless wobbling dugouts" a cow, "being ferried somewhere to be married," stands placidly chewing her cud. The culmination of this traveler's extraordinary appreciation of the ordinary is "an empty wasps' nest" given as a reward for admiration of it: "small, exquisite, clean matte white, / and hard as stucco" (186). The speaker's perceptual precision confutes the coarse indifference of Mr. Swan, who reveals his deficiency by demanding, "What's that ugly thing?"

Neither blindly self-serving nor distracted by domestic investment, the attentive narrator of "Santarem" is capable of the particularized attention that evades both accommodation and imperialism. In contrast to the heedless Mr. Swan, the minutely observant traveler who is the focal consciousness of all of Bishop's travel poems is always unnamed and literally self-less. This effaced narrator, who engages the phenomenal landscape with an eye and ear alerted to its ordinary wonders, resumes a style that looks backward to the naive presentation of the earliest accounts of travel. Distanced from the historical burdens of social identity, this traveler, unhindered by gendered conventions of male and female travel writing, is free to concentrate on travel as a form of constructive encounter with a genuinely new world.

DISPLACEMENT AS CONSTRUCTIVE PROCESS

The geographical practice[7] at the heart of Bishop's poetry emerges from the tension between emplacement and motion. The focus on place is obvious in many titles—*North & South*, "Brazil," "Elsewhere," *Geography III*, "Florida," "Cape Breton," "Varick Street," but a dialectics of movement is enacted in most of the poems. Let "The Bight" (60–61) from the 1955 volume *A Cold Spring* provide an example. The poem begins by ostensibly providing a view—a postcard perhaps—of a specific location, a beach and the harbor beyond it: "At low tide like this how sheer the water is." Even the visual adjective, however, dictates a further motion of the eye; if something is "sheer," one must look farther than the outside layer. The deeper vision structured by the poem begins in paradox and proceeds to a catalogue of activities marked by verbs.

Lines 2–4 suggest that the water scene is paradoxically dry:

> White, crumbling ribs of marl protrude and glare
> and the boats are dry, dry as matches.
> Absorbing rather than absorbed,
> the water in the bight doesn't wet anything.

The imagery of a decaying skeleton may indicate that the visual distance of the static perspective of conventional description is destructive; the insistence on dryness may also suggest that it is false. In addition to its literal meaning, the line suggests a perspective that is "absorbing," that is, interesting rather than deeply engaging, a quality of involvement suggested by the word *absorbed*. The possible reversal suggested by the wet-dry paradox and reinforced by the ironic distinction between degrees of absorption is realized in the extraordinary and continuous transformative activity catalogued by the rest of the poem, in which the static postcard is converted into a kaleidoscope of sensation. The color of the water turns into "a gas flame" an observer "can smell," the birds "soar" and "crash" like "pickaxes," the "frowsy sponge boats keep coming in," and even that which is literally inanimate acquires a kind of verbal vitality from participation in the ongoing process suggested by the rapid sequence of accumulating qualification:

> Some of the little white boats are still piled up
> against each other, or lie on their sides, stove in,
> and not yet salvaged, if they ever will be, from the
> last bad storm.

"All the untidy activity continues," the last lines of the poem assert, "awful but cheerful." Bishop's parenthetic insertion under the title that this is a poem "On my birthday" is both an insistence on the celebration of continuity and a playful presentation of a kind of credo of process, which although clearly not redemptive (a rebirth in the religious sense) may be a source of practical salvation or "salvage" in the diction of "The Bight." Proceeding through a series of imaginative Baudelaireian "correspondences,"[8] this insistent conversion of static scene to verbal motion provides the underlying rhetorical structure of many Bishop poems, whatever their subjects.

In "The Map," for example, which introduces *The Complete Poems*, the static placement of topographical features is modified by imaginative perception. In "The Sandpiper," the geography experienced by the bird is too immediate for myths of fixed representation: "The world is a mist," "The beach hisses like fat," while the moiling Atlantic is "dragging" off the small "grains" of the sandpiper's unstationary territory (131).[9] "Florida" is less a "state" than a noisy and active fusion of living and dying flora and fauna, and the "Cold Spring" of "Maryland" thaws under the power of a catalogue of natural and perceptual processes. This predominant geographical strategy of place superseded by process becomes an emotional strategy in such poems as the early "Letter to New York," in which the speaker requests that the possible differences between the letter writer and the speaker be displaced by an active account of "where you are going and what you are doing"; while in the later villanelle "One Art" the pain of loss is dissolved in the insistent circularity of the poem's formal repetition.

The extraordinary necessity for tactical displacement is signaled in such poems as "The Bight" by the pattern of allusions to death throughout the poem. The seriousness of this precept as an issue of travel finds expression in "Crusoe in England" (162–66). In Bishop's revision of the original story, the end of movement brings death. In Daniel Defoe's novel, Friday dies at the hands of savages during a subsequent voyage; in Bishop's poem Friday's death by measles is remembered from the lethal stasis of England. The suggestive contrast between survival and extinction latent in all Bishop's poetry is interpreted in "At the Fishhouses." The intensity of the poetic engagement with the scene in the poem (64–66) makes it easy to forget that the initial location is a shambles. As in "The Bight," the process of transfiguration is achieved through verb forms, as description spills over into participles, and through details of sensory experience and paradoxical reversal. Significantly, the poem begins with "Although": the word is a semantic signal that the reader is to experience an exception to what is apparent. Although the reader is invited to observe a location marked by signals of decay and decrepitude—rust in "melancholy stains, like dried blood" and inhabited by an "old man" who converses about "the decline in population"—the implicit stasis and sadness are countered first by the active and overwhelming odor—"it makes one's nose run and one's eyes water"—and then by transmogrified visual effect: "All is silver." The sea in the background, the trees near the beach, the aged wood of the fishhouse, and, most surprising, the very tubs and wheelbarrows used in processing the herring, as well as the clothing of the fisherman who scrapes the bodies of the fish, share an "apparent translucence" that is an effect of the fading evening light and a liberal coating of "sequins," the leftover scales from "unnumbered" dead fish.

If the first half of the poem insists on the active process of transfiguration, the second half elucidates it. Just as the old man is the representative spirit of the fishhouse, the "curious" seal is the emissary of the mutable Atlantic. He seems to respond to the speaker's sportive serenade of "Baptist hymns" with complementary playful movements: "he would disappear, then suddenly emerge / almost in the same spot" before returning to his element. Like the seal, the sea is characterized in terms of movement: "swinging above the stones, / icily free above the stones." The motion of the sea becomes the metaphor for "what we imagine knowledge to be: / dark, salt, clear, moving utterly free." Bishop's witty play with the religious notion of baptism as "total immersion" does not detract from the serious implicit reversal of death enacted by the poem and replicated in the repeated resurrection of the saucy seal. The possibility of transposition through free movement is underscored by the paradox of the ceremonial immersion in the penultimate lines of the poem. If you were to dip your hand into the frigid water, the poem insists, your "wrist" and "bones" would "ache and your hand would burn / as if the water were a transmutation of fire / that feeds on stones and burns with a dark gray flame."

The effect here is not the oxymoronic balance of two opposed properties in one image: cold fire. Rather than stationary equilibrium, the lines achieve an active antithesis of limitation, and, just as the cold is converted to heat, death, represented as static location, is subject to "transmutation" through the freedom purchased by metaphoric motion. This principle of vital movement is the basis for "knowledge" throughout Bishop's oeuvre.

POSTMODERN EPISTEMOLOGY

"Over 2,000 Illustrations and a Complete Concordance" (57–59), "Questions of Travel" (93–94), and "Santarem" (185–87), Bishop's central narratives of travel, pose questions and suggest answers about poetic practice and possibilities. "Over 2,000 Illustrations" begins the process of inquiry by presenting a reaction to the loss of the powerful authorization of the Christian narrative. The poem can be read as a story of Derridean supplementation, a theory that explains the emergence of textual replacement for lost originary presence. The haphazard perusal of the biblical illustrations by the traveler-narrator is four times removed from the originating events of Christ's death and resurrection, to which the Bible itself is a supplementary account and to which the photographs of hallowed sites add an additional supplement. From the perspective of the narrator, the powerful narrative of Christianity can no longer provide a legitimating structure for the encounter with the world represented as travel; thus the pilgrimage gives way to the postmodern journey. The poem details the experience of loss and tentatively introduces the liberation such loss may initiate.

The modifiers of the title "*Over 2,000* Illustrations and a *Complete* Concordance" stress the theme of failed overcompensation: "The Seven Wonders of the world are tired." What is at stake is not the ineffectuality of representation, but a problem of interpretation. Instead of responding to the iconic values the scenes are supposed to establish, the narrator is aware of all their distracting particularities: the gesturing "Arab" rather than the "Tomb, the Pit, the Sepulcher" he is pointing out; the mountings—the "cattycornered rectangles / or circles set on stippled gray"—rather than the engravings. It is this concentration on details instead of order, effects instead of cause, that disturbs the speaker in travels that are presented as a series of contrasts of the sacred to the irrelevant. The pattern is introduced with place names. "Entering the Narrows of *St. Johns*" the travelers are aware only of the sound and sight of the "goats." Proceeding to *St. Peter's*, they notice the sun and the wind and the motion of "the Collegians" who crisscross "the great square with black, like ants." Metaphoric "Easter lilies" give way to "jukebox" music at a Mexican funeral; the hint of blessed birth is absorbed in vapid conversation at a British tea party. This pattern of inferred degradation culminates in the frightening emptiness of a "holy grave," which conveys not only the loss of religion but the absolute vulnerability the narrator fears as the consequence of that loss. "Open to every wind from the pink desert," the sacred site is merely a "gritty marble trough" as yellow as "scattered cattle-teeth." The gaping tomb is "half-filled with dust" that must be a natural result of the desert wind, for it is evidently not the hallowed "dust / of the poor paynim prophet who once lay there." Even in this poem, however, the unacknowledged counterpart to the loss of security conveyed through the imagery of death is the immediacy and vitality of experience: the "bleating goats" which appear "reddish" on the distant hillsides, "leaping up the cliffs / among the fog-soaked weeds and butter and eggs" and the "little pockmarked prostitutes" of Marrakesh "who balanced their tea trays on their heads / and did their belly dances."

In "Over 2,000 Illustrations" the nostalgia for certainty is displaced by the recognition of uncertainty, a move described by Thomas J. Travisano as a critique "of one of the great themes of modernism, the necessity of what Ezra Pound called a 'live tradition' as a means of ordering and giving value to experience" (114). The poem gives narrative structure to the existential shift from modern to postmodern sensibility. Erkkila defines Bishop as a "fundamentally postmodern" poet who uses "traditional form" to "set off and simultaneously control the scenes of desolation, unbelief, and exhaustion that are the subject of her poems" (120). Without the powerful traditional narrative to hold it together, experience, as the speaker observes in "Over 2,000 Illustrations," becomes discontinuous—"Everything only connected by 'and' and 'and'"—but Bishop's travel poems do not present this circumstance in the negative light of Erkkila's interpretation. The nativity invoked at the conclusion of the poem introduces a new birth of consciousness in place of the unwavering illumination of the Christian vision, a strangely inert "unbreathing . . . colorless, sparkless" flame associated with static domesticity ("lulled within, a family with pets"), a topos which in Bishop's poems connotes loss. To return again and again—the regressive action suggested by "looked and looked"—to the ineffectual supplementation of an empty legend is unproductive and must be finally depleted of effect by being "looked away." Caught in the frightening loss of certainty the poem plots, the narrator is only subliminally conscious of the advantage of the loss of ingenuous "infant sight."

Yet the postmodern turn may be understood in terms of challenging opportunity. While the hyperbolic formulations of contemporary theorists exceed the implied claims of Bishop's reticent traveler, Jean-Francois Lyotard's optimistic conception of postmodern epistemology is relevant. According to Steven Best and Douglas Kellner, for Lyotard "Postmodern knowledge is against metanarratives and foundationalism; it eschews grand schemes of legitimation; and it is for heterogeneity, plurality, constant innovation, and pragmatic construction of local rules" (165). The foregrounding of the processes of perception, the dissolution of narrative identity, and the discontinuous sequence of encounter are marks of postmodern practice in Bishop's poetry, and the heterogeneity, innovation, and pragmatism of her vision suggest an affirmative postmodern epistemology.

If the modern travel of "Over 2,000 Illustrations" is an engagement with loss, the postmodern journey of "Questions of Travel" is an inquiry into what may be found. Like "Over 2,000 Illustrations," "Questions of Travel" begins with the inscription of doubt. "Thus should have been our travels" is the objection raised by the narrator of the first poem. In the second, the speaker worries, "There are too many waterfalls here." At issue in the first poem is the rejection of the stereotyped role of pilgrim; in the second the role of tourist is interrogated. For it is the tourist lacking "imagination" who must run off to "imagined places" to "see the sun the other way round." Tourism so defined, like pilgrimage, is a supplemental activity designed to remedy an absence. As such, as the first line implies, it is an embarrassing excess, which rightly provokes the narrator's anxious series of questions in the second stanza. If the object of travel is merely the distraction of scenery, it is not surprising that the initial series of *de trop* images proceeds to sadness and culminates in shipwreck, a symbol of the destruction of travel:

> There are too many waterfalls here; the crowded streams
> hurry too rapidly down to the sea,
> and the pressure of so many clouds on the mountaintops
> makes them spill over the sides in slow-motion,
> turning to waterfalls under our weary eyes.
> —For if those streaks, those mile-long, shiny, tearstains,
> aren't waterfalls yet,
> in a quick age or so, as ages go here,
> they probably will be.
> But if the streams and clouds keep travelling, travelling,
> the mountains look like the hulls of capsized ships,
> slime-hung and barnacled.

Unlike the failure of pilgrimage, which the narrator fears may lead to frenetic meaningless activity, tourism once exhausted results in static domesticity.

The poem, however, introduces another way of thinking about travel: as peripatetic, nonlinear, inconclusive, vivid "connection" not authorized in advance but created in the distinct acts of encounter generated by the journey. The baroque appeal of disparate experience produces a species of "knowledge" introduced in "At the Fishhouses." The connections in "Questions of Travel," though "blurr'dly and inconclusively" produced, are, nevertheless, culturally constitutive: "history" is available in "the weak calligraphy of songbirds' cages" and the tropical "rain" better defines the relentless "oratory" of politics.

The special virtue of processual connection is asserted in "Santarem" through the metaphor of the convergence of the two rivers:

> . . . Hadn't two rivers sprung
> from the Garden of Eden? No, that was four
> and they'd diverged. Here only two
> and coming together. Even if one were tempted
> to literary interpretations
> such as life/death, right/wrong, male/female
> —such notions would have resolved, dissolved, straight off
> in that watery, dazzling dialectic.

The traveler again discounts the authorization of biblical narrative for the geographical dissolution represented by the moving rivers presented as the symbol for the "dazzling" obliteration of the restrictive binary categories of a static epistemology. It is this quotation that explains the abdication of gender in the personification of the traveling consciousness at the center of Bishop's poems. All categorical restrictions are declined in favor of perambulatory encounters through which new relations constantly emerge. Travel, so defined, is the pattern for a new way of being in the world. And, as in "At the Fishhouses," freedom and motion are essential to knowledge.

DISSOLUTION AND PROCESS

The primary metaphors of dissolution and process also find expression in Bishop's prose travel writing, "To the Botequin & Back," "A Trip to Vigia," and the account of the trip to the Dimantina region included in "*The Diary of Helena Morley*: The Book and Its Author," descriptions of excursions in Brazil included in *The Collected Prose*. The characteristic self-dissolution of Bishop's poetry, while literally impossible in pieces that recount her own experience, is expressed as her unwillingness to impose American priorities on the people or landscapes she encounters. In "A Trip to Vigia," for example, Bishop recounts an expedition organized by a poor Brazilian poet of her acquaintance. The car that they are to travel in is evidently unreliable, she begins by explaining. "But what could we do? I couldn't very well flaunt my dollars in his face and hire a better one" (111). Although the trip is arranged to see a famous church, the climax of the journey is not the impression made by the building; it is a human relationship negotiated en route. Bishop is interested in the social transition to intimacy marked by the shift in address from "'Dr. Ruy' to 'you.'" "That morning I asked M. to let me know when the mystic moment arrived" (112). The use of the word *mystic*, also repeated in describing the instance of change in address (114), shifts the scale of what counts as miraculous from the religious to the human. It is significant that unlike the imperial traveler, Bishop abdicates a position of power in both the provision of conveyance and within the personal exchange between the Brazilians she is accompanying. Besides rejecting personal aggrandizement as the object of journeying, a position of humility also facilitates the shift of focus in this account from the tourist spectacle to the engaged observation typical of her poems.

It is this transposition that motivates "To the Botequin & Back," in which the trip is not even nominally to a famous attraction. In this piece Bishop recounts a twenty-minute trip to the grocery store for cigarettes in the style of an annotated journey. She describes in rich exactitude everything she encounters from the "two kinds of morning glories" beautifying a "ruined house" (73) to the barber's "speckled mirror" (75) to the items she purchases—a Pepsi Cola, razor blades, and some "cheap candies" that the storekeeper "spills out all over the dirty counter for me to make my selection." She is most interested in the local men gathered in the store to drink and listen to the dramatic account of "an awful fight last night" (76). Her mundane adventure favorably contrasts the two topics that conclude the piece: an invitation from the local "Department of Tourism" to attend an official event and a description of a picturesque landscape with a waterfall.

An exemplary passage from the introduction to her translation of *The Diary of Helena Morley*,in which Bishop details a visit to the abandoned diamond mines of Boa Vista, is a summary instance of her practice and purpose. At the conclusion of this journey she describes the native expedience that has replaced the technology of the defunct colonial mines:

> Near there we stopped again to watch a group of men looking for diamonds in a stream beside the road. The head of the group had four men, black and white, working for him; he gave me his name and asked me to print it; here it is: Manuel Benicio de Loyola, "diamond-

> hunter of Curralinho." They were shoveling in the shallow, sparkling water, damming it up, releasing it, and arranging piles of gravel on the bank. One of them took up a small quantity of gravel in the wide round sieve and held it just beneath the surface of the water, swirling it skillfully around and around. In a few minutes he lifted it out in one thin layer. With the gesture of a quick-fingered housewife turning out a cake, he turned the whole thing upside down on the ground intact. Senhor Benicio de Loyola then put on horn-rimmed glasses, lowered himself to his knees in the wet mud, and stared, passing a long wooden knife over the gravel from side to side. In a second, he waved his hand, got up, and put his glasses back in his pocket, and his assistant got ready to turn out another big gravel pancake, while he and Seu Antonio Cicero talked about a large blue diamond someone had found a day or two before. (98)

In contrast to the Victorian male travel authors of the distanced "promontory view" described by Mary Louise Pratt as an exercise in European exploitation (202–207),[10] Bishop's narrative places her as a close and respectful observer in a foreign land. Significantly, she credits Richard Burton—the writer who for Pratt best exemplifies the "monarch-of-all-I-survey" perspective—for his account of the formerly active mines run by foreign companies, but her own journey culminates in an alternative location, stressing native agency over imported technology. While she maintains her stance as an outsider in the three narratives of travel in Brazil included in *The Collected Prose*, her meticulous descriptions characteristically respect the local and celebrate native adaptations to the stringencies of circumstance.

As in many of the poems, the elements of earth and water here convey her interest in process. "Click. Click. Goes the dredge, / and brings up a dripping jawful of marl" (60–61), Bishop brightly reports in "The Bight." Similarly, in this passage human modification of the world is observed with fascination. Although the records of Bishop's travels may begin with representation of geographical features, they often proceed to the approving notation of energetic human alteration.

This passage makes use of the figure of dissolution to emphasize the practical workings of transformation on several levels. In describing the actual procedure of dissolving the earth around the residue of stones, Bishop erases the distinction between male work and female work and erodes the separation of the races. The figurative masculine invasion of nature for gain in mining is replaced by the constructive feminine metaphor of a housewife making a pancake, and the miners are equally divided between white and black. Although it is always a mistake to overburden Bishop's precise observations with generalizations, it is possible to discern here something of her special sense of the role of history and the purpose of narrative. Her formal naming of the "head" of the workers, at his request, pokes sympathetic fun at the pride of self central to masculine travel narratives at the same time it memorializes this ordinary scene as an assertion of its genuine significance. If the workers do not find diamonds in this example, encouraged by stories of other local discoveries, they do continue to try. In Bishop's unsentimental presentation, the role of narrative, played out on the scale of rumor rather than epic, is to lay out the pattern of wonder that ensures continuous modification of an often unyielding world.

The purpose of travel, the narrative at the heart of Bishop's poetry, is to decline all forms of restriction through dissolving the limiting patterns of personal and social practice. Bishop's traveler—feminine only in the sense that her subversive vision replaces that of masculine domination—enacts a postcolonial ethics of travel.[11] Rejecting narrative figures of appropriation for a moral aesthetics, she discovers the constitutive conditions of a new history that dreams of evading the limits of previous stories of gender: the unimperial self, absorbed in the motion and renewal of a voyage to engage the serial marvels (the actual diamonds of legendary possibility) of an unredeemed, redeemable world.

CONCLUSION

Orpah's Journey: Reading the Constructive Narrative

A definitive text of women's travel is the Old Testament Book of Ruth. "[W]hither thou goest, I will go; where thou lodgest, I will lodge: thy people shall be my people, and thy God my God"—Ruth's famous declaration to her mother-in-law, Naomi—marks the text as more than a narrative of women's travel; it is also a story of feminine assimilation and acculturation. After the death of her husband and her two sons in the land of Moab, Naomi leaves for her native Judah to pursue economic survival in her own homeland, accompanied by the young Moabite widows of her two sons. Ruth's story portrays not only her loyal attachment to Naomi but her education in the ways of Naomi's community. Under her mother-in-law's tutelage, she secures the financial and social protection of Naomi's kinsman Boaz and finally becomes his wife to bear him the son who initiates the lineage of David. But there is another important character who makes a brief appearance in the story. The second daughter-in-law, Orpah, also begins the journey, only to yield to Naomi's urging to pursue her own destiny. As Orpah sets out, presumably toward her native land, she drops out of the story. Whereas Ruth's continuing narrative outlines the acceptable form of the woman's travel narrative subsumed under the patriarchal plot of dominant culture, Orpah's opposing absence may be appropriated to suggest a different version.[1] By remaining essentially secret, untold, it retains the possibility for alternative emplotment. Orpah's absent journey can signify the possible rejection of the customary alignment of women with cultural stereotypes that is realized in Ruth's narrative enactment of her mother-in-law's advice:

> Wash thyself therefore, and annoint thee, and put thy raiment upon thee, and get thee down to the threshingfloor: but make not thyself known unto the man, until he shall have done eating and drinking.
>
> And it shall be, when he lieth down, that thou shalt mark the place where he shall lie, and uncover his feet, and lay thee down; and he will tell thee what thou shalt do.

Naomi's advice to Ruth on securing Boaz's favor outlines the appropriate cultural pattern for the traditional deployment of feminine power through sexuality and subservience. Similarly, the account of a traveling woman may afford its protagonist the opportunity to observe and practice familiar feminine behaviors in new surroundings. Orpah's obscured story, however, evades accommodation. Like Leed's differentiation between women's travels under the auspices of men and those that remain "secret" (221), the difference between Ruth's accommodation and the alternative I ascribe to Orpah is the fundamental distinction upon which this study is based.

My purpose has been to begin to tell the secrets of Orpah's journey of deviation from convention as they are inscribed in American literature. But reading obscured inscriptions presents obvious problems of interpretation. The critical methodology of this study combines a battery of practices that reveal rather than conceal alternative meanings. The first chapter exemplifies the deconstructive strategy employed throughout: to examine the anomalous figure of the traveling woman as a challenge to the binary structures through which societies codify privileged evaluations. Between the ideological mobility of the man and the socially defined sessility of the woman, the woman traveler exists as a species of scandal that rewrites the travel narrative and disputes the social values it structures in a variety of contexts. Succeeding chapters concentrate on the elucidation of reconstructive alternatives. Chapter 2 introduces the cognitive model of narrative revolution more fully developed below. Chapter 3 applies Pierre Macherey's political theory of narrative revision; chapter 4 extends Michel de Certeau's description of political subversion in everyday life to the practice of narrative revision; chapter 5 expands the implications of genre criticism to mark the alteration of ethical structures; chapter 6 makes use of French Feminist tactics of narrative subversion; chapter 7 illustrates the narrative project of transformation from the perspective of influential theories of anthropology, history, and psychological criticism; and chapter 8 defines a postmodern epistemological practice. The differences in approach are appropriate to the analysis of texts widely separate in historical circumstances, style, and specific meanings, but both texts and approaches participate in the same narrative project: the articulation of the possibility of change.

Narrative, as this study conceives it, implies much more than the name for the arrangement of incidents in literary composition. Like a growing number of cognitive psychologists, I assume that narrative is a basic mental process through which people plot dynamic relationships with the exigencies of human experience. Telling or hearing a story, writing or reading a narrative, is an active practice of evaluation that connects experience to the schemes of interpretation that form the substance of culture. Through narrative, people align personal events with social meaning. In *Metaphors We Live By* George Lakoff and Mark Johnson argue that experiential metaphors organize the social meanings codified by culture and that metaphors of spatial orientation are central to this process. For this reason, travel, as the quintessential narrative trope of spatial orientation, has provided the basis for the organization of primary aspects of Western social and political practice. Citing Stephen Pepper's theory of "root metaphors," Theodore R. Sarbin explains that a suggestive metaphor may, in fact, become reified into a metaphysical system that patterns expectations and actions, and studies like Mary Louise Pratt's *Imperial Eyes* confirm that narratives of travel have configured the dangerous beliefs that have sanctioned centuries of Western imperialism. Because men have been the principal travelers, their stories of aggressive conquest and disconnection from community have been deeply influential, but, as this study argues, the root narrative of travel may find and foster alternative visions and values.

Donald E. Polkinghorne explains that the "ordering of events by linking them into a plot comes about through an intermixing of the various elements of the cultural repertoire of sedimented stories and innovations" (20). But such "emplotment is not the imposition of a ready-made plot structure on an independent set of events: instead it is a dialectic process that takes place between the events themselves and a theme which discloses their significance as parts of one story." While this story-making often replicates existing ideologies by matching individual experiences with existing plots, it may also "generate unique and novel configurations" (19–20). Lakoff and Johnson theorize the subversion and reconstruction of meaning through several related comparative practices: (1) developing awareness of the conceptual choices implicit in the metaphors that structure understanding, (2) noting dissimilar experiences that can provide a basis for the development of alternative organizing structures, and (3) "[e]ngaging in an unending process of viewing" experience "through new alternative metaphors" (233). Within this processual model the study of the narrative trope of women's travel, which stands for contradiction, articulates uncodified possibilities, and repeatedly enacts the advantage of alternatives, assumes significance as a signal instance of the narrative invention of transformation and a literary model of the cognitive processes of political and social revolution.

Since "human beings think, perceive, imagine, and make moral choices according to narrative structures" (Sarbin 8), to contest the structural implications of root narratives may be to change the world. Thus the trope of women's travel—and the study of its narrative challenges and revisions of the dominant order—acquires its radical power. A feminist practice of critical otherness locates the representations of and by women as sites of dialectical challenge, resistance, and subversion. Because travel literature has frequently transmitted patriarchal values by scripting the passage to manhood as the rewards of colonial exploitation, it certainly does invite rereading from the political perspective of "the disruptive liminality of women," as George Van Den Abbeele suggests in *Travel as Metaphor* (xxvi). But the trope of women's travel can also move us beyond deconstruction to a feminist theory of *construction* grounded in the psychology of narrative.

This study of the trope of women's travel as constructive feminist practice is based on Hayden White's "tropics of discourse" and in propositions about the convergence of narrative and cognition by psychologists and literary critics. According to psychologists John A. Robinson and Linda Hawpe, narrative as a psychological process is a creative response to the need for "understandable order in human affairs," which "requires a cognitive analysis of action in the social context" (111–12). Because the "instantiation of the models we carry in our own minds" is, according to Jerome Bruner, only fully expressed through "the cultural tool kit" (*Actual Minds, Possible Worlds* 7, 15) of literature, we must attend to its characteristic forms of expression to understand the connection between the social world and the story in order to imagine the reconstruction of either. There is a primary tension for Hayden White between what we know and what we are trying to understand that is addressed through tropological discourse, which "moves 'to and fro' between received encodations of experience and the clutter of phenomena which refuses incorporation into conventionalized notions of 'reality,' 'truth,'or 'possibility'" (4). Such discourse consists of description of what is known, putative argument or narrative threading through the descriptive material, and a combination of these two categories expressed as trope: "the rendering of the unfamiliar into the familiar is a troping that is generally figurative," according to White (5). In *Reading for the Plot* Peter Brooks, citing Roman Jakobson's basic linguistic categories, identifies the two literary features of this process as metaphor and metonomy. Narrative is the metonymic "acting out of the implications of metaphor" (26) through which a series of posited paradigmatic equivalencies is projected spatially and temporally in story form: "in every case of narrative, it seems fair to say, there must be enactment in order to produce transformation: the plotting-out of initial givens so that their uses may be transformed" (27).

The secret journeys of this study are metaphors for deviation as a constructive response to gendered social and political restriction. The implications of the restrictions and the effects of alternative social and political arrangements are plotted as events in the story of a particular woman's movement in space and time. To read the narrative of reconstruction within the trope of women's travel it is necessary, first, to determine what social and political expectations are coded by ideologies of women's stability and men's movement within a specific historical situation; second, to review the patterns of representation that organize these meanings within a given culture; and, third, to analyze the trope of women's travel to discover what possibilities of alternative meaning are conveyed through its deviation from social and representational norms.

The description of gendered expectations in the Puritan New England of Mary Rowlandson in chapter 2 is a good example of the first procedure. The analysis of representations of masculine travel narrative forms available to John Greenleaf Whittier in chapter 1 exemplifies the second. In both of these operations, I have made use of a variety of psychological, anthropological, and political theories that articulate patterns of experience and representation. In *Psychoanalysis and Feminism*, Juliet Mitchell argues that "psychoanalysis is not the recommendation *for* a patriarchal society, but an analysis *of* one" (xiii). Similarly, I have assumed that the theories I have made use of are descriptive of distinct conditions to which the literature under consideration also responds. Thus, for example, Lacanian psychology, which defines the content of the unconscious as having the structure of languages provides a way of understanding the texts of Edith Wharton, who deliberately fashioned her own response to personal circumstance out of her competent absorption of cultures organized by literature and language. To make use of Lacanian theory is not to assume that Lacan is telling eternal truths applicable in all circumstances, but it is to assert that he is explaining conditions that have bearing on Wharton's uses of culture. Likewise, Carol Gilligan's description of the moral component of female psychological development has bearing on Jewett's creation of narrative structures to define women's ethical development. Just as Wharton and Jewett create different narratives in response to differing social, political, and psychological conditions in different circumstances, different scholars present different theories to account for inevitably varying conditions. A broad range of hypothetical explanations is appropriate to the analysis of changing relations between selves and worlds negotiated by differing tropes of women's travel.

In the literature of women's journeys of this study, the transformative project of the third step—the discovery of alternative meanings—may be observed by comparing contradictory representations of male and female travelers. In many of the works considered, figures of masculine travel suggest the deficiency of the social strategies and values that they traditionally encode. The male traveler frequently, as in Willa Cather's, Elizabeth Bishop's, and Sarah Orne Jewett's works, epitomizes the defects of imperial acquisition. In *The Professor's House*, for example, as Tom Outland reports, Roddy Blake explains as business as usual his sale of the Pueblo artifacts treasured by Outland. In so doing he defines commercial exploitation as the unquestionable end result of masculine exploration: "he knew I cared about the things, and was proud of them, but he'd always supposed that I meant to 'realize' on them, just as he did, and that it would come to money in the end. 'Everything does,' he added" (244). And if the male traveler sometimes represents moral defect, he routinely exemplifies functional failure. John Greenleaf Whittier's *Snow-Bound* invokes the traditional stories of American male travel to finally undercut their contemporary validity. The British soldiers deeply challenge the certainties that organize Mary Rowlandson's world precisely because they *cannot* cross the river. Neither Tom Outland nor the professor in Cather's novel "realizes" the achievement of an alternative pattern of male travel. Despite his rhetorical power, Lawyer Royall in Edith Wharton's *Summer* is defined by what he could *not* achieve. On the basis of his own history he admonishes the audience at the Old Home Week Celebration "to look at things as they are. Some of us have come back to our native town because we'd failed to get on elsewhere" (194). From within the literal confinement imposed by slavery, Harriet Jacobs's protagonist provokes her master's expensive and futile trips to the North to recover her. And Jewett and Welty both demote professional male wanderers to pathetic comic figures. In many periods and differing conditions the literature of women's travel presents the root metaphor of the male journey as a symbol of defective internal values and detrimental external achievement in contrast to the woman traveler's redemptive revisions of both interior and exterior conditions through deconstruction and reconstruction.

The scandalous narrative of women's travel presents or invents alternative arrangements to controvert the dominant social order. The binary dissolution of Bishop's "Santarem," for instance, contradicts many stationary categories of public meaning, just as Harriet Livermore disturbs the arrangements Whittier seems to endorse in *Snow-Bound*. And these deconstructive challenges to the protagonist's social world may also dissolve the static categories of her psychological situation. The journeys in *Housekeeping* enact this process, and the complex freedom experienced by Virgie during her swim in Eudora Welty's "The Wanderers" is another example. Similarly, by opposing the ideal of feminine virtue to the reality of female slavery, Jacobs deconstructs the relevance of the first category, and through her effort to reconstruct the meaning of virtue in her public life, she also revises the equally contradictory category of motherhood in her private experience. In addition to escaping the slave conditions that restrict her actual mothering, Jacobs must redefine her inherited concept of motherhood to recognize active, sometimes solitary, initiative as well as stationary domestic loyalty as balanced necessities for the slave mother. The psychological recognition of the emotional contradiction in the gender arrangements of the family is also the effect of the gothic journey as introduced in Cather's *The Professor's House* and developed in Wharton's *Summer*.

Reconstructions of gendered family relationships at the social and psychological levels are also the respective achievements of Sarah Orne Jewett and Marilynne Robinson. In *The Country of the Pointed Firs*, Jewett's women travelers fashion a mature relation of mothers and daughters that reconfigures domestic relations as patterns for ethical social arrangements in the outer world. In Robinson's *Housekeeping*, the psychological acceptance of the death of the mother, and the concomitant rejection of the domestic stasis associated with the earliest experiences of the mother-child tie, opens the way for a revised female family relation based on mutuality and mobility. In both of these works this revision of female bonds confutes the influential psychoanalytic interpretation of mother-daughter experience as preoedipal and, therefore, necessarily irrational and confining. The combined representations of family by Jacobs, Cather, Wharton, Jewett, and Robinson suggest that because detrimental relationships result from social strictures, they may be confronted through the trope of the gothic journey and recreated as alternative patterns of social and psychological development through the trope of women's travel.

The transformative patterns of such reconstruction of psychology, society, and culture are developed in Welty's short fiction as the complex revision of self and world that her stories of travel reiterate. For Bishop the particularized experience of the world experienced as travel in her poetry rejects the traditional accounts of masculine travel as dangerous egotism and feminine travel as detrimental accommodation. Like Jewett, Welty, and Robinson, Bishop reconceives the encounter with nature as an opportunity to redefine and reverse the social assumptions out of which literary conventions develop. All of these writers exchange static domesticity for differing definitions of dynamic relationship to family, community, the natural world, political power, and social convention.

The narrative trope of women's travel, as we have observed it, serves to reconceptualize the world and the woman's private and public role within it. The travel narrative structure in such diverse works as Rowlandson's colonial memoir and Cather's and Wharton's modern novels even constructs a discourse that exceeds what is socially or literally available to consciousness or intention. Through trope, the woman's travel narrative can articulate possibilities that are not yet socially, culturally, or psychologically coded: what may not be known may be depicted as incidents in a journey. As Bishop's poetry demonstrates, the journey of the woman traveler can establish an alternative epistemology.

In his study of literature and imperialism, *Dreams of Adventure, Deeds of Empire*, Martin Green describes the imperial adventurer as a romanticized and militant mercantile hero, who, free from "classical precedent" (39), feels the lure of excessive plunder, which he realizes because of his moral stature and technological superiority. In his American form, a frontier identity made him large, violent, rapacious, and aggressively antiaristocratic. In contrast to the vast overseas English empire formed through the subjugation of native populations and the imposition of British institutional structures on existing native cultures, the predominantly continental imperialism of the United States proceeded through the eradication and removal of indigenous peoples and the replacement of their cultures. Central to Sara Mills's analysis of British women's travel writing is the complex interplay between the "discourses of femininity and colonialism." Women travel writers "were at one and the same time part of the colonial enterprise, and yet marginalized within it" (106). We may, therefore, understand British women's travel narrative as presenting a dialectic between acceptance and rejection of acculturation, positions represented by Ruth and Orpah. On the other hand, American literature of the trope of women's travel I define is different in kind. It imposes a relation of contradiction between the two terms: Orpah's journey rejects Ruth's accommodation and reconfigures the circumstances which promote it. By projecting societal norms onto the rejected representative of male travel, American writers of this study use the trope of women's travel to impose a separation from various imperial effects—greed in Cather, egocentrism in Bishop, isolation in Welty and Wharton, and exploitation in Jacobs and Robinson.

Through the articulation of contradictive difference, the trope of the woman traveler demonstrates the implications of the conceptual choices against which the moving woman is defined. Like the root metaphor of male travel, this alternative trope organizes meanings differently in differing contexts. Thus, for example, in texts from the same century by Whittier, Jacobs, and Jewett, feminine stasis represents, respectively, feminine propriety, sexual submission to slave owners, and passive acceptance of isolation and hardship. In these same texts male movement expresses, I have argued, psychological and ideological contradiction, intolerable exploitation, or confused isolation, and the trope of women's travel stands for the violation of communal norms in *Snow-Bound*, the empowerment of the black woman in *Incidents in the Life of a Slave Girl*, and the establishment of female community in *The Country of the Pointed Firs*. Viewing the range of alternatives available through the operation of the trope of the woman traveler suggests that different structures of value, social arrangement, and understanding are imaginable and, therefore, possible. Although varying with regard to historical context and authorial representation, the deconstructive and reconstructive trope of the woman traveler contravenes dominant ideological values, presents conceptual values unavailable in dominant culture, develops the mature social arrangements of women, and defines modes of transformation. To read the constructive texts of women's travel challenges and reconstitutes psychological and epistemological, familial and communal, and social and political conventions.

The woman traveler, as this study reveals her, functions as the trope described by White that is realized through narrative as described by Brooks. Her movement beyond the known limits, a metaphor enacted as the narrative of journey, is a vehicle for conceptualizing alterations and realizing change. She also provides the occasion for observing the use of narrative as the vehicle for personal and social change. As the Orpah figure moves out of her traditional position as object of masculine culture to become her own subject, she goes beyond subversion to construction. Her active career controverts an historically recurrent opposition: masculine mobility in an exterior area and feminine restriction to a domestic space. Thus the narrative trope of women's travel does nothing less than create an effectual feminine self and define a place for women in a reconceived world. Although the agent of control and influence is lost in feminist theories of victimization and only incompletely realized in feminist theories of resistance, to trace the trajectory of the woman traveler throughout American literature is to tell a vital secret about a revolutionary paradigm of female agency that in an array of conformations has been there all along.

NOTES

INTRODUCTION

1. See, for example, such classic texts as Henry Nash Smith's *Virgin Land* and R. W. B. Lewis's *The American Adam*.

2. See also Annette Kolodny's *The Land before Her: Fantasy and Experience of the American Frontiers, 1630–1860* (1984) for an account of the woman's perspective in formative American literature of imperial expansion.

3. Of course, many American women, particularly upper-class white women in the nineteenth century, traveled outside the boundaries of their national communities. See, for example, the collection *Telling Travels: Selected Writings by Nineteenth-Century American Women Abroad*, edited by Mary Suzanne Schriber. In contrast to the secret journeys of this study, according to Scriber's introduction, the texts of these travelers have much in common with their British counterparts: "Often marshaling the discourse of colonialism, these travel writers 'produced' in their texts the European, African, and Middle Eastern, among 'Other' natives, particularly the native Woman, and then reveled in the privileges and superiority of American womanhood" (xxii). The trope of women's travel I define, however, deconstructs and reconstructs rather than reinforces political, social, and epistemological patterns negotiated by American gender codes. Although Leed's classification is, no doubt, a simplification of the many conditions of women's travel, a focus on the "secret" journey has allowed me to emphasize the radical revision possible through representation of women's travel rather than the complicities central to Schriber's description.

4. See Lawrence, who considers the diverse forms and effects of women's travel in the British literary tradition and emphasizes, as I do, women's travel as a complex trope of agency. See also the general introduction of William L. Andrews's *Journeys in New Worlds: Early American Women's Narratives*, which interprets the journey motif in colonial texts by women as "exploration beyond the frontiers of woman's sphere" and "discovery within uncharted borders of the self" (5).

5. "A feminist critique of the metaphorical significance of travel would highlight gender inequality imposed by patriarchal power and authority," according to Alison Blunt in "Mapping Authorship and Authority: Reading Mary Kingsley's Landscape Descriptions." Further, she argues that "feminist spatiality can stimulate a reinterpretation" of other forms of the "position" of women's texts (65).

6. See also critical studies of the American canon cited by Fetterly: Baym's "Early Histories of American Literature," Greenspan's "Evert Duyckink and the

History of Wiley and Putnam's Library of American Books," Lauter's *Canons and Contexts*, Oliver's "Theodore Roosevelt, Brander Matthews, and Campaign for Literary Americanism," Renker's "Resistance and Change: The Rise of American Literature Studies," Tompkins's "Susanna Rowson, Father of the American Novel," and Spengemann's *A Mirror for Americanists*.

7. In her 1992 dissertation "American Women's Travel Narratives," which analyzes accounts of actual experiences, Maureen Ellen St. Laurent observes that women's travel writing typically reflects "a sense of transgressing the boundaries of gender codes" (27). I extend this observation to consider how the transgression of gender codes by the trope of woman's travel affects social experience.

CHAPTER 1. THE NOT UNFEARED, HALF-WELCOME GUEST

1. Throughout Emerson's poem at least sixteen verbs and gerunds depicting the unchecked motion of the snow storm overwhelm the motif of temporary interruption of activity expressed in three verbs in the first stanza.

2. See also James E. Rock's opposing traditional reading in "Whittier's *Snow-Bound: 'The Circle of Our Hearth' and the Discourse on Domesticity*." For Rock, *Snow-Bound* "affirms the domestic economy of lWhittier's] time and the personal values and family history of his Quaker heritage and defines the redeemed American family, lately broken apart by the Civil War but now ready for consolation and renewal." In this interpretation, Harriet serves as the "masculine" counterfigure to "the eternal feminine" represented by the other women portrayed, a characterization that lends "depth and complexity" to the poem (350).

3. All citations from Whittier's poetry are from *The Complete Poetical Works of John Greenleaf Whittier*, Cambridge Edition (Boston: Houghton Mifflin, 1891).

4. By Kennedy's biased account, Harriet Livermore traveled four or five times to Jerusalem beginning in 1836. She was known to have accepted food from Protestant missionaries there, and was not, according to Dr. Selah Merill, the American Consul in 1883 who is supposed to have interviewed people who knew Harriet, permitted to preach on the streets of the city (32).

5. Lady Hester Stanhope lived in her mountain villa of Djoun in Syria, where she died in 1829. An English eccentric, she recounted her adventures and beliefs in her *Memoirs and Travels*. Like Harriet, she believed in the Second Advent, that is the return of Christ during her lifetime (Kennedy 33).

6. These horses apparently generated controversy. Kennedy cites a physician who attended Lady Stanhope in Syria and compiled her memoirs, and Dr. Wm. M. Thompson, who made the arrangements to bury her, as the sources of an accurate portrayal which corrects some of the mistaken details of Whittier's account: "It appears from the Memoirs that a village doctor named Meta, on Mt. Lebanon, predicted that on the coming "Mahendi" he would ride a horse born saddled, and that 'a woman would come from a far country to partake in the mission.'" For this reason Lady Hester kept two horses as pampered pets, but

neither was white, as in the Whittier poem; nor did either bear the distinctive red marks he mentions. One of the mares, chestnut in color, was swaybacked. This characteristic was interpreted by Lady Hester as the portended natural saddle (34–35).

7. Kennedy contends that this statement is undoubtedly mistaken: "A poor and obscure fanatic, living almost wholly on charity in Jerusalem, would not have been accepted by Arabs as their chief" (35).

8. Generally basing his analysis on Freudian theory, Poster cites Francois Basch, *Relative Creatures: Victorian Women in Society and the Novel*, trans. A. Rudolf (New York, 1979), 3–15 on this specific point. He is describing Viennese family relationships in this passage.

9. In *Whittier: A Portrait in Paradox*, Edward Wagenknect describes *Margaret Smith's Journal* as Whittier's "one prose work of the first rank," which is "one of the inexplicably neglected classics of American literature" (7).

10. As Birgitta Maria Ingemanson observes in "Under Cover: The Paradox of Victoran Women's Travel Costume," "The women travelers of these times were seldom outwardly flamboyant, but their very decision to travel challenged accepted norms and invited retribution. Along with the Bachelor Girl and the Old Maid, they became the butt of jokes; traveling heroines in novels often met unfortunate ends" (7).

CHAPTER 2. MOVING TARGETS

1. I quote Rowlandson throughout from VanDerBeets anthology *Held Captive by the Indians* because, unlike many of the available sources, this version retains unmodernized spelling, capitalization, and punctuation.

2. See also Vaughn and Clark, 1–28.

3. In his influential 1973 *Regeneration through Violence*, Richard Slotkin defines the captivity narrative as the typological representation of a passive Puritan society "awaiting rescue by the Grace of God" (94). Jane Tompkins contends in 1985 that Rowlandson, in fact, suppresses anything that doesn't conform to the Puritan vision of the world. Several contemporary scholars do, however, consider the contradictions in Rowlandson's text. Susan Howe's 1985 poststructuralist encounter evokes Rowlandson's poetics of omission. In a 1988 article Kathryn Zabelle Derounian examines the split between psychological symptoms and religious aspiration. Mitchell Robert Breitwieser's 1990 *American Puritanism and the Defense of Mourning: Religion, Grief, and Ethnology in Mary White Rowlandson's Captivity Narrative* posits the unresolved mourning of Rowlandson as a project antithetical to the Puritan argument. And Maureen L. Woodward's 1996 study of "Female Captivity and the Deployment of Race in Three Early American Texts" observes both construction and deconstruction of "dominant white identity" according to the "European Protestant norm" (116). Christopher Castiglia's 1996 *Bound and Determined: Captivity, Culture Crossing, and White Womanhood* explains the captivity narrative originating with Rowlandson as producing "radical epistemology" (6) that challenges gendered orders of masculine independence and feminine community building to

"increase women's social mobility" (5). In "'My Outward Man': The Curious Case of Hannah Swarton" (1996), Lorrayne Carroll claims that although "Rowlandson's journey begins and ends within the pale of Puritan practices," her movement across New England and her encounter with King Philip authorize the public speech of the text that is debarred for women within the church (45).

4. See Drimmer 8–20 on popular reception, Vaughn and Clark 11–15 on ethnographic record.

5. Ann Stanford's "Mary Rowlandson's Journey to Redemption" (1976) pursues this trope in support of a religious reading. Similarly, Amy Lang's introduction to Rowlandson's text notes that the account "carefully records the physical and social details of he 150-mile trek," but she interprets the actual journey as a symbol for the spiritual salvation: "Rowlandson's real journey is an interior one" (21). In "Stepping Out: Writing Women's Travel" (1996) Nancy A. Walker notes that the captivity narrative is an early form of American travel writing (145). The one sustained discussion of Rowlandson's memoir as a travel text is to be found in Maureen Ellen St. Laurent's dissertation "American Women's Travel Narratives: Gender and Genre," which interprets Rowlandson's journey as a confrontation of "self-understanding" and a test of the "boundaries of [Rowlandson's] social roles" (41).

6. Vaughn and Clark list John Winthrop's "Christian Education," Thomas Shepard's "My Birth and Life," Anne Bradstreet's "To My Dear Children," and Edward Taylor's "Spiritual Relation" as evidence of the popularity of the autobiographical form as model (4).

7. I retain Rowlandson's designation of Native Americans as Indians.

8. I intend the designation *Rowlandson* to refer to the historical author, Mrs. Mary Rowlandson, and the designation *Mary* to indicate the character, Mary Rowlandson, the protagonist of the narrative.

9. For example, Rowlandson quotes Job: *"Naked came I out of my Mothers Womb, and naked shall I return: The Lord gave, and the Lord hath taken away, Blessed be the Name of the Lord"* (57) and *"Have pitty upon me, have pitty upon me , O ye my Friends, for the Hand of the Lord has touched me"* (64).

10. Just as Rowlandson's experience exceeds the cultural categories for its containment, it also resists standard critical approaches. A twentieth-century reader might discover a dialectical or deconstructive relation between the two separate accounts. In the dialectical strategy derived from Socrates, both arguments contend from a position of seeming initial equality until the superior argument finally predominates by dint of logic. This is not the case in Rowlandson's narrative. While the Christian view is emphatically stated, an alternative perspective cannot be realized through direct presentation, hence the literal and figurative indirection of the travel text. Thus there is no balanced dialectical engagement.

Dialectical materialism, especially as the Marxist method is reinterpreted by Fredric Jameson in *The Political Unconscious*, is closer to the case of Rowlandson's text. Basing his system of dialectical analysis, in part, on the Althusserian argument that ideology represents "not the system of real relations which govern the existence of individuals, but the imaginary relation of those individuals to the real relations in which they live" (Althusser 165), Jameson posits literature as an "imaginary" system that struggles to resolve the predicaments posed in "real relations" through the creation of elaborate ideological analogues. In *The Captivity and Restauration*, however, the historical and material "real" remains virtually inexpressible.

The practice of Derridean deconstruction poses one solution to this conundrum. Under the manifest text, to borrow convenient Freudian terminology, there is a contradictory text, which, like the unconscious, can be approached through a series of "slips of the tongue" on the surface of the text. Yet in *A Narrative of the Captivity and Restauration of Mrs. Mary Rowlandson* the contradictory text, the travel account that provides the main body of the work, *is* the manifest text. Further, deconstruction as technique rests on a philosophy of supplementarity in which the "real" does not exist but is invented as text. Rowlandson's difficulty is not the absence of reality, but its surfeit. Her accomplishment is to approximate the "real" through the trope of travel from within a system that makes any such approximation unimaginable.

11. The specifics of composition are undetermined. Most recently, according to Frances Roe Kestler, Rowlandson "composed her single, momentous work either while waiting to be reunited with her children or more probably while in Boston" (16), whereas for Richard Diebold "internal evidence suggests" that the narrative was written "in Wethersfield either in 1677 or 1678" after the Rowlandsons left their temporary home in Boston (1246).

12. Rowlandson's narrative enjoyed extraordinary popularity. Kestler lists four editions published during her lifetime, thirty-nine altogether (68).

13. These troops were Massachusetts and Connecticut forces under the command of Captain Thomas Savage. VanderBeets, *Held*, 53, n. 16.

14. A good review is provided in Smyth 239–60.

15. Most historians believe there were forty-two people in the house at the time of the attack (Kestler 12), although Rowlandson puts the number at thirty-seven, one of whom escaped, twelve of whom died in the raid, and twenty-four of whom were taken captive (44–45).

16. See VanDerBeets, *Indian*, 1–4 for a summary of pertinent primary references.

17. Quonopin's generosity here may be a result of the imminence of Mary's ransom, but that is not the tone of its presentation.

18. Rowlandson's humanization of the Indian, however incomplete, is a significant accomplishment. Citing J. Hammond Trumball, ed., *The Public Record of the Colony of Connecticut*, I, 78, Vaughn and Clark note, "Puritan society had abundant legal and social strictures against imitating or admiring the Indian's 'profane course of life.' Indian ways were to be shunned; 'savagery' was feared and despised" (17).

19. In fact, according to Vaughn and Clark, "no ethnographic evidence indicates that northeastern Indians ever raped their captives" (14). But so strong was the taboo against miscegenation, that returning female captives apparently needed to reassure their communities on this score. Rowlandson is admirably direct: "not one of them ever offered me the least abuse of unchastity to me in

word or action. Though some are ready to say I speak it for my own credit; But I speak it in the presence of God, and to his Glory" (84–85). See also *An Account of the Captivity of Elizabeth Hanson.*

CHAPTER 3. "THE PERILOUS JOURNEY THROUGH THE HUMAN HOUSE"

1. See the essays on Wharton's travel experience and her travel writing collected in *Wretched Exotic*, edited by Katherine Joslin and Alan Price and the anthology of Wharton's travel writings *Edith Wharton Abroad*, with a useful preface by Shari Benstock and introduction by Sarah Bird Wright, the editor of the collection.

2. For an extensive discussion of both writers' representations of interiors and landscapes, see Judith Fryer's *Felicitous Space: The Imaginative Structures of Edith Wharton and Willa Cather.*

3. Kate Ferguson Ellis, author of *The Contested Castle: Gothic Novels and the Subversion of Domesticity*, confesses, "Initially I had intended to write about the literary use of the home as a place of security and concord, but found myself writing about the home as a place of danger and imprisonment. Any enclosed space seemed to present this paradox, which links the 'safe' sphere of home inseparably to its dark opposite, the gothic castle" (x). This account of conversion, captures for me the effect of the paradoxical shift from possibility to diminishment in the gothic features of *The Professor's House* and *Summer.*

4. Juliann E. Fleenor provides a pertinent definition for the Female Gothic:

> It is essentially formless, except as a quest; it uses the traditional spatial symbolism of the ruined castle or an enclosed room to symbolize both the culture and the heroine; as a psychological form, it provokes various feelings of terror, anger, awe, and sometimes self-fear and self-disgust directed towards the female role, female sexuality, female physiology, and procreation; and it frequently uses a narrative form which questions the validity of narrative itself. It reflects a patriarchal paradigm that women are motherless yet fathered and that women are defective because they are not males. (15)

5. See Rosowski for a general discussion of the gothic elements in some of Cather's other works, especially *Lucy Grayheart* and *Sapphira and the Slave Girl*, 207–45.

6. See Hoffman 67–68.

7. According to Macherey, the "fable which shapes the narrative does not correspond to the initial project until that project has been subjected to a reversal" (190).

8. Susan Wolstenholme observes of Willa Cather, George Eliot, and Ann Radcliffe: "a woman writer may clearly assume a masculine perspective which she invites the reader to share. . . . But the writer's role . . . need not be read simply as a man's role" (12).

9. For a different discussion of Cather's deployment of gothic devices see Naomi E. Morgenstern's "'Love is Home-Sickness': Nostalgia and Lesbian Desire in *Sapphira and the Slave Girl*," which argues that Cather uses elements of gothic convention to contain violence and sexuality.

10. See MacAndrews's discussion of these traditional elements, 7–8, 10–11.

11. See also Katherine Joslin's "Finding the Self at Home: Chopin's *The Awakening* and Cather's *The Professor's House*." Joslin argues that Cather's novel explores the conflict between the romantic male quest for identity and the communal priorities of domesticity. Favoring a combination that favors the creation of social identity, she reads "ultimate failure" (179) in the quest theme. I am arguing for the positive interpretation of the travel motifs of the novel as the achievement of expression of the complex gendered priorities Cather was attempting to negotiate.

12. See also Marilyn Chandler's *Dwelling in the Text: Houses in American Fiction* in which she argues that the feminine house opposes the masculine desire for freedom in this novel and others.

13. Susan Rubin Suleiman in *The Female Body in Western Culture* insists that the "significance of the female body is not only (not even first and foremost) that of a flesh and blood entity, but that of a *symbolic construct*" (2).

14. Benstock notes that for Wharton the journey was an opportunity to assert feminine independence: "Every trip followed a trajectory of desire for expanding horizons that she could not resist" (xx). And like Charity, Wharton also combined travel with the pursuit of sexual fulfillment during a 1909 motor trip with Morton Fullerton. One result of this combination of movement and desire was *Summer*, which Benstock argues replicates the "seduction, secrecy, and adventure" of her affair (xxi). "*Summer*," according to Benstock, "derives as much from her experience as a travel writer as it does from her work as a novelist" (xxii). Because actual travel served Wharton as a means of feminine expansion into new realms of cultural, social, psychological, even sensual experience, the revocation of its promise in Charity's gothic journey is especially poignant.

15. Wharton's intention in this scene may have been to provide a dark vision of the degradation of the modern world. As Frederick J. Hoffman argues, World War I inspired in both Cather and Wharton a strong defense of cultural tradition: "Art and religion on one side, vulgarity and militarism on the other: this was the issue in all its bare simplicity of meaning" (67–68). And in *Pioneers and Caretakers*, his 1961 study of female American authors, Louis Auchincloss affirmed that "women writers," among them Willa Cather and Edith Wharton, have characteristically "struck an affirmative note" (3). When Mr. Royall appealed to those gathered to celebrate the history of their shared hometown heritage to consider coming home "for *good*" (194), it is likely he is speaking his author's values, yet *Summer* includes a Machereyan conflict, most clearly evidenced in the gothic journey and incest allusion of the concluding section of the novel. These features are best read, I am arguing, as representations of gender restriction. To read Wharton's novel as a Machereyan struggle between what she wanted to say and what needed to be said suggests to me that the related narrative tropes of the woman traveler and the gothic journey signal the emerging

modern consciousness of conflict between women's opportunities and their social restrictions. The troubling gothic journey of Charity Royall, whose potential is evident in her propensity for movement, symbolizes the secret of female limitation Wharton must have known well—and may not have wanted to tell.

16. In *Gender and the Gothic in the Fiction of Edith Wharton* Kathy A. Fedorko discovers in Charity's encounter with her dead mother a positive confrontation with repressed aspects of her own sexuality and feminine identity. This "triumph" (79), which is not fully cancelled by her passive acceptance of Royall's rescue, is the cornerstone of an interpretation of the gothic project in this novel as an incomplete process of feminine empowerment rather than the expression of the societal structure of feminine disempowerment I define.

17. Tania Modleski stresses the interrelationship of "separation anxiety and oedipal conflicts" as the basis of the contemporary gothic (73), and for Cynthia Griffin Wolff, Edith Wharton's achievement in *Summer* is the portrayal of "the necessary sexual components of the search for adult identity as it is experienced by a young woman" on her "journey toward maturity" (Introduction xii). But Wolff's Freudian reading of *Summer* as Wharton's "hymn to generativity and marriage" (*Feast* 293) does not adequately explain the conversion of the life journey metaphor into the trope of the gothic journey in the last chapters; nor does her dismissal of the incest theme, Charity's marriage to her adoptive father, as "not a 'bad' thing" (*Feast* 306) account for the negative effect of that reversal.

18. The New England location of Charity's subjugation may suggest that her story has particular reference to American societal norms. In "The New Frenchwoman," an article published in *The Ladies Home Journal* in 1917, Wharton explains that the American wife has been "withdrawn from circulation," a spatial metaphor Charity enacts literally (qtd. by Benstock 31).

19. See also Wolff's discussion of Wharton's "Beatrice Palmato" fragment, an unpublished pornographic episode of incest Wharton developed as the motivating secret in a ghost story treating multiple suicides in a family, 299–310.

20. See O'Brien, Wolff, and Lewis.

CHAPTER 4. A WOMAN'S PLACE

1. See Yellin xxxi–xxxiv, Washington 10–12.

2. See also Bonnie Frederick and Susan L. McLeod who briefly discuss the implications of reading Jacobs's text as travel narrative in their introduction to *Women and the Journey: The Female Travel Experience* (xx–xxi).

3. "O, why was I born a man, of whom to make a brute!" Douglass exclaims (294).

4. Writing years after the publication of Douglass's book, Jacobs would undoubtedly have been familiar with his famous example. She had also worked in an abolitionist reading room in Rochester, N.Y., which was located in the same building as Douglass's newspaper. See Jean Fagan Yellin's introduction for details of Jacobs' biography. Mary Helen Washington provides analysis of the gendered differences between male and female slave narratives (3–4).

5. Douglass used his ability to write to forge "protections" for an attempted escape to the north, which certified that he and his fellow slaves were traveling alone by permission of a slave owner (307).

6. Both Dr. Flint and Mr. Sands articulate their sexual interest in letters written to Linda (364, 385).

7. The duties of female slaves, rarely involving the transportation of goods or the practice of crafts, did not give them access to the world outside the plantation that was enjoyed by some male slaves. Further, men were more likely to be sold away from their families, whereas women often retained access to their young children; therefore the more mobile male produced a record of an individualized rather than collective identity (Valerie Smith, xxviii) out of his own institutionally imposed experience. See also Deborah Gray White's history of female slavery, which also defines the practice of "abroad marriage" as another factor contributlng to differences in mobility between male and female slaves (75–76).

8. The code of purity and domestic virtue of the white Northern Christian women Jacobs addresses rhetorically is also the genuine achievement of Linda's grandmother. Thus, the bimodal choices of Linda's earliest statements are considerably complicated by Linda's familial experience and her struggles against gender and racial confinement in the course of the narrative. One of the most significant achievements of her journey may be the rejection in the final paragraphs of the generic marriage ending, a critique that indicates its power to redefine received forms.

9. See Frederic Jameson's literary applications in *Marxism and Form* 383–85 and *The Political Unconscious* 77–80.

10. See "Beyond the Pleasure Principle" in which Freud discusses the repetition-compulsion of veterans who repeatedly dream their battle traumas.

CHAPTER 5. THE GENTEEL PICARA

1. In her preface to the 1925 Houghton Mifflin reissued volume of Jewett's 1896 novel, Willa Cather recollects that "Jewett had once laughingly told me that her head was full of dear old houses and dear old women, and when an old house and an old woman came together in her brain with a click, then a story was underway" (n. pag.).

2. See also "Art and Archetype: Jewett's *Pointed Firs* and the Dunnet Landing Stories," in which Michael E. Holstein designates the voyage as one of three central topoi in Jewett's work.

3. I make use of Barbara H. Solomon's arrangement, which presents Jewett's original version and adds the "Four Related Stories"—"A Dunnet Shepherdess," "The Foreigner," "The Queen's Twin," and "William's Wedding."

4. See also Catherine Petroski's *A Bride's Passage: Susan Hathorn's Year under Sail*, the transcription of a diary of a wife who lived this pattern in 1855 aboard her husband's whaling vessel.

5. Fields, *Letters*, 185.

6. See Donovan, *Sarah Orne Jewett*, chapter 1.

7. "My dear father used to say to me very often, 'Tell things *just as they are*!' and used to show me what he meant in *A Sentimental Education*" (qtd. by Donovan *Sarah Orne Jewett*, 5).

8. Love, they explain "is tied to the activities of relationship and premised, like attachment, on the responsiveness of human connection, the ability of people to engage with one another in such a way that the feelings of the other come to be experienced and taken on as *part of the self*" (120).

9. Essentially, this female counterpart of the unrealistic Don Quixote is an exaggeration of the book-befuddled, impractical, hence powerless, heroine of the sentimental novel. Donovan traces her development in the works of Maria Edgeworth, Jane Austen, Charlotte Lennox, whose *The Female Quixote* was published in 1752, and many others. See chapters 1 and 2, *New England Local Color Literature.*

10. Tabitha Tenney, whose *Female Quixotism* appeared in 1801, was a relative of Sarah Orne Jewett, and Donovan implies her direct influence in Jewett's short story "The Dulham Ladies" (*Local Color* 27).

11. See, in addition to Sherman, Joseph Church's "Absent Mothers and Anxious Daughters: Facing Ambivalence in 'The Foreigner "' and Louis Renza's discussion in chapter 2 of *"A White Heron" and the Question of Minor Literature*, 73–115.

12. William Todd is constantly criticized for his lack of spunk and energy by his sister, and he has, in fact, assumed the traditional role of the daughter as a companion for an aging mother. Elijah Tilley, the old fisherman, whom the narrator visits at the end of her stay in Dunnet Landing has, out of admiration and longing for his "poor dear" dead wife, assumed many of her duties, habits, and tastes.

13. This metaphor, with some wit, suggests the narrator's own situation in the encounter, but it also invokes the predicament of women suggested by bird imagery in nineteenth-century writing. See the extended discussion in Cheryl Walker's *The Nightingale's Burden.*

14. *A History of Their Own* by Bonnie S. Anderson and Judith P. Zinsser provides compelling and repeated evidence of this thesis throughout European history.

15. Chodorow adapts the term and the concept from Harry Guntrip.

16. For an intelligent discussion of the theoretical difficulties of the accomplishment of the articulation of the postoedipal mother, see Marianne Hirsch's *The Mother/Daughter Plot: Narrative, Psychoanalysis, Feminism*, especially chapter 5, "Feminist Discourse/Maternal Discourse," 162–99.

CHAPTER 6. SISTERS OF THE ROAD

1. Nels Anderson cites the classic distinction between classes of wanderers: "There are three types of genus vagrant: the hobo, the tramp, and the bum. The hobo works and wanders, the tramp dreams and wanders and the bum drinks and wanders" (87).

2. See *The Hobo as an American Cultural Hero* by Frederick Feied.

3. The nostalgia for intact domestic arrangements is a commonplace in hobo songs: "The freezin' ground was my foldin' bed last night," complains a Black blues singer; "I'm a poor boy, a long way from home" (qtd. by Allsop 273). "Now I'm eatin' wild berries and I'm sleepin' on the ground / I'm broken down and disgusted, and I'm tired of trampin' around," laments another (qtd. by Allsop 279).

4. According to Roger A. Bruns in *Knights of the Road: A Hobo History*, "[the term *hobo*] was first used by soldiers returning home after the Civil War who, when asked where they were headed, would reply, "*ho*meward *bound*" (12). In William Kennedy's 1983 novel *Ironweed*, the bum-hero Francis Phelan is not defined by his escapades on the open road but through his home-seeking journey. Engaged in an imaginative Odyssey, he returns physically and emotionally to the people and places of his origin.

5. In a related example, as an active participant in the Women Hoboes Convention, Bertha enthusiastically helps plan proposed way stations for "sisters of the road" to include kitchens, laundries, sewing rooms, facilities for writing and reading "books and magazines particularly specializing in the problems of women," and counseling services geared to the predicaments of "love and economics and birth control and pregnancy" (240). This project, while focusing on assumed feminine interests, also meets genuine female needs.

6. From a speech, "*Le corps à corps avec la mere*" (Montreal: Les editions de la pleine lune, 1981) p. 23, translated and cited by Kukendall, (266).

7. Both Phyllis Lassner and Elizabeth A. Meese also suggest the applicability of Irigaray.

8. Phylliss Lassner observes, "In Sylvie and Ruth, [Robinson] develops fully realized female characters who never express any urge that resembles sexual passion toward another" (56). Further, the husbands of both Sylvie and Helen are absent, and Grandmother Foster is a widow.

9. "All of Western culture rests on the murder of the mother" ("*Le Corps-à-corps avec la mere*," 81). This is a central contention of Luce Irigaray. See also "The Bodily Encounter with the Mother," and "Women-Mothers, the Silent Substratum of the Social Order" in Whitford.

10. Anderson attributes the term, which he uses broadly to suggest the places, practices, and culture of the itinerant class to a 1917 article in the *Chicago Daily News* (3).

11. It would be useful to compare Robinson's reconstitution of feminine nature through elemental tropes to Irigaray's challenge to the philosophical tradition through the mediation of the natural elements. As she explains,

> When I wrote *Amante marine*, *Passions elementaires*, *L'oubli de l'air*, I intended to make a study of our relation to the elements: water, earth, fire, air. I wanted to return to these natural materials which constitute the origin of our body, our life, our environment, the flesh of our passions. (qtd. by Whitford, Introduction, 9)

12. In *The Feminization of the Quest Romance*, Dana A. Heller defines the conversion through journey in terms of a literary transformation: *Housekeeping* changes "the 'lighting-out' motif traditionally reserved for male protagonists

into a feminized quest toward a self-naming, or self-mapping, of the female questing ground" (93).

13. In her reading of *Housekeeping* as the revision of the American Western, Sheila Ruzycki O'Brien also notes that in this scene Sylvie guides Ruth to "accept her losses" (223).

14. See also Chandler's discussion of domestic symbolism in this novel.

15. Meese describes the lake as a "Walden-like pond" (63).

CHAPTER 7. THE DEVELOPMENTAL JOURNEY

1. Carol Porter Smith's 1971 dissertation, "The Journey Motif in the Collected Works of Eudora Welty," conclusively demonstrates through explication the centrality of the journey in Welty's fiction. In a 1987 article, "'The Way to Get There': Journeys and Destinations in the Short Stories of Eudora," Gail L. Mortimer argues the allegorical significance of the travel motif in several key stories.

2. In *One Writer's Beginnings*, Welty acknowledges the importance of travel in her own development: "Through travel," she explains, "I first became aware of the outside world; it was through travel that I found my introspective way into becoming a part of it" (76).

3. In "Death of a Traveling Salesman" from the early *A Curtain of Green* (1941), R. J. Bowman, a commercial traveler, discovers an alternative system of values in the home of a poor country couple he goes to for help when his vehicle slides into a ravine: "He was shocked with knowing what was really in this house. A marriage, a fruitful marriage. That simple thing" (129). The force of this discovery seems to precipitate the heart attack that kills him.

4. Clytie's quest takes the form of disconcerting stares at the people she encounters: "The first thing she discovered about a face was always that she had never seen it before. When she began to look at people's actual countenances there was no familiarity in the world for her" (83). When she finally finds what she is seeking in her own reflection in the cistern, Clytie is punished by both the plot and the diction of the story: "she had fallen forward into the barrel with her poor ladylike black-stockinged legs upended and hung apart like a pair of tongs" (90). The absurdity of this description of Clytie's death suggests no easy resolution of the problem posed by a woman who is seeking something the community cannot provide.

5. Welty's stories of the woman traveler typically feature a conservative complement. The orphan Easter of "Moon Lake" is matched by the rooted Nina. In "Kin" from *The Bride of Innisfallen* (1955), Dicey, the Northern young woman returning to revisit her "home place" (539), is doubled by her stationary Jackson cousin Kate. And even Virgie, Welty's most complete portrayal of the self-transforming woman traveler, is furnished with an alterego throughout her life. In her childhood, Cassie Morrison, a lesser talent who competes with Virgie at the piano, learns to use her musical ability to please others. In adolescence, Cassie's conventional relations with boys contrast Virgie's flagrant display. In adulthood, Cassie consecrates much of her effort to honoring her dead

mother's memory, while Virgie gives away her mother's belongings in preparation for moving on.

6. See Patricia Yaeger's "The Case of the Dangling Signifier: Phallic Imagery in Eudora Welty's 'Moon Lake.'"

7. The apparition of the "bruise at her temple" that she "felt . . . come out like an evil star" has been variously interpreted. Vande Kieft suggests that the bruise is from her absent lover (127–28), while Peter Schmidt temporizes: "The female protagonist . . . has a bruise on her face—possibly from her lover—and is mistreated by the story's other main character . . . in a way that psychically bruises her a second time" (52). I believe Welty indicates that the source is the protagonist's traveling companion through internal dialogue: "Let it [the sight of the bruise] pay him back, then, for the hand he had stuck in her face when she'd tried once to be sympathetic, when she'd asked about his wife" (477).

8. See Ruth M. Vande Kieft's fine chapter "Shades of Comedy: Outside Stories" on the range of comic effects in Welty's fiction (53–69) in which she reads "The Wide Net" as comic ritual (57–58).

CHAPTER 8. THE POSTMODERN JOURNEY

1. All page references for Bishop's poems are to *The Complete Poems: 1927–1979*.

2. See Goldensohn on the explicit episode in lizard courtship to which the poem's imagery alludes (64).

3. Citing Todorov, Campbell estimates "the native population of the Americas fell from eighty million to ten million over the course of the sixteenth century (7).

4. Mills stresses that the proscriptive social definition of the feminine self was a constant problem for the woman travel writer: "whereas men could describe their travel as individuals and as representatives of the colonial power, women could only travel and write as gendered individuals with clearly delineated roles" (Mills 103).

5. The refusal of feminine placement in static domesticity is also an evasion of masculine subjugation, for it is, in fact, literature defined by men's journeys that is most dependent on the mythos of the domestic, according to the two recent critics. In *Transgressions of Reading: Narrative Engagement as Exile and Return*, Robert A. Newman argues the loss of "home" is the basis for narrative process: "Readers engaged by a text function much like exiles, viewing the narrative as a type of homeland in which they can no longer live" (2). Georges Van Den Abbeele, in *Travel as Metaphor*, defines the travel narrative as one in which "the transgression of losing or leaving the home is mediated . . ." (xix). In both of these theories, travel writing is the paradoxical replacement for the lost home. As we have observed in Bishop's parodic presentation of the armed invaders of Brazil, "home" is necessary to male adventure as the authorizing configuration for the aggrandizing attainments of the master "self" in a new location.

6. This interpretation contradicts the feminist argument that places Bishop in the tradition of modernist female "reticence," the abdication of self in

reaction to masculine disapproval of self-assertion. See Ostriker 48–55. Bishop's traveling consciousness is certainly assertive as well as particularized. Her rejection of gendered identity, as I see it, is a rejection of the limits of gendered discourse. It also treats gender as a public rather than private issue. The definitive gendering of "Crusoe in England" and "At the Fishhouses, for example, have been interpreted as issues of Bishop's personal experience by influential critics. The issueless union of Crusoe and Friday in the first poem has been interpreted as a commentary on Bishop's homosexuality (Diehl 20–23). The cold hard breasts of the mother earth in the second have been ascribed to Bishop's early loss of her own mother (Goldensohn 65, Erkkila 108). But the gendered attributes of these poems—read sociologically rather than psychologically—also serve to introduce the implicit distinction between masculine and feminine deployments of travel writing.

7. Dennis Porter stresses the literal meaning of the term *geography* as a form of earth writing (3).

8. See Travisano 105–108 for more on Bishop's treatment of Baudelaire in these lines.

9. In an acceptance speech for a literary award Bishop noted her own affinity with the little bird of this poem: "Yes, all my life I have lived and behaved very much like that sandpiper—just running along the edges of different countries, 'looking for something'" (qtd. by Giroux viii).

10. See my discussion of this concept, pp. 72–74, 90.

11. Bishop is a good illustration of Lawrence's observation: "women writers of travel have tended to mistrust the rhetoric of mastery, conquest, and quest that has funded a good deal of male fictional and nonfictional travel" (20).

CONCLUSION

1. Recent scholarship freely adapts Orpah's absent story to the consideration of issues of immigration and women's studies of religion. See Bonnie Honig's "Ruth the Model Emigree: Mourning and the Symbolic Politics of Immigration," Cynthia Ozick's "Ruth," and other essays collected by Judith A. Kates and Gail Twersky Reimer in *Reading and Reading Ruth: Contemporary Women Reclaim a Sacred Story*, and Bonnie J. Miller-McLemore's *Also a Mother: Work and Family as a Theological Dilemma.*

WORKS CITED

Adams, Percy G. *Travel Literature and the Evolution of the Novel.* Lexington: University of Kentucky Press, 1983.

Allsop, Kenneth. *Hard Travellin': The Hobo and His History.* New York: New American Library, 1967.

Althusser, Louis. *Lenin and Philosophy and Other Essays.* Trans. Ben Brewster. New York: Monthly Review Press, 1971.

Ammons, Elizabeth. "Going in Circles: The Female Geography of *The Country of the Pointed Firs.*" *Studies in the Literary Imagination* 16 (Autumn 1983): 83–92.

Anderson, Bonnie S., and Judith P. Zinsser. *A History of Their Own: Women in Europe from Prehistory to the Present.* Vol. 1. New York: Harper, 1978.

Anderson, Nels. *The Hobo: The Sociology of the Homeless Man.* 1923. Chicago: University of Chicago Press, 1961.

Andrews, William L. et al., eds. *Journeys in New Worlds: Early American Women's Narratives.* Madison: University of Wisconsin Press, 1990.

———. *To Tell a Free Story: The First Century of Afro-American Autobiography, 1760–1865.* Chicago: University of Illinois Press, 1986.

Auchincloss, Louis. *Pioneers and Caretakers: A Study of Nine American Women Novelists.* Minneapolis: University of Minnesota Press, 1961.

Babcock, Barbara A. "'Liberty's a Whore': Inversions, Marginalia, and Picaresque Narrative." *The Reversible World: Symbolic Inversion in Art and Society.* Ithaca, N.Y.: Cornell University Press, 1978.

Baker, Houston A. *Blues, Ideology, and Afro-American Literature: A Vernacular Theory.* Chicago: University of Chicago Press, 1984.

Baym, Nina. "Early Histories of American Literature." *American Literary History* 1 (Fall 1989): 123–39.

———. "Melodramas of Beset Manhood: How Theories of American Fiction Exclude Women Authors. *American Quarterly* 33. 2 (Summer 1981): 123–39.

Beckson, Karl, and Arthur Ganz. *A Reader's Guide to Literary Terms.* New York: Farrar, Strauss, and Cudahy, 1960.

Benstock, Shari. Preface. *Edith Wharton Abroad: Selected Travel Writings, 1888–1920.* Ed. Sarah Bird Wright. New York: Oxford University Press, 1987.

Berthoff, Warner. "The Art of Jewett's *Pointed Firs.*" *Appreciation of Sarah Orne Jewett.* Ed. Richard Cary. Waterville, Minn.: Colby College Press, 1973.

Best, Steven, and Douglas Kellner. *Postmodern Theory: Critical Interrogations.* New York: Guilford Press, 1991.

Bishop, Elizabeth. The *Complete Poems 1927–1979*. New York: Farrar, Straus, Giroux, 1987.

———. *Elizabeth Bishop: The Collected Prose*. Ed. Robert Giroux. New York: Farrar, Strauss, Giroux, 1984.

Blunt, Alison. "Mapping Authorship and Authority: Reading Mary Kingsley's Landscape Descriptions." *Writing Women and Space: Colonial and Postcolonial Geographies*. Ed. Alison Blunt and Gillian Rose. New York: Guilford, 1994.

Bowman, Barbara. "Victoria Holt's Gothic Romances: A Structuralist Inquiry." *The Female Gothic*. Ed. Juliann E. Fleenor. Montreal: Eden Press, 1983.

Box-Car Bertha. *Sister of the Road*. 1937. New York: Harper & Row, 1975.

Bradford, William. *Of Plymouth Plantation 1620–1647*. New York: Modern Library, 1981.

Braxton, Joanne M. *Black Women Writing Autobiography: A Tradition within a Tradition*. Philadelphia: Temple University Press, 1989.

Breitwieser, Mitchell Robert. *American Puritanism and the Defense of Mourning: Religion, Grief, and Ethnology in Mary White Rowlandson's Captivity Narrative*. Madison: The University of Wisconsin Press, 1990.

Brooks, Peter. *Reading for the Plot: Design and Intention in Narrative*. Cambridge, MS: Harvard University Press, 1984.

Bruner, Jerome. *Actual Minds, Possible Worlds*. Cambridge, Mass.: Harvard University Press, 1986.

———. "Narrative Construction of Reality." *Critical Inquiry* 18 (Autumn 1991): 1–21.

Bruns, Roger A. *Knights of the Road: A Hobo History*. New York: Methuen, 1980.

Caldwell, Patricia. *The Puritan Conversion Narrative: The Beginnings of American Expression*. New York: Cambridge University Press, 1983.

Campbell, Mary B. *The Witness and the Other World: Exotic European Travel Writing, 400–1600*. Ithaca, N.Y.: Cornell University Press, 1988.

Carby, Hazel V. *Reconstructing Womanhood: The Emergence of the Afro-American Woman Novelist*. New York: Oxford University Press, 1987.

Carroll, Lorrayne. "'My Outward Man': The Curious Case of Hanna Swarton" *Early American Literature* 31.1 (1996): 45–62.

Carter, Paul. *The Road to Botany Bay: An Exploration of Landscape and History*. Chicago: University of Chicago Press, 1989.

Cary, Richard, ed. *Appreciation of Sarah Orne Jewett: Twenty-nine Interpretive Essays*. Waterville, Minn.: Colby College Press, 1973.

———. Introduction. *Deephaven and Other Stories*. Ed. Sarah Orne Jewett. Albany: New College and University Press, 1966.

Castiglia, Christopher. *Bound and Determined: Captivity, Culture Crossing, and White Womanhood*. Chicago: University of Chicago Press, 1996.

Cather, Willa. Preface. 1925. *The Country of the Pointed Firs and Other Stories*. Ed. Sarah Orne Jewett. Garden City, N.Y.: Doubleday, 1956.

———. *The Professor's House*. New York: Vintage, 1973.

Cawelti, John G. *The Six-Gun Mystique*. Bowling Green, Ohio: Bowling Green Popular Press, 1984.

Chafetz, Jane Saltzman. "Society Determines Sex Roles." *Male/Female Roles.* Ed. Bruno Leone and M. Teresa O'Neill. St. Paul, Minn.: Greenhaven Press, 1985.

Chandler, Marilyn R. *Dwelling in the Text: Houses in American Fiction.* Berkeley, Calif.: University of California Press, 1991.

Chodorow, Nancy. "Family Structure and Feminine Personality." *Woman, Culture, and Society.* Ed. Michelle Zimbalist Rosaldo and Louise Lamphere. Stamford: Stamford University Press, 1974.

———. *The Reproduction of Mothering: Psychoanalysis and the Sociology of Gender.* Los Angeles: University of California Press, 1978.

Church, Joseph. "Absent Mothers and Anxious Daughters: Facing Ambivalence in Jewett's 'The Foreigner.'" *Essays in Literature* 17 (Spring 1990): 52–68.

Clifford, James. "Traveling Cultures." *Cultural Studies.* Ed. Lawrence Grossberg, Cary Nelson, and Paula Treichler. New York: Routledge, 1992.

Conger, Sydney McMillen. "The Reconstruction of the Gothic Feminine Ideal in Emily Bronte's *Wuthering Heights.*" *The Female Gothic.* Ed. Juliann E. Fleenor. Montreal: Eden Press, 1983.

Davies, Miranda, and Natania Jansz. *Women Travel: Adventures, Advice, and Experience.* London: Rough Guides, 1993.

———. *Half the Earth.* London: Rough Guides, 1990.

de Certeau, Michel. *The Practice of Everyday Life.* Trans. Steven Rendall. Berkeley: University of California Press, 1988.

Defoe, Daniel. *The Life and Strange Surprising Adventures of Robinson Crusoe. Collected Works of Daniel Defoe.* New York: Greystone Press, n.d.

DeLamotte, Eugenia. C. *Perils of the Night: A Feminist Study of Nineteenth-Century Gothic.* New York: Oxford University Press, 1990.

de Laurentis, Theresa. *Alice Doesn't: Feminism, Semiotics, and Cinema.* Bloomington: Indiana University Press, 1984.

Derounian, Kathryn Zabelle. "Puritan Orthodoxy and the 'Survivor Syndrome' in Mary White Rowlandson's Indian Captivity Narrative." *Early American Literature.* 22. 1 (Spring 1987): 82–93.

Derrida, Jacques. *Of Grammatology.* Trans. Gayatri Spivak. Baltimore, Md.: Johns Hopkins University Press, 1974.

Diebold, Robert K. "Mary Rowlandson." *American Writers before 1800: A Biographical and Critical Dictionary.* Ed. James A. Levernier and Douglas R. Wilmes. Westport, Conn.: Greenwood Press, 1977.

Diehl, Joanne Feit. "Bishop's Sexual Politics." *Elizabeth Bishop: The Geography of Gender.* Ed. Marilyn May Lombardi. Charlottesville: University of Virginia Press, 1993.

Donovan, Josephine. *Sarah Orne Jewett.* New York: Ungar, 1980.

———. *New England Local Color Literature: A Woman's Tradition.* New York: Ungar, 1983.

Douglas, Ann. *The Feminization of American Culture.* New York: Knopf, 1977.

Douglass, Frederick. *Narrative of the Life of Frederic Douglass.The Classic Slave Narratives.* Ed. Henry Louis Gates, Jr. New York: Penguin, 1987.

Drimmer, Frederick, ed. "Introduction: Captured by the Indians." *Captured by the Indians: Fifteen Firsthand Accounts, 1750–1870.* New York: Dove, 1961.

Dunn, Mary Maples. "Saints and Sisters: Congregational and Quaker Women in the Early Colonial Period." *Women in American Religion*. Ed. Janet Wilson James. Philadelphia: University of Pennsylvania Press, 1980.

Ehrenreich, Barbara, and Deirdre English. *For Her Own Good*. New York: Doubleday, 1989.

Ellis, Kate Ferguson. *The Contested Castle: Gothic Novels and the Subversion of Domestic Ideology*. Chicago: University of Chicago Press, 1989.

Emerson, Ralph Waldo. *Selections from Ralph Waldo Emerson*. Ed. Stephen Whichler. Boston: Houghton Mifflin, 1960.

Erkkila, Betsy. *The Wicked Sisters: Women Poets, Literary History and Discord*. New York: Oxford University Press, 1992.

Erdrich, Louise. *The Beet Queen*. New York: Bantam, 1987,

Fedorko, Kathy A. *Gender and the Gothic in the Fiction of Edith Wharton*. Tuscaloosa: University of Alabama Press, 1995.

Feied, Frederick. *No Pie in the Sky: The Hobo as American Cultural Hero in the Wake of Jack London, John Dos Passos, and Jack Kerouack*. New York: Citadel Press, 1964.

Fetterly, Judith. "'Not in the least American': Nineteenth-century Literary Regionalism." *College English* 56.8 (December 1994): 877–88.

Fiedler, Leslie. "Come Back to the Raft Ag'in, Huck Honey!" *An End to Innocence: Essays and Culture*. New York: Stein and Day, 1972.

Fields, Annie Adams, ed. *The Letters of Sarah Orne Jewett*. Boston: Houghton, 1911.

Fike, John. "An Interpretation of *Pointed Firs*." *Appreciation of Sarah Orne Jewtt*. Ed. Richard Cary. Waterville, Minn.: Colby College Press, 1973.

Fiske, John. *Television Culture*. London: Routledge, 1987.

Fleenor, Juliann E., ed. "Introduction: The Female Gothic." *The Female Gothic*. Montreal: Eden Press, 1983.

Frederick, Bonnie, and Virginia Hyde. Introduction. *Women and the Journey: The Female Travel Experience*. Ed. Bonnie Frederick and Susan L. McLeod. Pullman: Washington State University Press, 1993.

Frederick, Bonnie, and Susan L. McLeod, eds. *Women and the Journey: The Female Travel Experience*. Pullman: Washington State University Press, 1993.

Freeman, Mark. *Rewriting the Self: History, Memory, Narrative*. New York: Routledge, 1993.

Freud, Sigmund. *Beyond the Pleasure Principle: The Complete Psychological Works of Sigmund Freud* Vol. 18. Ed. and trans. James Strachey. London: Hogarth, 1955.

———. "Some Psychical Consequences of the Anatomical Distinction between the Sexes." *The Standard Edition of the Complete Works of Sigmund Freud*. Vol. 19. Ed. and trans. James Strachey. London: Hogarth, 1961.

Fryer, Judith. *Felicitous Space: The Imaginative Structures of Edith Wharton and Willa Cather*. Chapel Hill: University of North Carolina Press, 1986.

Gates, Henry Louis, Jr. "Binary Oppositions in Chapter One of *Narrative of the Life of Frederick Douglass Written by Himself*." *Afro-American Literature*. Ed. Dexter Fisher and Robert B. Stepto. New York: Modern Language Association, 1979.

Gates, Henry Louis, Jr., ed. Introduction. *The Classic Slave Narratives*. New York: Penguin, 1987.

Gilligan, Carol. "Exit-Voice Dilemmas in Adolescent Development." *Mapping the Moral Domain*. Ed. Carol Gilligan et al. Cambridge: Harvard University Press, 1988.

———. "Prologue: Adolescent Development Reconsidered." *Mapping the Moral Domain*. Ed. Carol Gilligan et al. Cambridge: Harvard University Press, 1988.

Gilligan, Carol et al., eds. *Mapping the Moral Domain: A Contribution of Women's Thinking to Psychological Theory and Education*. Cambridge: Harvard University Press, 1988.

Gilligan, Carol, and Grant Wiggins. ""The Origins of Morality in Early Childhood Relationships." *Mapping the Moral Domain*. Ed. Carol Gilligan et al. Cambridge: Harvard University Press, 1988.

Giroux, Robert. Introduction. *Elizabeth Bishop: The Collected Prose*. Ed. Robert Giroux. New York: Farrar, Strauss, Giroux, 1984.

Goldensohn, Lorrie. *Elizabeth Bishop: The Biography of a Poet*. New York: Columbia University Press, 1992.

Green, Martin. *Dreams of Adventure, Deeds of Empire*. New York: Basic Books, 1979.

Greenspan, Ezra. "Evert Duyckink and the History of Wiley and Putnam's Library of American Books, 1845–47." *American Literature* 64 (December 1992): 677–93.

Harmon, William, and C. Hugh Holman. *A Handbook to Literature*, 7th ed. Upper Saddle River, N.J.: Prentice-Hall, 1996.

Heller, Dana A. *The Feminization of the Quest Romance: Radical Departures*. Austin: University of Texas Press, 1991.

Hirsch, Marianne. *The Mother/Daughter Plot: Narrative, Psychoanalysis, Feminism*. Bloomington: Indiana University Press, 1989.

Hoffman, Frederick J. *The Twenties: American Writing in the Postwar Decade*. New York: Free Press, 1962.

Holstein, Michael E. "Art and Archetype: Jewett's *Pointed Firs* and the Dunnet Landing Stories." *Nineteenth-Century Literature* 42 (Sept. 1987): 188–202.

Homans, Margaret. *Bearing the Word: Language and Female Experience in Nineteenth-Century Women's Writing*. Chicago: University of Chicago Press, 1986.

Honig, Bonnie. "Ruth the Model Emigree: Mourning and the Symbolic Politics of Immigration." *Political Theory* 25.1 (Feb. 1997): 112–27.

Howe, Susan. "The Captivity and Restoration of Mrs. Mary Rowlandson." *Tremblor* 2 (1985).

Ingemanson, Birgitta Maria. "Under Cover: The Paradox of Victorian Women's Travel Costume." *Women and the Journey: The Female Travel Experience*. Ed. Bonnie Frederick and Susan L. McLeod. Pullman: Washington State University Press, 1993.

Irigaray, Luce. "The Bodily Encounter with the Mother." *The Irigaray Reader*. Ed. Margaret Whitford. Cambridge, Mass.: Blackwell, 1991.

———. "Women-Mothers, the Silent Substratum of the Social Order." *The Irigaray Reader*. Ed. Margaret Whitford. Cambridge, Mass.: Blackwell, 1991.

Jacobs, Harriet. *Incidents in the Life of a Slave Girl: The Classic Slave Narratives.* Ed. Henry Louis Gates, Jr. New York: Penguin, 1987.

———. *Incidents in the Life of a Slave Girl.* Ed. Jean Fagan Yellin. Cambridge, Mass.: Harvard University Press, 1987.

James, William. *The Varieties of Religious Experience.* 1902. New York: Collier Books, 1961.

Jameson, Fredric. "Cognitive Mapping." *Marxism and the Interpretation of Culture.* Chicago: University of Chicago Press, 1988: 347–57.

———. *Marxism and Form: Twentieth-Century Dialectical Theories of Literature.* Princeton, N.J.: Princeton University Press, 1971.

———. *The Political Unconscious: Narrative as a Socially Symbolic Act.* Ithaca, N.Y.: Cornell University Press, 1981.

Jennings, Francis. *The Invasion of America: Indians, Colonialism, and the Cant of Conquest.* Chapel Hill: University of North Carolina Press, 1975.

Jewett, Sarah Orne. *The Country of the Pointed Firs. Short Fiction of Sarah Orne Jewett and Mary Wilkins Freeman: Including* The Country of the Pointed Firs. Ed. Barbara H. Solomon. New York: NAL, 1979.

Johnson, Barbara. *A World of Difference.* Baltimore, Md.: Johns Hopkins University Press, 1987.

Joslin, Katherine. "Finding the Self at Home." *Kate Chopin Reconsidered.* Ed. Lynda S. Boren and Sara deSaussaure Davis. Baton Rouge: Louisiana University Press, 1992.

Joslin, Katherine, and Alan Price, eds. *Wretched Exotic: Essays on Edith Wharton in Europe.* New York: Peter Lang, 1993.

Kates, Judith A., and Gail Twersky Reimer. *Reading and Rereading Ruth: Contemporary Women Reclaim a Sacred Story.* New York: Ballantine, 1994.

Kennedy, William Sloane. *John G. Whittier: The Poet of Freedom.* New York: Funk & Wagnalls, 1892.

Kestler, Frances Roe. *The Indian Captivity Narrative: A Woman's View.* New York: Garland, 1990.

Kibbey, Ann. *The Interpretation of Material Shapes in Puritanism: A Study of Rhetoric, Prejudice, and Violence.* New York: Cambridge University Press, 1986.

Kolodny, Annette. *The Land Before Her: Fantasy and Experience of the American Frontiers, 1630–1860.* Chapel Hill: University of North Carolina Press, 1984.

———. *The Lay of the Land: Metaphor as Experience and History in American Life and Letters.* Chapel Hill: University ofNorth Carolina Press, 1975.

Kribbs, Jayne K., ed. Introduction. *Critical Essays on John Greenleaf Whittier.* Boston: G. K. Hall, 1980.

Kuykendall, Eleanor H. "Toward an Ethic of Nurturance: Luce Irigaray on Mothering and Power." *Mothering: Essays in Theory.* Ed. Joyce Trebilcot. Savage, Md.: Rowman & Littlefield, 1983.

Lakoff, George, and Mark Johnson. *Metaphors We Live By.* Chicago: University of Chicago Press, 1980.

Lang, Amy Schraeger, ed. Introduction. "A True History of the Captivity and Restoration of Mrs. Mary Rowlandson." *Journeys in New Worlds.* Ed. William L. Andrews et al. Madison: University of Wisconsin Press, 1990.

Lassner, Phyllis. "Escaping the Mirror of Sameness: Marilyne Robinson's *Housekeeping.*" *Mother Puzzles: Daughters and Mothers in Contemporary American Literature.* Ed. Mickey Pearlman. Westport, Conn.: Greenwood Press, 1989.

Lauter, Paul. *Canons and Contexts.* New York: Oxford UP, 1991.

Lawrence, Karen R. *Penelope Voyages: Women and Travel in the British Literary Tradition.* Ithaca, N.Y.: Cornell University Press, 1994.

Leed, Eric J. *The Mind of the Traveler: From Gilgamesh to Global Tourism.* New York: Basic Books, 1991.

Leverenz, David. *Manhood and the American Renaissance.* Ithaca, N.Y.: Cornell University Press, 1989.

Levernier, James, and Hennig Cohen, eds. Introduction. *The Indians and Their Captives.* Westport, Conn.: Greenwood Press, 1977.

Levi-Strauss, Claude. *Triste Tropiques.* Trans. John Weightman and Doreen Weightman. NewYork: Atheneum, 1974.

Lewis, R. W. B. *The American Adam: Innocence, Tragedy and Tradition in the Nineteenth Century.* Chicago: University of Chicago Press, 1955.

———. *Edith Wharton: A Biography.* New York: Harper & Row, 1975.

Lifton, Robert Jay. *The Broken Connection.* New York: Simon & Schuster, 1979.

Lifton, Robert Jay, and Eric Olson. *Living and Dying.* New York: Bantam, 1973.

Lombardi, Marilyn May. *Elizabeth Bishop: The Geography of Gender.* Charlottesville: University of Virginia Press,1993.

Lowell, James Russell. "Review of *Snow-Bound. A Winter Idyll,* 1866." *Critical Essays on John Greenleaf Whittier.* Ed. Jayne K. Kribbs. Boston: G. K. Hall, 1980.

MacAndrews, Elizabeth. *The Gothic Tradition in Fiction.* New York: Columbia University Press, 1979.

Macherey, Pierre. *A Theory of Literary Production.* Trans. Geoffrey Wall. New York: Routledge, 1986.

Malin, Irving. *New American Gothic.* Carbondale: Southern Illinois University Press, 1962.

Masse, Michelle A. *In the Name of Love: Women, Masochism, and the Gothic.* Ithaca, N.Y.: Cornell University Press, 1992.

Masserand, Anne. M. "Eudora Welty's Travellers: The Journey Theme in Her Short Stories." *The Southern Literary Journal* 3 (1971): 39–48.

Masson, Margaret W. "The Typology of the Female as a Model for the Regenerate: Puritan Preaching, 1690–1730." *Signs: Journal of Women in Culture and Society* 2 (1976): 304–15.

Mather, Cotton. *Magnalia Christi Americana,* vol. I. New York: Russell & Russell, 1967.

Matthieson, F. O. *Sarah Orne Jewett.* Boston: Houghton, 1929.

McNall, Sally. *Who Is in the House? A Psychological Study of Two Centuries of Women's Fiction in America 1795 to the Present.* New York: Elsevier, 1981.

Meese, Elizabeth A. "A World of Women: Marilynne Robinson's *Housekeeping.*" *Crossing the Double-Cross.* Chapel Hill: University of North Carolina Press, 1986.

Mills, Sara. *Discourses of Difference: An Analysis of Women's Travels and Colonialism*. New York: Routledge, 1993.

Miller, Perry. "John Greenleaf Whittier: The Conscience in Poetry." *Critical Essays on John Greenleaf Whittier*. Ed. Jayne Kribbs. Boston: G. K. Hall, 1980.

Miller-McLemore, Bonnie J. *Also a Mother: Work and Family as a Theological Dilemma*. Nashville, Tenn.: Abington, 1994.

Mitchell, Juliet. "Introduction I." *Feminine Sexuality: Jacques Lacan and the* école freudienne. Ed. Juliet Mitchell and Jacqueline Rose. New York: Norton, 1985.

———. *Psychoanalysis and Feminism: Freud, Reich, Laing and Women*. New York: Vintage, 1975.

Mobley, Marilyn. "Rituals of Flight and Return: The Ironic Journeys of Sarah Orne Jewett's Female Characters." *Colby Literary Quarterly* 22 (March 1986): 36–42.

Modleski, Tania. *Loving with a Vengeance: Mass-Produced Fantasies for Women*. New York: Routledge, 1982.

Morgenstern, Naomi E. "'Love Is Home-Sickness': Nostalgia and Lesbian Desire in *Sapphira and the Slave Girl*." *Novel* 29.2 (Winter 1996): 184–99.

Morison, Samuel Eliot, ed. Introduction. *Of Plymouth Plantation by William Bradford*. New York: Knopf, 1963.

Morris, Mary, ed. *Maiden Voyages: Writings of Women Travelers*. New York: Vintage, 1993.

Mortimer, Gail L. "'The Way to Get There': Journeys and Destinations in the Short Stories of Eudora Welty." *Southern Literary Journal* 19.2 (Spring 1987): 61–69.

Mulvey, Laura. "Visual Pleasure and the Narrative Cinema." *Screen* 16 (1975), 6–18.

Neisser, Ulrich. *Cognition and Reality: Principles and Implications of Cognitive Psychology*. San Francisco: W. H. Freeman, 1976.

Newman, Robert D. *Transgressions of Reading: Narrative Engagement as Exile and Return*. Durham, N.C.: Duke University Press, 1993.

O'Brien, Sharon. *Willa Cather: The Emerging Voice*. New York: Fawcett Columbine, 1987.

O'Brien, Sheila Ruzycki. "*Housekeeping* in the Western Tradition: Remodeling Tales of Western Travelers." *Women and the Journey: The Female Travel Experience*. Ed. Bonnie Frederick and Susan L. McLeod. Pullman: Washington State University Press, 1993.

Oliver, Lawrence. "Theodore Roosevelt, Brander Matthews, and the Campaign for Literary Americanism." *American Quarterly* 41 (March 1989): 93–111.

Ostriker, Alicia Suskin. *Stealing the Language: The Emergence of Women's Poetry in America*. Boston: Beacon, 1986.

Ozick, Cynthia. "Ruth." *Reading and Rereading Ruth: Contemporary Women Reclaim a Sacred Story*. Ed. Judith A. Kates and Gail Twersky Reimer. New York: Ballantine, 1994.

Page, Barbara. "Off-Beat Claves, Oblique Realities: The Key West Notebooks of Elizabeth Bishop." *Elizabeth Bishop: The Geography of Gender*. Ed. Marilyn May Lombardi. Charlottesville: University of Virginia Press, 1993.

Pearlman, Mickey. Introduction. *Mother Puzzles: Daughters and Mothers in Contemporary American Literature.* Westport, Conn.: Greenwood Press, 1989.

Petrowski, Catherine. *A Bride's Passage: Susan Hathorn's Year under Sail.* Boston: Northeastern University, 1996.

Poe, Edgar Allan. *The Narrative of A. Gordon Pym of Nantucket: Complete Stories and Poems of Edgar Allan Poe.* Garden City, N.Y.: Doubleday, 1966.

Polkinghorne. *Narrative Knowing and the Human Sciences.* Albany: State University of New York Press, 1988.

Porter, Dennis. *Haunted Journeys: Desire and Transgression in European Travel Writing.* Princeton, N.J.: Princeton University Press, 1991.

Poster, Mark. *A Critical Theory of the Family.* New York: Seabury Press, 1978.

Pratt, Mary Louise. *Imperial Eyes: Travel Writing and Transculturation.* New York: Routledge, 1991.

Radway, Janice A. *Reading the Romance: Women, Patriarchy, and Popular Literature.* Chapel Hill: University of North Carolina Press, 1984.

Renker, Elizabeth. "Resistance and Change: The Rise of American Literary Studies." *American Literature* 64 (June 1992): 347–65.

Renza, Louis. *"A White Heron" and the Question of Minor Literature.* Madison: University of Wisconsin Press, 1984.

Robinson, John A., and Linda Hawpe. "Narrative Thinking as a Heuristic Process." *Narrative Psychology: The Storied Nature of Human Conduct.* Ed. Theodore R. Sarbin. New York: Praeger, 1986.

Robinson, Marilynne. *Housekeeping.* New York: Bantam, 1984.

Rock, James E. "Whittier's *Snow-Bound*: 'The Circle of Our Hearth' and the Discourse of Domesticity." *Studies in the American Renaissance.* Ed. Joel Myerson. Charlottesville: University of Virginia Press, 1993.

Romines, Ann. *The Home Plot: Women, Writing and Domestic Ritual.* Amherst: University of Massachusetts Press, 1992.

Rose, Jacqueline."Introduction—II." *Feminine Sexuality: Jacques Lacan and the* école freudienne. Ed. Juliet Mitchell and Jacqueline Rose. New York: Norton, 1982.

Rosowski, Susan. *The Voyage Perilous: Willa Cather's Romanticism.* Lincoln: University of Nebraska Press, 1986.

Rowlandson, Mary. "A Captivity and Restauration of Mrs. Mary Rowlandson." *The Indian Captivity Narrative: A Woman's View.* Ed. Frances Roe Kestler. New York: Garland, 1990.

Ruddick, Sara. "Maternal Thinking." *Mothering: Essays in Theory.* Ed. Joyce Treblicot. Savage, Md.: Rowman & Littlefield, 1983.

Russ, Joanna. "Somebody's Trying to Kill Me and I Think It's My Husband: The Modern Gothic." *The Female Gothic.* Ed. Juliann E. Fleenor. Montreal: Eden Press, 1983.

Said, Edward W. "Yeats and Decolonization." *Nationalism, Colonialism, and Literature.* Ed. Terry Eagleton, Fredric Jameson, and Edward W. Said. Minneapolis: University of Minnesota Press, 1990.

Sarbin, Theodore R., ed. *Narrative Psychology: The Storied Nature of Human Conduct.* New York: Praeger, 1986.

Schmidt, Peter. *The Heart of the Story: Eudora Welty's Short Fiction.* Jackson: University of Mississsippi Press, 1991.

Schriber, Mary Suzanne, ed. *Telling Travels: Selected Writings by Nineteenth-Century American Women Abroad.* DeKalb: Northern Illinois University Press, 1995.

Schweitzer, Ivy. *The Work of Self-Representation: Lyric Poetry in Colonial New England.* Chapel Hill: University of North Carolina Press, 1991.

Sherman, Sarah Way. *Sarah Orne Jewett: An American Persephone.* Hanover: University of New Hampshire Press, 1989.

Silverman, Kaja. *The Subject of Semiotics.* New York: Oxford, 1983.

Slotkin, Richard. *Regeneration through Violence: The Mythology of the American Frontier, 1600–1860.* Middletown, Conn.: Wesleyan University Press, 1973.

Smith, Carol Porter. "The Journey Motif in the Collected Works of Eudora Welty." Dissertation. University of Maryland, 1971.

Smith, Henry Nash. *Virgin Land: The American West as Symbol and Myth.* New York: Vintage Books, 1950.

Smith, John. *The Complete Works of Captain John Smith (1580–1631)*, 3 vols. Ed. Philip L. Barbour. Chapel Hill: University of North Carolina Press, 1986.

Smith, Valerie, ed. Introduction. Harriet Jacobs. *Incidents in the Life of a Slave Girl.* New York: Oxford University Press, 1988.

Smyth, Mary M., et al. *Cognition in Action.* Hillsdale, N.J.: Lawrence Erlbaum, 1987.

Solomon, Barbara H., ed. *Short Fiction of Sarah Orne Jewett and Mary Wilkins Freeman: Including* The Country of the Pointed Firs. New York: NAL, 1979.

Spengemann, William. *A Mirror for Americanists; Reflections on the Idea of American Literature.* Hanover: University Press of New England, 1989.

Stanford, Ann. "Mary Rowlandson's Journey to Redemption." *Ariel: A Review of International English Literature* 7.3 (1976): 27–37.

St. Aubin de Teran, Lisa. *Indiscreet Journeys: Stories of Women on the Road.* Boston: Faber & Faber, 1991.

St. Laurent, Maureen Ellen. "American Women's Travel Narratives: Gender and Genre." Diss. Vanderbilt University, 1992.

Stepto, Robert B. "Narration, Authentication, and Authorial Control in Frederick Douglass' Narrative of 1845." *Afro-American Literature.* Ed. Dexter Fisher and Robert B. Stepto. New York: Modern Language Association, 1979.

Stout, Janis P. *The Journey Narrative in American Literature.* Westport, Conn.: Greenwood Press, 1983.

———. *Strategies of Reticence: Silence and Meaning in the Works of Jane Austen, Willa Cather, Katherine Anne Porter, and Joan Didion.* Charlottesville: University of Virginia Press, 1990.

Suleiman, Susan Rubin, ed. *The Female Body in Western Culture: Contemporary Perspectives.* Cambridge, Mass.: Harvard University Press, 1986.

Terkleni, Theano S. "Home as Region." *Geographical Review* 85.3 (July 1995): 324–31.

Thoreau, Henry David. *Walden. The American Tradition in Literature.* Ed. George Perkins et al. New York: McGraw-Hill, 1990.

Tomkins, Jane. "'Indians': Textualism, Morality, and the Problem of History." *Race, Writing, and Difference*. Ed. Henry Louis Gates, Jr. Chicago: University of Chicago Press, 1985.

———. "Susanna Rowson, Father of the American Novel." *The (Other) American Traditions: Nineteenth-Century Women Writers*. Ed. Joyce E. Warren. Brunswick: Rutgers University Press, 1993.

Travisano, Thomas J. *Elizabeth Bishop: Her Artistic Development*. Charlottesville: University of Virginia Press, 1988.

Turner, Victor J. "Social Dramas and Stories about Them." *On Narrative*. Ed. W. J. T. Mitchell. Chicago: University of Chicago Press, 1981.

Vande Kieft, Ruth M. *Eudora Welty: Revised Edition*. Boston: G. K. Hall, 1987.

Van Den Abbeele, Georges. *Travel as Metaphor from Montaigne to Rousseau*. Minneapolis: University of Minnesota Press, 1992.

VanDerBeets, Richard. *Held Captive by the Indians: Selected Narratives 1642–1836*. Knoxville: University of Tennessee Press, 1973.

———. *The Indian Captivity Narrative: An American Genre*. (New York: University Press of America, 1984.

Vaughn, Alden T., and Edward W. Clark, eds. "Cups of Common Calamity: Puritan Captivity Narratives." *Puritans among the Indians*. Cambridge: Harvard University Press, 1981.

Vendler, Helen. "Elizabeth Bishop: Domestication, Domesticity, and the Otherworldly." *Part of Nature, Part of Us: Modern American Poets*. Cambridge, Mass.: Harvard University Press, 1981.

Voelker, Paul D. "*The Country of the Pointed Firs*: A Novel by Sarah Orne Jewett." *Appreciation of Sarah Orne Jewett*. Ed. Richard Cary. Waterville, Minn.: Colby College Press, 1973.

Wagenknecht, Edward. *John Greenleaf Whittier: A Portrait in Paradox*. New York: Oxford, 1967.

Walker, Cheryl. *The Nightingale's Burden: Women Poets and American Culture Before 1900*. Bloomington: Indiana University Press, 1982.

Walker, Nancy A. "Stepping Out: Writing Women's Travel." *Annali d'Italianista* 14 (1996): 145–51.

Warren, Robert Penn. *John Greenleaf Whittier's Poetry*. Minneapolis: University of Minnesota Press, 1971.

Washington, Mary Helen. *Invented Lives: Narratives of Black Women*. New York: Doubleday, 1987.

Welty, Eudora. *The Collected Stories*. New York: Harcourt, Brace, Jovanovich, 1980.

———. *The Eye of the Story: Selected Essays and Reviews*. New York: Random House, 1970.

———. *One Writer's Beginnings*. Cambridge, Mass.: Harvard, 1983.

Wharton, Edith. *Summer*. New York: Harper & Row, 1979.

White, Deborah Gray. *Ain't I a Woman?: Female Slaves in the Plantation South*. New York: Norton, 1985.

White, Hayden. *Tropics of Discourse*. Baltimore, Md.: Johns Hopkins University Press, 1978.

Whitford, Margaret, ed. *The Irigaray Reader*. Cambridge, Mass.: Blackwell, 1991.

Whittier, John Greenleaf. *The Complete Poetical Works of John Greenleaf Whittier*. Boston: Houghton Mifflin, 1891.

———. *The Letters of John Greenleaf Whittier* vol. 3. Ed. John B. Pickard. Cambridge, Mass.: Harvard University Press, 1975.

———. *Whittier's Prose Works: Margaret Smith's Journal, Tales and Sketches*. Boston: Houghton Mifflin, 1889.

———. "Snow-Bound." *The Complete Poetical Works*. Boston: Houghton Mifflin, 1891.

Wicks, Ulrich. *Picaresque Narrative, Picaresque Fictions: A Theory and Research Guide*. Westport, Conn.: Greenwood Press, 1989.

Wolff, Janet. "On the Road Again: Metaphors of Travel in Cultural Criticism." *Cultural Studies* 7.2 (1987): 224–39.

Wolff, Cynthia Griffin. *A Feast of Words: The Triumph of Edith Wharton*. New York: Oxford University Press, 1977.

———. Introduction. *Summer*. Edith Wharton. New York: Harper & Row, 1979.

Wolstenholme, Susan. *Gothic (Re)Visions: Writing Women as Readers*. Albany: State University of New York Press, 1993.

Woodward, Maureen L. "Female Captivity and the Deployment of Race in Three Early American Texts." *Papers on Language and Literature* 32.2 (Spring 1996): 115–31.

Wright, Sarah Bird, ed. *Edith Wharton Abroad: Selected Travel Writings, 1888–1920*. New York: St. Martin's, 1995.

Yaeger, Patricia. "The Case of the Dangling Signifier: Phallic Imagery in Eudora Welty's 'Moon Lake.'" *Twentieth-Century Literature* 28.4 (Winter 1982): 431–52.

Yellin, Jean Fagan, ed. Introduction. Harriet A. Jacobs. *Incidents in the Life of a Slave Girl*. Ed. Cambridge, Mass.: Harvard University Press, 1987.

INDEX